Role of Sustainable Development in Environmental Conservation

Editors

Dr. Mamta Sharma   Dr. Hukam Singh

Dr. Upendra Singh

Pustak Bharati
Toronto Canada

Editors : Dr. Mamta Sharma
Dr. Hukam Singh
Dr. Upendra Singh

Book Title : Role of Sustainable Development in Environmental Conservation

Cover Picture : By Dr. Anil Kumar Chhangani, D.Sc

Published by :
Pustak Bharati (Books India)
180 Torresdale Ave, Toronto Canada M2R3E4
email : pustak.bharati.canada@gmail.com
Web : www.pustak-bharati-canada.com

Published for
Raj Rishi Government Autonomous College,
Alwar, Rajasthan, India

Financial Assistance
Rashtriya Uchchatar Shiksha Abhiyan
(RUSA-2.0)

Copyright ©2023

ISBN : 978-1-989416-46-4

ISBN 978-1-989416-46-4
90000

9 781989 416464

Preface

"Our planet is slowly dying, and if we don't do anything about it soon enough, it would eventually begin to deteriorate and everything would be used. The world would become a barren place without any resources. We need to cater to the needs of our planet, and we need to change our life styles so that it becomes beneficial to the planet. We need to become much more eco-friendly, so that no harm is dealt to the planet by our existence. Many people don't realize that they waste large amounts of energy and other resources in various unnecessary things that could otherwise be saved."

This series of books is an extension of the 3 days international conference on **Multidisciplinary Approach Towards Sustainable Development and Climate Change for A Viable Future (ICMSDC-2022)** held from 12th-14th August 2022 at Raj Rishi Government Autonomous College, Alwar, Rajasthan.

We are very happy and delighted to publish our series of books which are accumulation of research papers of knowledgeable experts in the field of sustainable development and climate change.

Climate change is the most significant challenge to achieving sustainable development, and it threatens to drag millions of people into grinding poverty. At the same time, we have never had better know-how and solutions available to avert the crisis and create opportunities for a better life for people all over the world. Climate change is not just a long-term issue. It is happening today, and it entails uncertainties for policy makers trying to shape the future.

There is a dual relationship between sustainable development and climate change. On the one hand, climate change influences key natural and human living conditions and thereby also the basis for social and economic development, while on the other hand, society's priorities on sustainable development influence both the greenhouse gas emissions that are causing climate change and the vulnerability.

Climate policies can be more effective when consistently embedded within broader strategies designed to make national and regional development paths more sustainable. This occurs because the impact of climate variability and change, climate policy responses, and associated socio-economic development will affect the ability of countries to achieve sustainable development goals. Conversely, the pursuit of those goals will in turn affect the opportunities for, and success of, climate policies.

With these books, we aim to reach to as many people as we can, and spread awareness about sustainable development and climate change and its in-depth analysis through our didactic research papers. We hope that the thought with which ICMSDC-2022 was executed is taken forward through this series of books and the inception of an idea of saving the environment is rooted in the minds of our readers. The articles in these books have been contributed by eminent research scholars, scientists, academicians and industry experts whose contributions have enriched this book series. We thank our publisher, Pustak Bharati, Toronto, Canada for joining us in this initiative and helped in publishing this series of books.

Finally, we will always remain indebted to all our well-wishers for their blessings, without which ICMSDC-2022 and series of these book would have not come into existence.

Financial Assistance provided by Rashtriya Uchchatar Shiksha Abhiyan (RUSA-2.0) is gratefully acknowledged.

Dr. Mamta Sharma
Dr. Hukam Singh
Dr. Upendra Singh

Contents

1. High time to Save the Biological Diversity

Dr. Mamta Sharma*,
Dr. Hukam Singh**
Dr. Upendra Singh ***

Introduction

Biodiversity refers to the variety of living organisms present on earth, including all the species of plants, animals, fungi, and microorganisms that inhabit the planet. The environment, on the other hand, encompasses all the physical and natural systems that support life on earth, including the air, water, land, and climate. Biodiversity and environment conservation are two intertwined concepts that are crucial for sustaining life on earth. Biodiversity is essential for the functioning of ecosystems, which provide a range of services that support human wellbeing, such as air and water purification, pollination of crops, and climate regulation. The loss of biodiversity can have devastating impacts on these services, leading to reduced agricultural yields, increased air pollution, and more severe weather events. Furthermore, biodiversity is important for human health, as many of the medicines and foods we rely on come from plants and animals. It is estimated that up to 50% of modern drugs are derived from natural compounds found in plants and animals. Biodiversity is also crucial for cultural, spiritual, and recreational purposes, as it forms the basis of many traditional practices and indigenous knowledge systems. However, biodiversity is under threat from a range of human activities, including habitat destruction, overexploitation of natural resources, pollution, and climate change. These activities have led to the extinction of many species, with up to one million species at risk of extinction in the coming decades.

The term biodiversity refers to the wealth of plants, animals and microorganisms that contain precious genes and formulate delicate ecosystems. Biodiversity is the variety and variability of life on Earth. Biodiversity is typically a measure of variation at the genetic, species, and ecosystem level. Biodiversity refers to variety and variability among the living organisms and ecological complexes in which occur. This includes diversity within species, between species and of the ecosystem. It is defined as the totality of genes, species and ecosystems of a region. Biodiversity or Biological diversity comprises Genetic diversity, Species diversity and Ecosystem diversity (level of biodiversity).

Genetic Diversity :

It refers to the variation of genes within the species stores as immense amount of genetic information. Genetic variation is seen among the individuals within a species. For instance, in cattle there are many varieties with respect to colour, milk yield, size or disease resistance. The genetic variation may be in alleles, entire genes or in chromosomal structures. It leads to better adaptation of species to the changed environment. New species are formed due to genetic variation.

Species Diversity :

It refers to the various species found within a region. Variability found within a species or between different species of a community. Species diversity is measured by species richness (number of species per unit area) and evenness or equitability (evenness in the number of individuals of a species). In the case of species richness, higher species diversity represents greater species diversity. In the second case, evenness of species represents higher species diversity.

Ecosystem Diversity :

It refers to the variations in the biological communities in which the species live. The diversity within a community is called alpha diversity. The diversity between communities is called Beta diversity. Examples are Tropical Rain Forest and Boreal Forest. The present diversity has developed over millions of years of evolution and therefore ecological balance should not be disturbed. The diversity of the habitats over total landscape or geological area is referred to as Gamma diversity (or) Landscape diversity. For example, Forest ecosystem, aquatic ecosystem, Grasslands, Deserts, mangroves etc. Alpha diversity refers to the average species diversity in a habitat or specific area. Alpha diversity is a local measure.

Beta diversity refers to the ratio between local or alpha diversity and regional diversity. This is the diversity of species between two habitats or regions. It is calculated by the following equation: (number species in habitat1 (H1) - number of species habitat 2 (H2) & 1 have in common) +(number of species in H2- number of species H1 & H 2 have in common).

Gamma diversity is the total diversity of a landscape and is a combination of both alpha and beta diversity.

Biodiversity Conservation

Environment conservation refers to the efforts to protect and restore the natural systems that support life on earth. This includes actions to reduce pollution, mitigate climate change, and conserve habitats and species. Environment conservation is crucial for maintaining the services that ecosystems provide, as well as for preserving biodiversity and the benefits it provides to human health and wellbeing. One of the key strategies for biodiversity and environment conservation is protected areas, such as national parks, wildlife reserves, and marine sanctuaries. These areas provide habitats for species to thrive, while also serving as important sources of ecological and cultural value. Protected areas are also important for promoting sustainable tourism, which can provide economic benefits to local communities while supporting conservation efforts.

The enormous value of biodiversity emphasizes the need to conserve biodiversity. Biodiversity is a natural reservoir with tremendous economic potential. Wildlife is a gift of nature to be nurtured. Biodiversity is an important resource for man and nation. So, its conservation and rational use are the need of the hour to achieve sustainable development.

World wide fund for Nature (WWF 1994) works to conserve biological diversity as follows.
➢ Creating and maintaining systems of effective and sustainable protected areas.
➢ Promoting practices of sustainable development
➢ Conserving certain species of special concern.
➢ Promoting environmental education to enable people to manage the natural resources sustainably

Methods of Conservation

There are two methods of conservation of biodiversity.

- In-situ conservation (within habitat)
- Ex-situ conservation (outside habitats)

Biodiversity and its Conservation Methods

Biodiversity refers to the variability of life on earth. It can be conserved in the following ways:

- In-situ Conservation
- Ex-situ Conservation

In-situ Conservation :

In-situ conservation of biodiversity is the conservation of species within their natural habitat. In this method, the natural ecosystem is maintained and protected. The in-situ conservation has several advantages. Following are the important advantages of in situ conservation:

1. It is a cost-effective and convenient method of conserving biodiversity.
2. A large number of living organisms can be conserved simultaneously.
3. Since the organisms are in a natural ecosystem, they can evolve better and can easily adjust to different environmental conditions.

Certain protected areas where in-situ conservation takes place include national parks, wildlife sanctuaries and biosphere reserves.

Ex-Situ Conservation :

Ex-situ conservation of biodiversity involves the breeding and maintenance of endangered species in artificial ecosystems such as zoos, nurseries, botanical gardens, gene banks, etc. There is less competition for food, water and space among the organisms.

Ex-situ conservation has the following Advantages :

1. The animals are provided with a longer time and breeding activity.
2. The species bred in captivity can be reintroduced in the wild.
3. Genetic techniques can be used for the preservation of endangered species.

Conclusion :

One of the most important strategies for biodiversity and environment conservation is sustainable management of natural resources. This involves using resources in a way that meets the needs of the present without compromising the ability of future generations to meet their own needs. For example, sustainable forestry practices can help to maintain forest ecosystems while providing timber for construction and other uses. Similarly, sustainable agriculture practices can help to conserve soil and water resources while producing food for human consumption. Reducing pollution and mitigating climate change are also important for biodiversity and environment conservation. Pollution can have harmful effects on both human health and the environment, leading to reduced biodiversity and ecosystem services. Mitigating climate change is also crucial, as it can lead to changes in weather patterns and the distribution of species, as well as more severe weather events such as hurricanes, floods, and droughts. Finally, education and awareness-raising are crucial for biodiversity and environment conservation. This includes teaching people about the importance of biodiversity and the environment, as well as providing them with the knowledge and skills needed to support conservation efforts. Public participation and engagement are also important, as they can help to build support for conservation initiatives and ensure that they are effective and sustainable. In conclusion, biodiversity and environment conservation are essential for sustaining life on earth. Biodiversity provides a range of services that support human wellbeing, while environment conservation is crucial for maintaining the natural systems that provide these services. Protected areas, sustainable resource management, pollution reduction, climate change mitigation, and education and awareness-raising are all important strategies for achieving biodiversity and environment conservation goals. By working together to protect and restore our planet's natural systems, we can ensure a healthy and sustainable future for ourselves and for future generations.

References

Source of knowledge is the internet and it is highly acknowledged.

*Associate Professor (Zoology)
**Professor
*** Associate Professor (Chemistry)
Raj Rishi Government (Autonomous) College
Alwar, Rajasthan 301001,India.
email : <u>mamta810@gmail.com</u>;
<u>drhukamsingh63@gmail.com</u>;
<u>dr.usingh09@gmail.com</u>

2. Potential of Waste Plastic as Fuel : A Review

Farmaan Mushtak[1*],
Surjit Singh Katoch[2]
Adarsh Singh[3]

Abstract

Production of plastic is estimated to skyrocket in the near future, with an estimated 3.8% growth worldwide by 2030. This surge in plastic production is because of its versatility and cost-effectiveness as a material. Unfortunately, these waste plastic materials often end up discarded or disposed of improperly, leading to environmental damage. Transformative techniques such as waste plastic to fuel conversion could potentially be a substantial source for alternative fuels. As the global population continues to grow, the demand for energy and resources is increasing. This makes it necessary to look for sustainable solutions that can reduce our dependence on traditional sources of energy. Waste plastic to fuel conversion can convert waste plastics into liquid fuels that can be used in vehicles and generators. Converting plastics to fuel involves breaking down the polymers in plastic into smaller molecules, which are then converted into a liquid form. This liquid form of fuel has several advantages over traditional fuels, including lower emissions, higher efficiency, and lower cost. Besides being beneficial for the environment, this process can also limit the amount of plastic that goes to landfill or ocean. Thus, it helps prevent wastage of resources and protects our environment.

Keywords : plastic, alternative energy, fuel, sustainable, environment

1. Introduction

Plastic is a game-changing innovation that has significantly altered the way in which we go about our daily lives. It is a man-made substance that gets its start in the chemical lab as polymers and other organic compounds. It is much more durable and versatile than other materials, which makes it easier to use in a variety of applications because of its superior characteristics. The use of plastic in everyday items such as packaging, furniture, and even medical equipment is now practically unavoidable. Because of how easy it is to use and how versatile it is, it is an excellent option for a wide variety of products and industries. The rise in production of plastics can be attributed to the increased demand for their utilization in a diverse array of applications, such as in homes, electronics, automobiles, agriculture, packing materials, toys, and many more. This consumption is so vast because of the versatility, durability, and lower production cost. Data from PlasticsEurope, 2021 (Plastics Europe, 2021) shows that the world has seen an average 8.6% increase in plastic production every year since 1950, culminating in 367 million tons in 2020. These plastics don't break down very quickly, which makes it more difficult to dispose of them and raises the stakes for the risk they present. Due to the high durability of waste plastics, the most common method for getting rid of them is to dump them in landfills, which is why this method is so detrimental to the environment. Because of this, there is a risk that this will affect the surrounding environment. In this discussion, we will go over the various processes that can be utilised in order to convert waste plastic into fuel.

1.1 Source and Properties of Plastic Wastes

Plastics come in two forms: municipal and industrial waste. Both have distinct characteristics that require varied management approaches for effective disposal.

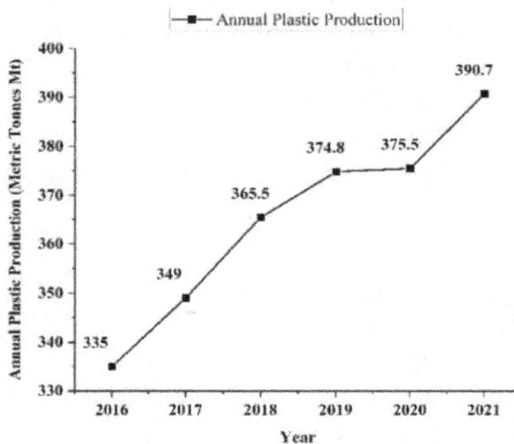

Figure 1. Annual Plastic Production from previous years. Data source: (Plastics Europe, 2021)

Municipal waste has a higher composition of household plastics, while industrial waste comprises heavier materials from manufacturing processes. An alarming amount of plastic waste has been created in the world, with less than 10% being recycled. This is a huge environmental problem that needs to be addressed soon. Out of 9000 million tonnes of plastic produced from 1950-2017, over 7000 million tonnes have become waste and been disposed of in landfills or dumped (Environment, 2022). Cigarette butts, which contain small plastic fibers, are the most frequent form of plastic waste encountered in the environment. Other common offenders include food wrappers, grocery bags, bottle caps and plastic bottles, stirrers and straws. Rivers and lakes are often overlooked sources of ocean pollution since they carry plastics from inland locations to the seas. They play a major role in polluting the seas with plastic waste (*Visual Feature | Beat Plastic Pollution*, 2022).

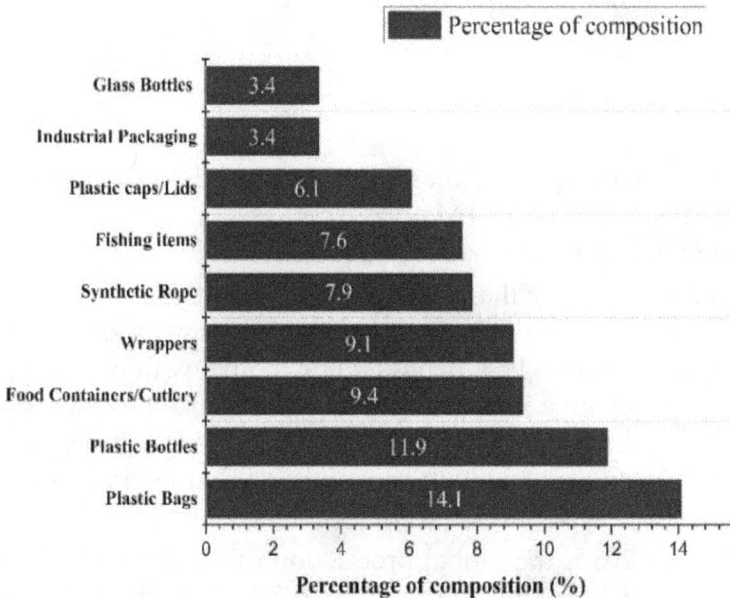

Figure 2. Major plastic Items dominating the Ocean garbage. Source (Morales-Caselles et al., 2021)

Plastics are divided into two categories: thermoplastics, which makes up 80% of plastic products, and thermoset, which makes up the remaining 20% (Phanisankar et al., 2020). Thermoplastics are the most commonly used plastic and account for a significant chunk of the global plastic waste. This is causing a monumental environmental issue due to their large numbers and consistently growing quantity.

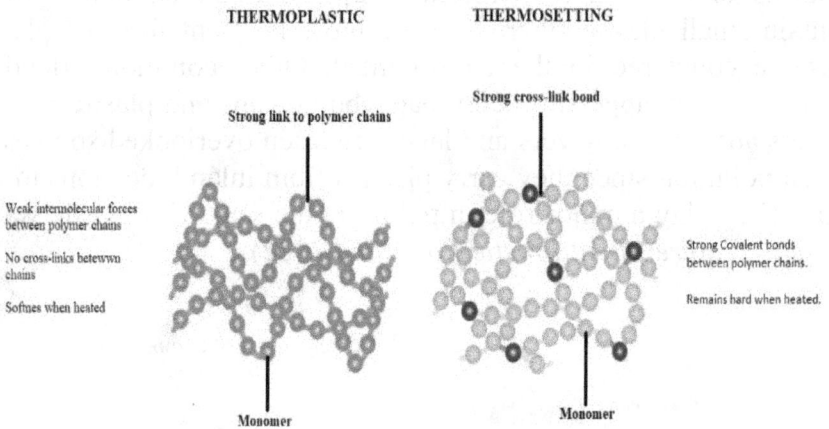

THERMOPLASTIC   THERMOSETTING

Strong cross-link bond

Strong link to polymer chains

Weak intermolecular forces
between polymer chains

No cross-links betewwn
chains

Softnes when heated

Strong Covalent bonds
between polymer chains.

Remains hard when heated.

Monomer   Monomer

Figure 3. Schematics of thermoplastics and thermoset. Source (Melito, 2022)

2. Approaches to Plastic Waste Management

During the last century there has been an exponential increase in the use of plastics, and it does not appear to be slowing down soon as this trend continues. The benefits that come with using plastics outweigh the negative impacts that have been linked to their use and way of disposal. Effective disposal of plastic waste is a big hurdle in solid waste management, with repercussions on energy utilization, environmental conservation, politics, and the economy.

From 1950 to 2015, the global production of plastic was 8.3 billion metric tonnes (BMTs). Of this amount, 6.3 BMTs, about 80 percent, was left as waste. Out of the 6300 million metric tonnes of waste produced, only a little fraction was recycled (9%), some was incinerated (12%) and the majority was dumped into landfills, oceans, or water bodies (79%) (*NITI AAYOG*, 1988). There are mainly two ways of plastic waste management, the first is to recycle or reprocess the plastic waste into secondary usable material and the second option is incineration of plastic waste. However, if not done properly, incineration is costly and pollutes the environment.

According to the data that has been gathered, the two most effective strategies for plastic waste management are road construction and tar and concrete production. These techniques are more beneficial than the other four methods—landfills, recycling, pyrolysis, and liquefaction—because of their ability to reduce plastic pollution while providing useful products or materials (Huang et al., 2022; Wong et al., 2015).

3. Process of Fuel Generation

Producing fuel from plastic is an area of research that is garnering attention worldwide. The most common techniques used to convert plastic into fuel involve hydrocracking, thermochemical and catalytic conversion (Passamonti & Sedran, 2012). Researchers around the world favor thermochemical conversion, also known as pyrolysis, when producing fuel from plastic.

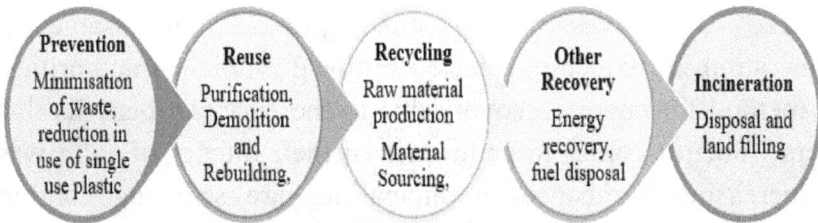

Figure 4. Plastic waste management Strategies.

Colours show the sustainability of the strategies used, green being the safest and red being the least safe.

Pyrolysis is a process used to break down higher polymers into lower hydrocarbons with different numbers of carbons and boiling points. It is usually done in an inert or air-free environment that is kept at a higher temperature than usual (Panda et al., 2010). Motor gasoline can be obtained from hydrocarbons with the boiling points in between 35°C and 185°C, diesel 185°C and 290°C, while the ash residue is produced above 538°C (Sharma et al., 2014). The ratio of fractions produced from thermal degradation of plastics can be adjusted by selecting the correct temperature, type of plastic, duration, and catalyst. Combination of these parameters will determine the yield and properties of the degraded products (Elordi et al., 2009; Syamsiro et al., 2014). The amount of gas, liquid, and residue produced varies as the input polymer being used, the degradation temperature, and the atmosphere it is being exposed to.

3.1 Incineration

Waste incineration is a method of burning of wastes i.e., carbon compounds in the presence of oxygen, also known as complete combustion, that releases H_2O and CO_2. This method can generate energy, which is known as fuel. Incinerating plastic waste is an effective way to generate energy, substituting fossil fuels with hydrocarbon polymers in the waste (Phanisankar et al., 2020). According to table 1, polyethylene has a comparable level of calorific value to that found in fuel oil.

Because it involves turning waste plastics into usable fuel, incineration is frequently selected by local municipal authorities as the method for energy recovery due to the financial benefits that it offers. When it comes to getting rid of their municipal solid waste, an increasing number of municipalities are selecting combined incineration as the method of choice. When it comes to getting rid of their municipal solid waste, an increasing number of municipalities are selecting combined incineration as the method of choice. The elevated calorific value of the plastic, which helps in the process of generating energy, is the primary benefit of employing this strategy. In addition to the provision of additional energy to fuel municipal solid waste incineration, municipal authorities are able to utilize incineration as a source of energy in their operations.

Table 1. Calorific Value of plastic versus some hydrocarbons.
Source: (Passamonti et al, 2012)

Fuel	Calorific value (MJ/kg)
Coal	27
Polyethylene	46
Polypropylene	45
Methane	53
Municipal solid waste	10
PVC	19
PET	21.6

3.2 Recycling/ Recovery of Plastic Wastes

Plastic waste recycling is a modern technology in which there is a break down complex molecular structures of plastics into much smaller particles as liquid or gas. This converted material can then produce new types of petrochemicals and plastics. According to International Standards like ISO, Recycling Plastic is referred to as a Recovery Process. There are various methods for plastics recovery as discussed in table 2.

Table 2. Various methods of plastics recovery

S.no	Method	Description
1.	Primary Recycling	Waste plastic is converted into products with performance almost similar to that of original product first made.
2.	Secondary Recycling	Waste plastics are converted into items with a performance level lower than the original material
3.	Tertiary Recycling	Conversion of waste plastics to produce fuels, chemicals, and similar products
4.	Quaternary Recycling	Energy recovery from plastic waste by incineration.

There are two categories of Plastic waste recovery i.e., Material Recovery and Energy Recovery.

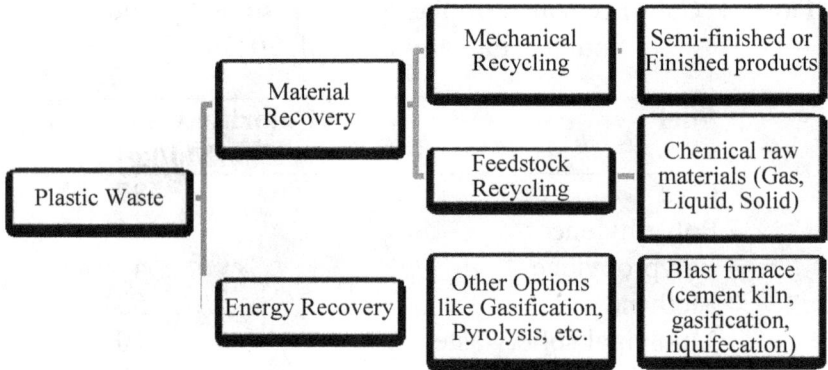

Figure 5. Flowchart for recovery process of plastics

Currently, 39.5% of plastic waste is being put to energy recovery, with about 30% each for recycling and landfill disposal (Ragaert et al., 2017). As per Sogancioglu M, 2017 (Sogancioglu et al., 2017) LDPE (low density polyethylene) yielded the most energy when subjected to pyrolysis, with 75% of the energy being converted into oil. Polyethylene is being considered as the raw material for several technologies that can produce fuel (gasoline) (Mohd. Wasif Quadri et al., 2020). Research studies have shown that when polyethylene is thermally cracked, it breaks down into several different categories, including gasses, liquids, waxes, aromatics, and char. This process comprises 5 primary reactions and 2 secondary reactions that result in 5 compounds are shown in figure 6.

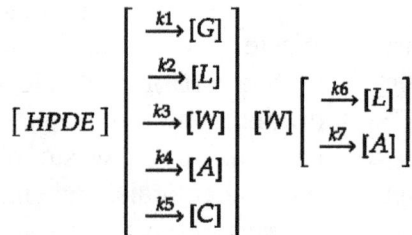

$$[HPDE]\begin{bmatrix} \xrightarrow{k1} [G] \\ \xrightarrow{k2} [L] \\ \xrightarrow{k3} [W] \\ \xrightarrow{k4} [A] \\ \xrightarrow{k5} [C] \end{bmatrix} [W]\begin{bmatrix} \xrightarrow{k6} [L] \\ \xrightarrow{k7} [A] \end{bmatrix}$$

Figure 6. Decomposition of polyethylene

HDPE (high-density polyethylene) has five letters that each stand for a different fraction- G (gases), L (liquids), W (waxes) and A (aromatics) and C (char).

Chemical recycling offers the advantage of being able to handle diverse, complex, and contaminated polymers with minimal pre-treatment required. Waste processing plants that want 40% or higher target for their recycling scheme should consider the cost involved in separating and processing these tough materials.

Table 3 Extracted oil percentages from various plastics. Source: (Phanisankar et al., 2020)

Plastic Polymer type	Temperature at which testing was done	End Product		
		Oil (% by weight)	Gas (% by weight)	Solid (% by weight)
Polyethylene terephthalate PET	500	23.1	76.9	0
Polyethylene terephthalate PET	500	38.89	52.13	8.98
High-Density Polyethylene HDPE	350	80.88	17.24	1.88
High-Density Polyethylene HDPE	400	82	16	2
High-Density Polyethylene HDPE	500	85	10	5
High-Density Polyethylene HDPE	550	84.7	16.3	0
High-Density Polyethylene HDPE	650	68	31.5	0
PolyVinyl Chloride PVC	500	12.3	87.7	0
Low-Density Polyethylene LDPE	425	89.5	10	0.5
Low-Density Polyethylene LDPE	500	80.41	19.43	0.16
Low-Density Polyethylene LDPE	500	95	5	0
	550	93.1	14.6	0
	600	51	24.2	0
	300	69.82	28.84	1.34
	380	80.1	6.6	13.3
	400	90	6	4

Low-Density
Polyethylene LDPE
Low-Density
Polyethylene LDPE
Polypropylene PP
Polypropylene PP
Polystyrene PS

3.3 Pyrolysis/Cracking

Pyrolysis is a process in which thermal decomposition of plastic waste takes place at various temperatures ranging from 300°C to 900°C in an oxygen free environment. Argon or nitrogen gas is typically used to create the inert atmosphere during pyrolysis. End products of this process are, biochar, bio-oil, and gases (Rehan et al., 2016; Zaman et al., 2017).

Pyrolysis is a cost-effective and energy-efficient method of transforming plastic waste into hydrocarbons. This process helps to reduce our reliance on oil while also reducing landfill waste. Substituting fossil fuel with this type of alternative energy resource could prove to be a major breakthrough in the fight against climate change.

3.4 Hydrocracking

It is a chemical process that is commonly used for transformation of heavier molecules (high boiling) into lighter ones (lower boiling point) like diesel, petrol etc. with pressure range 35 to 200 kg/cm^2 and temperature range 260-425°C. It involves breaking carbon-carbon bonds, as well as hydrogenating unsaturated hydrocarbons, in presence of hydrogen (Bhutani et al., 2006; Scherzer & Gruia, 1996; Weitkamp, 2012). Primarily, the aim is to produce of very good quality gasoline from diverse range of feedstocks, like polyvinyl chloride (PVC), polystyrene (PS), polyether terephthalate (PT-ET), polypropylene (PP) and many kinds of mixed plastics. Refineries employ transition metals and acid solids such as zeolites, silica-alumina, and sulfated zirconia to catalyze hydrocracking reactions. These catalysts take part both in pyrolysis and hydrogenation activities to produce good end products such as gasoline.

3.5 Thermal Cracking

Crude is naturally found in the Earth and comprises a blend of hydrocarbons with different molecular weights. Separation or refining of these hydrocarbons based on features like boiling point has been deemed profitable for the marketplace ("Crude Oil," 2021; Miller & Sorrell, 2014). Thermal cracking is a chemical process which breaks down large hydrocarbon molecules into smaller ones. In 1913, heavy hydrocarbons were successfully converted into motor gasoline and petroleum, revolutionizing technology and changing the way people live ("Thermal Cracking | Chemical Process | Britannica," 2023). Thermal cracking is breaking down polymeric materials which are heated in a low-oxygen environment within a temperature range of 350 to 900°C. The end products of this process are volume fraction condensable liquid hydrocarbons such as napthenes, aromatics, isoparaffins, paraffins, oelifins, non-condensable highly efficient combustion gas and carbonized char.

3.6 Catalytic Cracking

In 1836, the groundbreaking term catalysis was first introduced by the Swedish chemist Jons Jacob Berzelius and has since become an essential branch of chemistry. Catalysis is a process in which a substance called a catalyst is used to increase the rate of chemical reactions. Catalytic cracking is a proven technique for enhancing the productivity and economics of pyrolysis processes by selectively forming added amount of naphthenes and aromatics in presence of commercially-available fluid-cracking catalysts (FCC) (*(EPIC)*, 2004). Many everyday plastics such as PE and PP have undergone thorough testing, primarily using catalysts typically used in the petrochemical refinery business (*ENVIS,CPCB*, 1998).

3.7 Waste plastics Conversion to liquid Hydrocarbons by Pyrolysis

The effective conversion of plastic waste into light weight liquid hydrocarbons is determined by factors such as temperature, catalyst presence, and residence time among others. Pyrolysis reactions can either be done with a catalyst present or not. Based on this, pyrolysis

17

reactions can be classified as catalytic pyrolysis and thermal pyrolysis.

Conclusion

Production of fuel from plastics is an acceptable solution as it helps with waste management and development of substitute energy sources. It's essential to get the right combination of conversion parameters for efficient processing of combustible hydrocarbons and diesel grade fuel. These parameters include reactor design, pyrolysis temperature, catalyst selection and plastic-to-catalyst ratio - all of which can be properly optimized to maximize the production potential. Catalysts play a crucial role in making thermal conversion process more energy efficient. The type of catalyst chosen for the process is very important in order to achieve optimal fuel production.

Although there has been progress in conversion of plastic into fuel, many problems still exist. One key hurdle is PVC (polyvinyl chloride) which releases hydrochloric acid gas when it goes through pyrolysis. However, pretreatment using HCl adsorbents can reduce chlorine levels in plastics according to recent researches.

Finding the most efficient ways to produce fuel from mixed plastics is essential for protecting our environment. It's also important to filter out PET and PVC from the mix before pyrolysis takes place, which can help us harness this potential resource responsibly.

References :

A *newsletter from ENVIS Centre- Central Pollution Control Board CPCB*. (1998). Parivesh NewsLetter May 2001; Central Pollution Control Board. http://www.cpcbenvis.nic.in/cpcb_newsletter/PLASTIC%20WAST E%20MANAGEMENT.pdf

A Review of the Options for the Thermal Treatment of Plastics Prepared by: Environment and Plastics Industry Council (EPIC). (2004). http://www.resol.com.br/textos/A%20Review%20of%20the%20opti ons%20for%20the%20thermal%20treatment%20of%20plastics.pdf

Bhutani, N., Ray, A. K., & Rangaiah, G. P. (2006). Modeling, Simulation, and Multi-objective Optimization of an Industrial Hydrocracking Unit. *Industrial & Engineering Chemistry Research*, *45*(4), 1354–1372. https://doi.org/10.1021/ie050423f

Crude oil. (2021). In *Rural Electrification* (pp. 39–80). Elsevier. https://doi.org/10.1016/B978-0-12-822403-8.00003-5

Elordi, G., Olazar, M., Lopez, G., Amutio, M., Artetxe, M., Aguado, R., & Bilbao, J. (2009). Catalytic pyrolysis of HDPE in continuous mode over zeolite catalysts in a conical spouted bed reactor. *Journal of Analytical and Applied Pyrolysis*, *85*(1–2), 345–351. https://doi.org/10.1016/j.jaap.2008.10.015

Environment, U. (2022). *Plastic Pollution*. UNEP - UN Environment Programme. https://www.unep.org/plastic-pollution

Huang, S., Wang, H., Ahmad, W., Ahmad, A., Ivanovich Vatin, N., Mohamed, A. M., Deifalla, A. F., & Mehmood, I. (2022). Plastic Waste Management Strategies and Their Environmental Aspects: A Scientometric Analysis and Comprehensive Review. *International Journal of Environmental Research and Public Health*, *19*(8), 4556. https://doi.org/10.3390/ijerph19084556

Melito, S. (2022). *Thermoplastics vs. Thermoset Plastics | Material Properties | Fictiv*. Fictiv. https://www.fictiv.com/articles/thermoplastic-vs-thermoset-plastic-mechanical-properties-overview

Miller, R. G., & Sorrell, S. R. (2014). The future of oil supply. *Philosophical Transactions of the Royal Society A: Mathematical, Physical and Engineering Sciences*, *372*(2006), 20130179. https://doi.org/10.1098/rsta.2013.0179

Mohd. Wasif Quadri, Devendra Dohare, & Shri Govindram Seksaria Institute of Technology and Science Indore. (2020). A Study to Optimise Plastic to Fuel Technology-A Review. *International Journal of Engineering Research And*, *V9*(04), IJERTV9IS040137. https://doi.org/10.17577/IJERTV9IS040137

Morales-Caselles, C., Viejo, J., Martí, E., González-Fernández, D., Pragnell-Raasch, H., González-Gordillo, J. I., Montero, E., Arroyo, G. M., Hanke, G., Salvo, V. S., Basurko, O. C., Mallos, N., Lebreton, L., Echevarría, F., van Emmerik, T., Duarte, C. M., Gálvez, J. A., van Sebille, E., Galgani, F., … Cózar, A. (2021). An inshore–offshore sorting system revealed from global classification of ocean litter. *Nature Sustainability*, *4*(6), 484–493. https://doi.org/10.1038/s41893-021-00720-8

NITI Aayog -Undp Handbook on Sustainable Urban Plastic Waste Management. (1988). https://www.niti.gov.in/sites/ default/ files/ 2021-10/Final_Handbook_PWM_10112021.pdf

Panda, A. K., Singh, R. K., & Mishra, D. K. (2010). Thermolysis of waste plastics to liquid fuelA suitable method for plastic waste management and manufacture of value added products—A world prospective. *Renewable and Sustainable Energy Reviews*, *14*(1), 233–248. https://doi.org/10.1016/j.rser.2009.07.005

Passamonti, F. J., & Sedran, U. (2012). Recycling of waste plastics into fuels. LDPE conversion in FCC. *Applied Catalysis B: Environmental*, *125*, 499–506. https://doi.org/10.1016/j.apcatb. 2012.06.020

Phanisankar, B. S. S., Vasudeva Rao, N., & Manikanta, J. E. (2020). Conversion of waste plastic to fuel products. *Materials Today: Proceedings*, *33*, 5190–5195. https://doi.org/10.1016/j.matpr. 2020.02.880

Plastics Europe, 2021. (n.d.). *Plastics—The Facts 2021 An analysis of European plastics production, demand, and waste data*. Plastics Europe. Retrieved October 21, 2022, from https://plasticseurope.org/knowledge-hub/plastics-the-facts-2021/

Ragaert, K., Delva, L., & Van Geem, K. (2017). Mechanical and chemical recycling of solid plastic waste. *Waste Management*, *69*, 24–58. https://doi.org/10.1016/j.wasman.2017.07.044

Rehan, M., Nizami, A. S., Shahzad, K., Ouda, O. K. M., Ismail, I. M. I., Almeelbi, T., Iqbal, T., & Demirbas, A. (2016). Pyrolytic liquid fuel: A source of renewable electricity generation in Makkah. *Energy Sources, Part A: Recovery, Utilization, and Environmental Effects*, *38*(17), 2598–2603. https://doi.org/10.1080/15567036. 2016.1153753

Scherzer, J., & Gruia, A. J. (1996). *Hydrocracking Science and Technology* (0 ed.). CRC Press. https://doi.org/10.1201/ 9781482233889

Sharma, B. K., Moser, B. R., Vermillion, K. E., Doll, K. M., & Rajagopalan, N. (2014). Production, characterization and fuel properties of alternative diesel fuel from pyrolysis of waste plastic grocery bags. *Fuel Processing Technology*, *122*, 79–90. https://doi.org/10.1016/j.fuproc.2014.01.019

Sogancioglu, M., Yel, E., & Ahmetli, G. (2017). Pyrolysis of waste high density polyethylene (HDPE) and low density polyethylene (LDPE) plastics and production of epoxy composites with their pyrolysis chars. *Journal of Cleaner Production*, *165*, 369–381. https://doi.org/10.1016/j.jclepro.2017.07.157

Syamsiro, M., Saptoadi, H., Norsujianto, T., Noviasri, P., Cheng, S., Alimuddin, Z., & Yoshikawa, K. (2014). Fuel Oil Production from Municipal Plastic Wastes in Sequential Pyrolysis and Catalytic Reforming Reactors. *Energy Procedia*, *47*, 180–188. https://doi.org/10.1016/j.egypro.2014.01.212

Thermal cracking | chemical process | Britannica. (2023). In *Encyclopædia Britannica*. https://www.britannica.com/technology/thermal-cracking

Visual Feature | Beat Plastic Pollution. (2022). Unep.Org. https://www.unep.org/interactives/beat-plastic-pollution/#:~:text=%20butts%20%E2%80%94%20whose%20filters%20contain,the%20next%20most%20common%20items

Weitkamp, J. (2012). Catalytic Hydrocracking—Mechanisms and Versatility of the Process. *ChemCatChem*, *4*(3), 292–306. https://doi.org/10.1002/cctc.201100315

Wong, S. L., Ngadi, N., Abdullah, T. A. T., & Inuwa, I. M. (2015). Current state and future prospects of plastic waste as source of fuel: A review. *Renewable and Sustainable Energy Reviews*, *50*, 1167–1180. https://doi.org/10.1016/j.rser.2015.04.063

Zaman, C. Z., Pal, K., Yehye, W. A., Sagadevan, S., Shah, S. T., Adebisi, G. A., Marliana, E., Rafique, R. F., & Johan, R. B. (2017). Pyrolysis: A Sustainable Way to Generate Energy from Waste. In M. Samer (Ed.), *Pyrolysis*. InTech. https://doi.org/10.5772/intechopen.69036

[1,2,3]Department of Civil Engineering,
National Institute of Technology Hamirpur, H.P, India
email : 21mce406@nith.ac.in

3. Analyzing the Impact of Toxic Waste on the Environment

Subhadip Sarkar

Introduction

The background analysis of the impact of toxic wastes into atmosphere is evaluated in the section. Aim of the study defines the ill effect of Toxic industrial wastes on the health and safety of the population

Literature Review : Past researchers ideologies around the topic of the research is evaluated for designing strategies for waste management. Literature gap is identified for formulating the research framework for a suitable conclusion.

Methodology : Secondary qualitative

Findings : India has witnessed rapid industrialization over the past few decades, which has led to the generation of large amounts of hazardous waste. The enforcement of hazardous waste regulations is weak in India, which makes it easier for industries and individuals to dispose of waste improperly without facing any consequences. Toxic element leads to several health issues for human beings including, developmental disabilities, cancer, and birth defects.

Discussion : The government of India has not allocated adequate funding to address the issue of hazardous waste management, which has resulted in a lack of resources and infrastructure for proper waste disposal.

Conclusion and Recommendation: Timely collection of hazardous elements from the local places is able to maintain safety. On the other hand, reducing the use of toxic wastage-generating material is able to improve environmental health

Keywords : toxic wastes, India, Industrial sector, environment pollution, prevalence of toxic waste, prevention protocols

Introduction

The toxic waste from the industrial sector in India creates environment threats for a sustainable future. Pollution rate increases due to the emission rate of CO_2 in environment by the industrial development (Arabi et al. 2020). The managers needs to take decision on promoting sustainable practices in the firm net Zero the carbon emission rate using better waste management. The problem statement of the study is to analyse the impact of the toxic waste on the environment.

The rationale for the research identifies the strategies for waste management for reducing the threats over mankind. Moreover, the industrial development factors are analysed in the study for understanding the toxic materials extracted from the industries. Lack of sustainability practices is visible in the Indian industries that increase the toxic waste creating threats for future generation (Ramesh et al. 2022). Alternative eco friendly raw materials are needed to be selected by the company to reduce the toxic waste rates form the industries.

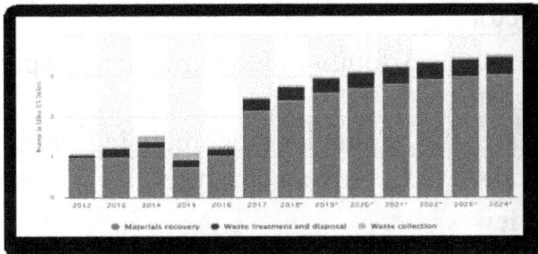

Figure 1: Waste management revenue
(Source: Statista, 2023)

Figure 1 shows the industry revenue structure generated form better waste management and disposal activities. The reputation of the industries is increased due to the systematic management of the toxic waste for a productive environment (Roosen et al. 2020). Recycled raw materials from waste management helps to improve the construction industry in India reducing the budget of project management. The study shows the approximately 3.5 billion US dollars generated will be generated from the waste treatment in India by 2024 (Statista, 2023). The study is highly significant to deal with the practices found in India for managing the wastes to improve the systems in future. Hence, additional funding is needed for the technological advancement in the industries for identifying and removing the toxic waste for sustainable growth and development.

Research Aim and Objectives The aim of the research is to provide an analysis of the impact of toxic waste on the environment.

The objectives of the study are as follows

RO1 : to examine the affect of toxic waste on environment

RO2 : To evaluate the causes of increased rate of pollution from Indian heavy industries

RO3 : To justify the practices found in India for managing the wastes

RO4 : To inspect new strategies for dealing with the toxic waste for increasing company reputation

Research Questions

RQ1 : How the toxic waste is affecting the environment?

RQ2 : What are the causes of the increasing rate of pollution from the industrial sector?

RQ3 : How the practices found in Industrial are incapable of dealing with the toxic waste?

RQ4 : What are the strategies for reducing toxic wastes and increasing reputation of the Indian company?

Literature Review

Discussing the Impact of Toxic Waste on the Environment

The toxic wastes impacts negatively on the health condition of the population creating long term health issues creating barriers for environmental sustainability. As stated by Sehnem et al. (2019), methane gas is generated from the industrial wastages creates respiratory systems related health issues in the population. On the other hand, Elmagrhi et al. (2019) have opined that the uncontrolled industrial wastes contaminates the ground water and surface water formulating threats for the human and environment. Hence, the waste control is necessary for reducing the global warming rate with reducing green house gases from the industrial sector.

Analysing the Causes for Increased Rate of Pollution from Industrial Sector

The industrial sector in India burns fossil fuel for generating energy to complete the tasks of manufacturing. As stated by Alsayegh et al. (2020), untreated liquid and gas wastes released in the environment by the industries, it creates threats for the future generation. On the contrary, Nguyen et al. (2019) have stated that improper ways of disposing the wastes increases the population rate in the atmosphere. Thus, the industrial activities of India are needed to be evaluated for formulating better mitigation techniques for environmental threats.

Strategies for Dealing with the Toxic Waste from Industrial Sector in India

The traditional techniques for waste collection are needed to be removed from Indian industries for preventing pollution rate. Moreover, the technologies used in the industries are needed to be improved for recycling the wastes for future usage. As commented by Wang et al. (2020), the renewable energy sources are needed to be used in the firms for operating the tasks minimising the pollution rate. Contradictorily, Jalaei, Zoghi & Khoshand (2021) have stated that usage of plastic in the firms is needed to be reduced to combat the toxic waste formulation. Hence, industrial pollution prevention ideologies are needed to be set for dealing with toxic waste in systematic way.

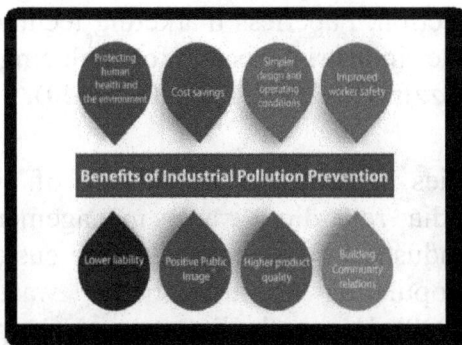

Figure 2: Industrial pollution prevention
(Source: Jalaei, Zoghi & Khoshand, 2021)

Figure 2 shows the benefits of the IPP for a sustainable development of the industrial sector increasing the reputation. The managers needs create strategies for protecting human health and environment collecting alternative resources (Jiang et al. 2019). A better community relation is created with waste recycling practices for satisfying the customers with environmental awareness.

Underpinning Theories : Waste Management Theory

The waste management theory is needed to be implemented in the industries of India for reducing the threats of environment pollution. Clean technologies are suggested by the WMT to process the wastes before disposing in the atmosphere (Aniyikaiye et al. 2019). Waste treatments are necessary for colleting the waste in a leak proof tank or location to increase the suitability of the environment.

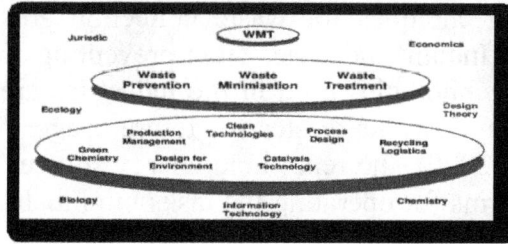

Figure 3: Waste management theory

(Source: Aniyikaiye et al. 2019)

Figure 3 shows the factors of waste management theory to instruct the managers for designing the waste prevention practices for environment protection. Paperless marketing techniques are needed to be used in the industrial sector for reducing wastes in the atmosphere (Magazzino Mele & Schneider, 2020).

Literature Gap

The study identifies a literature gap in lack of awareness in the population of India regarding waste management. Promotional activities of the industrial sector needed to be customer centric for attracting the population towards better waste management (Alsayegh et al. 2020). Hence, the literature gap helps the researcher to continue the study for finding solutions for increasing awareness of the Indian population for managing toxic wastes.

Methodology

Toxic wastages have a significant negative impact on the environment which has been discussed in this research. The study has collected the information through the secondary qualitative method. Through the secondary qualitative method, the collection of data has become easier. The extraction of information through existing information has explained the impact of various wastages like factory wastage, biomedical wastage, household wastage and many more, on the environment.

Findings

Theme 1 : Prevalence of Toxic Wastage on the Environment

The prevalence of toxic waste in the environment can vary depending on the type of waste, the quantity produced, and the disposal methods used. Inappropriate disposal of toxic waste is able to lead to environmental contamination, which can have serious consequences for both human health and the natural world (Navas et al. 2022). Toxic waste is able to contaminate soil, water, and air, leading to a range of health problems, including cancer, birth defects, and neurological damage. In this context, Shaikh & Shaikh (2021) explained, the prevalence of toxic waste in the environment is a growing concern worldwide, and many governments and organizations are taking steps to regulate and manage the production and disposal of hazardous waste. These efforts include implementing stricter regulations on industrial activities, promoting recycling and waste reduction, and encouraging the development of cleaner and safer technologies.

Theme 2 : Multiple causes Behind the High Rise of Toxic Wastage in India

India has witnessed rapid industrialization over the past few decades, which has led to the generation of large amounts of hazardous waste. Here, Sivalingam et al. (2019) mentioned, there is a severe lack of proper disposal facilities for hazardous waste in India. Many industries and households dispose of their waste in an unregulated and informal manner, leading to environmental contamination. Many people in India are not aware of the dangers of toxic waste and the proper methods for disposal. This leads to improper handling and disposal of hazardous waste (Sharma & Das, 2020). The enforcement of hazardous waste regulations is weak in India, which makes it easier for industries and individuals to dispose of waste improperly without facing any consequences.

Theme 3 : Waste Management Protocols by the Indian Government for Environmental Safety

The government of India has taken many steps to reduce the prevalence of hazardous waste. In September 2019, the government of India announced a ban on single-use plastics from 2nd October of this year (Cpcb.nic.in, 2023). During the pandemic of 2020, the government of India also actively managed biomedical wastage from hospitals by issuing guidelines. In March 2021, the government of India notified new EPR rules for e-waste management (Cpcb.nic.in, 2023).

Discussion

Toxic waste, also known as hazardous waste, is any material that poses a threat to human health or the environment if not properly disposed of. According to Rana & Sharma (2019), some common sources of toxic waste include industrial activities, such as manufacturing, mining, and chemical processing; agricultural practices, such as pesticide and fertilizer use. Household activities, such as the improper disposal of batteries, electronics, and cleaning products also considered the reason for the increase in toxic wastage in India. Turaga et al. (2019) mentioned, the government of India has not allocated adequate funding to address the issue of hazardous waste management, which has resulted in a lack of resources and infrastructure for proper waste disposal. The regulatory framework for hazardous waste management in India is weak, which makes it easier for industries and individuals to flout regulations and dispose of waste improperly (Awasthi et al. 2019). The high rise of toxic wastage in India, highlights the need for stronger regulations, increased awareness and education, and adequate funding for hazardous waste management,

Toxic element leads to several health issues for human beings including, developmental disabilities, cancer, and birth defects. It also can lead to neurological disorders and various negative conditions of the skin (Thakur et al. 2021). It has been found that the wastage is able to enter the food chain through the soil, water and air which can lead to bioaccumulation. On the other hand, toxic wastage can damage the ecosystem by destroying natural processes and reducing biodiversity. Toxic wastage can destroy the natural balance in the ecosystem and leads to the loss of natural resources like food, and minerals (Priyadarshini & Abhilash, 2020). In India, the pollution rate is increasing each year which has impacted humans, plants, animals and other living organisms poorly.

Conclusion and Recommendation

Conclusion

Managing toxic wastage is important to prevent fetal diseases from occurring. In India, the toxic wastages are causing damage to soil, water and air that cna directly enter the food chain of the human beings. The use of toxic wastages producing elements has increased, although the government has issued some serious guidelines to prevent the prevalence of waste. holding, and collecting the disposal of electronic wastages need to be done properly. There are various safety measures that need to be considered for the effective management of the toxic waste in India among which burning is the easiest solution. However, burning wastage can directly impact the health of the fieldwork. The use of the secondary qualitative process pof data collection has helped in collecting accurate information for this research.

Recommendation

Understanding the source of the toxic waste can help in managing it from generating in thye forts place. However, the government of India need to take some serious steps for controlling the prevalence of toxic waste (Navas et al. 2022). Timely collection of hazardous elements from the local places is able to maintain safety. On the other hand, reducing the use of toxic wastage-generating material is able to improve environmental health. Using specific areas for dumping the wastage and laminating it completely in a scheduled time period is able to reduce the chance of an increase in toxic wastage (Sharma & Das, 2020). The regulatory framework for hazardous waste management in India needs to be strong. Household activities, such as the improper disposal of batteries, electronics, and cleaning products also considered the reason for the increase in toxic wastage in India needs to be managed by issuing protocols.

References

Alsayegh, M. F., Abdul Rahman, R., & Homayoun, S. (2020). Corporate economic, environmental, and social sustainability performance transformation through ESGdisclosure. *Sustainability, 12*(9), 3910. Retrieved from: https://www.mdpi.com/2071-1050/12/9/3910/pdf [Retrieved on: 10/03/2023]

Aniyikaiye, T. E., Oluseyi, T., Odiyo, J. O., & Edokpayi, J. N. (2019). Physico-chemical analysis of wastewater discharge from selected paint industries in Lagos, Nigeria. *International journal of environmental research and public health, 16*(7), 1235. Retrieved from: https://www.mdpi.com/1660-4601/16/7/1235/pdf [Retrieved on: 10/03/2023]

Arabi, M., Ostovan, A., Bagheri, A. R., Guo, X., Li, J., Ma, J., & Chen, L. (2020). Hydrophilic molecularly imprinted nanospheres for the extraction of rhodamine B followed by HPLC analysis: A green approach and hazardous waste elimination. *Talanta, 215*, 120933. Retrieved from: http://ir.yic.ac.cn/bitstream/133337/25012/1/Hydrophilic%20molecularly%20imprinted%20nanospheres%20for%20the%20extraction%20of%20rhodamine%20B%20followed%20by%20HPLC%20analysis%20A%20green%20approach%20and%20hazardous%20waste%20elimination.pdf [Retrieved on: 10/03/2023]

Awasthi, A. K., Li, J., Koh, L., & Ogunseitan, O. A. (2019). Circular economy and electronic waste. *Nature Electronics, 2*(3), 86-89. DOI 10.1038/s41928-019-0225-2

Cpcb.nic.in, 2023 Waste management Retrieved from: https://cpcb.nic.in/waste-management/ On 10th march, 2023

Elmagrhi, M. H., Ntim, C. G., Elamer, A. A., & Zhang, Q. (2019). A study of environmental policies and regulations, governance structures, and environmental performance: The role of female directors. *Business strategy and the environment, 28*(1), 206-220. Retrieved from: https://eprints.soton.ac.uk/425077/1/Accepted_BSE_Manuscript_9_October_2018.pdf [Retrieved on: 10/03/2023]

Jalaei, F., Zoghi, M., & Khoshand, A. (2021). Life cycle environmental impact assessment to manage and optimize construction waste using Building Information Modeling (BIM). *International Journal of Construction Management*, *21*(8), 784-801. Retrieved from: https://www.researchgate.net/ profile/ Milad-Zoghi/publication/332068603_Life_cycle_environmental_impact_as sessment_to_manage_and_optimize_construction_waste_using_Buil ding_Information_Modeling_BIM/links/5d81fb85a6fdcc8fd6f14cde /Life-cycle-environmental-impact-assessment-to-manage-and-optimize-construction-waste-using-Building-Information-Modeling-BIM.pdf [Retrieved on: 10/03/2023]

Jiang, B., Adebayo, A., Jia, J., Xing, Y., Deng, S., Guo, L., ... & Zhang, D. (2019). Impacts of heavy metals and soil properties at a Nigerian e-waste site on soil microbial community. *Journal of hazardous materials*, *362*, 187-195. Retrieved from: https://www.academia.edu/download/87583419/j.jhazmat.2018.08.0 6020220616-1-sbb82w.pdf [Retrieved on: 10/03/2023]

Magazzino, C., Mele, M., & Schneider, N. (2020). The relationship between municipal solid waste and greenhouse gas emissions: Evidence from Switzerland. *Waste Management*, *113*, 508-520. Retrieved from: https://www.academia.edu/download/ 64541321/ Waste_fascia%20A.pdf [Retrieved on: 10/03/2023]

Navas, G., D'Alisa, G., & Martínez-Alier, J. (2022). The role of working-class communities and the slow violence of toxic pollution in environmental health conflicts: A global perspective. *Global Environmental Change*, *73*, 102474. https://doi.org/10.1016/ j.gloenvcha.2022.102474

Nguyen, B., Claveau-Mallet, D., Hernandez, L. M., Xu, E. G., Farner, J. M., & Tufenkji, N. (2019). Separation and analysis of microplastics and nanoplastics in complex environmental samples. *Accounts of chemical research*, *52*(4), 858-866. Retrieved from:https://escholarship.mcgill.ca/downloads/rx913t61w [Retrieved on: 10/03/2023]

Priyadarshini, P., & Abhilash, P. C. (2020). Circular economy practices within energy and waste management sectors of India: A meta-analysis. *Bioresource Technology*, *304*, 123018. https://www.academia.edu/download/89311518/j.biortech.2020.123 01820220806-1-1p7grnx.pdf

Ramesh, M., Deepa, C., Kumar, L. R., Sanjay, M. R., & Siengchin, S. (2022). Life-cycle and environmental impact assessments on processing of plant fibres and its bio-composites: A critical review. *Journal of Industrial Textiles*, *51*(4_suppl), 5518S-5542S. Retrieved from: https://journals.sagepub.com/doi/pdf/10.1177/1528083720924730 [Retrieved on: 10/03/2023]

Rana, R., & Sharma, M. (2019). Dynamic causality testing for EKC hypothesis, pollution haven hypothesis and international trade in India. *The Journal of International Trade & Economic Development*, *28*(3), 348-364. DOI: 10.1080/09638199.2018.1542451

Roosen, M., Mys, N., Kusenberg, M., Billen, P., Dumoulin, A., Dewulf, J., ... & De Meester, S. (2020). Detailed analysis of the composition of selected plastic packaging waste products and its implications for mechanical and thermochemical recycling. *Environmental science & technology*, *54*(20), 13282-13293. Retrieved from: https://pubs.acs.org/doi/pdf/10.1021/acs.est.0c03371 [Retrieved on: 10/03/2023]

Sehnem, S., Vazquez-Brust, D., Pereira, S. C. F., & Campos, L. M. (2019). Circular economy: benefits, impacts and overlapping. *Supply Chain Management: An International Journal*, *24*(6), 784-804. Retrieved from: https://pesquisa-eaesp.fgv.br/sites/gvpesquisa.fgv.br/files/arquivos/circular_0.pdf [Retrieved on: 10/03/2023]

Shaikh, I. V., & Shaikh, V. A. E. (2021). A comprehensive review on assessment of plastic debris in aquatic environment and its prevalence in fishes and other aquatic animals in India. *Science of the Total Environment*, *779*, 146421. https://doi.org/10.1016/j.scitotenv.2021.146421

Sharma, E., & Das, S. (2020). Measuring impact of Indian ports on environment and effectiveness of remedial measures towards environmental pollution. *International Journal of Environment and Waste Management*, *25*(3), 356-380. doi:10.2202/1446-9022.1049

Sivalingam, P., Poté, J., & Prabakar, K. (2019). Environmental prevalence of carbapenem resistance Enterobacteriaceae (CRE) in a tropical ecosystem in India: human health perspectives and future directives. *Pathogens*, *8*(4), 174. doi:10.3390/pathogens8040174

Statista (2023), Industry revenue of "Waste collection, treatment and disposal activities" in India from 2012 to 2024, Retrieved from: https://www.statista.com/forecasts/1054323/waste-collection-treatment-and-disposal-activities-revenue-in-india   [Retrieved on: 10/03/2023]

Thakur, V., Mangla, S. K., & Tiwari, B. (2021). Managing healthcare waste for sustainable environmental development: A hybrid decision approach. *Business Strategy and the Environment*, *30*(1), 357-373. https://onlinelibrary.wiley.com/doi/pdfdirect/10.1002/bse.2625

Turaga, R. M. R., Bhaskar, K., Sinha, S., Hinchliffe, D., Hemkhaus, M., Arora, R., ... & Sharma, H. (2019). E-waste management in India: issues and strategies. *Vikalpa*, *44*(3), 127-162. DOI: 10.1177/0256090919880655

Wang, C., Zhao, L., Lim, M. K., Chen, W. Q., & Sutherland, J. W. (2020). Structure of the global plastic waste trade network and the impact of China's import Ban. *Resources, Conservation and Recycling*, *153*, 104591. Retrieved from: https://pure.coventry.ac.uk/ws/files/26656601/Wang_et_al_Structure_Global_Plastic_Waste_RCR_A4.pdf [Retrieved on: 10/03/2023]

**Assistant Professor,
Department of Civil Engineering,
SEACOM Skills University, Bolpur,
Birbhum, West Bengal
email : Subhadipsarkar555@gmail.com**

4. Survival of Mammalian Diversity in and around Human Landscape, Thar Desert, Rajasthan

Aazad P. Ojha[1*],
L. S. Rajpurohit[1],
Mamta Sharma[2],
A. K.Chhangani [3]

Abstract

The present study was carried out in and around Jodhpur city in human landscape area, Thar desert of Rajasthan. This study emphasize on list out mammalian diversity in different sub habitat type in human landscape, which supports and play important role in ecosystem, maintaining food chain and sustaining desert biodiversity. We also listed the emerging threats, which causing drastic change in mammalian population and this also give an understanding how wild mammals survive in human landscape in the changing climate situation in the study area. Thar desert is characterized with low rainfall, high temperature, and many climatic events like dusty wind storms and rainy winters etc. Due to growing urbanization, many roads have been constructed to connect cities, towns and villages, which led to habitat destruction of wild areas. Due to variety of habitats and micro ecosystem, this desert area harbor many distinct consumer species including amphibian, reptilian, avian and mammalian species. The unique mammalian species of Thar desert includes- *Canis lupus* (Indian grey wolf), *Hyaena hyaena* (Hyaena), *Canis aureus* (Golden jackal), *Felis sylvestris* (Desert cat), *Gazelle bennetti* (Chinkara), *Boselaphus tragocamelus* (Blue bull), *Antelope cervicapra* (Black buck), *Sus scrofa* (Wild boar), *Hystrix indica* (Porcupine), *Lepus tibetanus* (Desert hare), *Semnopithecus entellus* (Hanuman langur) *etc.* Conservation of mammalian predator species is imperative to regulate the ecosystem and food chain.

Keywords : Mammals, human landscape, Prey-predator, Crop raiding, Conservation.

Introduction

Density and abundance of mammalian species play an important role in the ecosystem and to sustain the species population in the area. Availability of prey mammalian species like small mammals and other herbivore animals, which being listed further in the context, is the most important factor for determining carnivore distribution across habitat types and their overall abundance (Carbme&Gittleman, 2002). This study list out mammalian diversity in different sub habitat type in and around human landscape, which supports and play important role in ecosystem specially food chain and sustaining desert biodiversity. Development, growing urbanization, change in agricultural and land use, animal husbandry etc. has affected their population in the study area and human wildlife relation. In semiarid areas with high human density, the forests are highly fragmented with minimal water resources resulting in increased dependency on restricted available resources (Malagnoux*et al.* 2007; Gibbs, 2000). Thar desert Thar desert is characterized with low rainfall, high temperature (can exceed 50 °C during summer and below 5 °C in winters), and many climatic events like dusty wind storms and rainy winters etc. Due to growing urbanization, many roads have been constructed to connect cities, towns and villages, which led to habitat destruction of wild areas. Due to variety of habitats and micro ecosystem, this desert area harbor many distinct consumer species including amphibian, reptilian, avian and mammalian species. In this paper, we are presenting the findings on mammalian species diversity, their major threats, their interaction with other species including human and their conservational management in different human landscape of the Thar desert . The unique mammalian species of Thar desert includes- *Canis lupus* (Indian grey wolf), *Hyaena hyaena* (Hyaena), *Canis aureus* (Golden jackal), *Felis sylvestris* (Desert cat), *Gazelle bennetti*(Chinkara), *Sus scrofa* (Wild boar), *Boselaphus tragocamelus* (Blue bull), *Antelope cervicapra* (Black buck), *Semnopithecus entellus* (Hanuman langur) *Hystrix indica* (Porcupine), *Lepus tibetanus* (Desert hare), *etc.* The mammalian species observed in study area are surviving well in human landscape in the deserts (Prakash, 1994;1995), some of the species like Hanuman langurs are buffered against catastrophic die-off during ENSO-related drought in human landscape (Wait *et al.*,2007b). Rodents are numerically the most abundant species of desert lands around the world, and in Thar desert too (Prakash, 1975). Several species are facing problems in the wild for survive because of developmental activities, climate change, habitat loss, grazing pressure, illegal mining, etc. (Ojha *et al.* 2017).

Material and Methods

The Study was conducted in and around Jodhpur city (within 30-40 km area) in different areas like fellow lands, agricultural lands, rocky areas, sacred grooves (Oran and Gaucher land), and different community based rural areas. Jodhpur lies in semi-arid region of Thar desert between $26^{\circ},00'$ and 27°, 37' N latitude and $72^{\circ},55'$ and $73^{\circ},52'$ E longitude with fluctuated climate, winter being cold and some time with rain and summer are hotter. The altitudinal elevation of Jodhpur from sea level is of 250-300 meters above sea level. For the extensive survey and data collection, four sample areas were selected. The sites selected in terms of occurrence as high number of mammalian species, low and high human interference zone and various micro ecosystem. The sampling sites were named as site (A), site(B), site (C), and site (D) (*see figure 1*). This study was conducted from March 2016 to March 2020. Data were collected and recorded regarding population sighted, individual counts and samples like scats, palates, pug marks, hair etc. were collected to identify species. Further,the local people interviewed, a total 260 people of 18 - 75 year age group including male and female were interviewed and necessary information was gathered. For direct behavioral observation of mammalian species scan and Ad libitum methods were used (Altman, 1974), Photography with DSLR, camera trap etc. and scats, footmarks, body parts sample like hairs etc. for indirect evidences were followed. Indirect samples were collected on transects, tracks, and roads and off roads whenever encountered within the intensive study area. Mammalian diversity of the study area was calculated using Shannon Diversity Index (**H**). Formula for calculating value as follow-

$$H = \Sigma \, (pi)(\ln pi)$$

If there is only one species present or no diversity then the value of H = 0

To calculate the index, the first **relative abundance** of each species which denoted by symbol'*pi*'is calculated and expressed as =

$$pi = ni/\,N$$

Whereas**ni** = Number of individual species i

N = Total number of individuals of all species.

The maximum value for the Shannon index **(Hmax)**is calculated by

– Hmax = lnS

Where **S** is the **species richness** of a given sample or community and in is the natural logarithm.

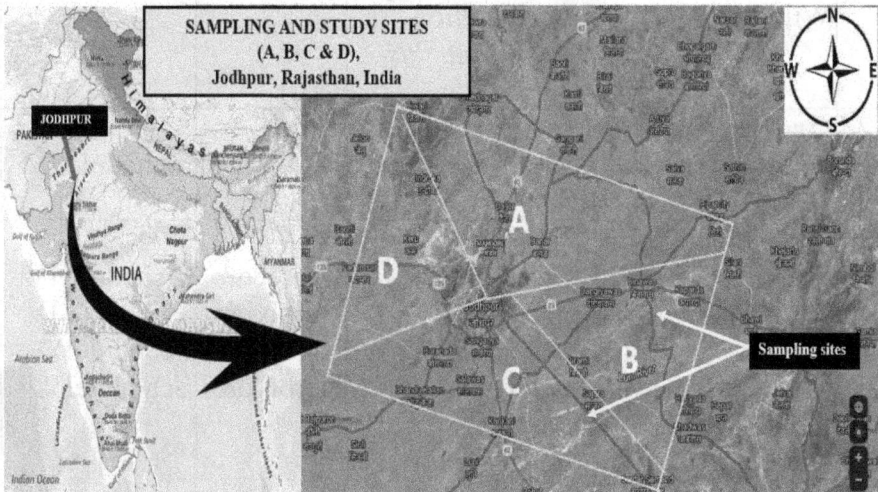

Figure 1: Map showing sampling and study sites A, B, C, and D, marked within rectangle line (green color line).

Map source 1. India map – surveyofindia.gov.in; 2. Satellite map view- Google map

Observation and Results

During study it was found that habitat under study has been adversely affected due to growing human population, change in landscapes, increasing dog population in highways and roads lies in the study area,as a result mortality of many wild species increased in recent past by road accidents, dogs predation, stuck in the farm fencing, diseases or poisoning etc. List of mammalian species recorded with their feeding habit and wildlife protection act, 1972 statusis given in *table-1*.

Table 1: List of Mammalian fauna with conservation status as per the Indian Wildlife Protection Act, 1972.

S N	Species Common Name	Zoological Name	Habit type	Status as Per WPA 1972
1	**Order:** **Artiodactyl** Chinkara Black buck Blue bull Wild boar	*Gazella* *bennetti* *Antilope* *cervicapra* *Boselaphus* *tragocamelus* *Sus scrofa*	Herbivore Herbivore Herbivore Omnivore	Schedule I Schedule I Schedule III Schedule III
2	**Order:** **Lagomorphs** Desert Hare	*Lepus tibetanus*	Herbivore	Schedule IV
3	**Order: Rodentia** Five stripped palm squirrels Indian crested porcupine Indian gerbils Desrtjird	*Funambuluspen nantii* *Hystrix indica* *Tatera indica* *Meriones hurrianae*	Herbivore Herbivore Herbivore Herbivore	Schedule IV Schedule IV ScheduleIV ScheduleIV
4	**Order:** **Insectivora** Hedgehog Grey musk shrews	*Hemiechinus collaris* *Suncusmurinus*	Insectivore Insectivore	ScheduleIV
5	**Order:** **Carnivora** Indian grey wolf Hyeana	*Canis lupus* *Hyaena hyaena* *Canis aureus*	Carnivore Carnivore Carnivore	Schedule I ScheduleIII Schedule II

	Golden jackal	*Vulpes*	Omnivore	Schedule I
	Desert fox	*vulpespussila*	Omnivore	Schedule II
	Indian fox	*Vulpes*	Carnivore	Schedule I
	Desert cat	*bengalensis*	Carnivore	Schedule II
	Jungle cat	*Felis sylvestris*	Carnivore	Schedule II
	Indian common	*Felis chaus*	Carnivore	Schedule II
	civet	*Viverricula*	Carnivore	Schedule II
	Indian small	*indica*	Carnivore	Schedule II
	mongoose	*Herpestes*		
	Ruddy mongoose	*javanicus*		
	Common	*Herpestes*		
	mongoose	*smithii*		
		Herpestes		
		edwardsii		
6	**Order: <u>Primates</u>**			
	Hanuman langur	*Semnopithecus entellus*	Herbivore	Schedule II
7	**Order: <u>Chiroptera</u>**			
	Indian flying fox	*Pteropusgigant us*	Herbivore	ScheduleIV

(Note :WPA- Wildlife Protection Act.)

The diverse mammalian fauna is found to be due to presence of many traditional conservational methods such as religious based, artificial feeding, sacred grooves and large population of mammals dependency on human subsidies. In recent studies, protection at community level on religious aspect plays important role in western Rajasthan. People do not kill and harm animals because animals is connected with Gods name and power in Hindu mythology. A good example of this system is protection in Oran lands. Oran lands are left over geographical areas on the name of local God or Goddess, where hunting, poaching, capturing of wild animals is strictly prohibited in these areas and no agricultural practices and cutting of trees are allowed here (Ojha *et al.* 2017). Other reason of this high diversity is due to Human subsidies. The type of human subsidies are artificial food provisioning, and water bodies localy called Kheli made by local people for their livestock directly benefit to wild animals in severe drought condition during summer season in the study area. In Kumbhalgarh wildlife sanctuary, the Hanuman langur population suffered a disastrous decline. Similarly, the langur population in an adjacent protected area, the Tadgahr-Raoli wildlife sanctuary, suffered a 20% reduction from 1999 to 2001 (Waite *et al.* 2007a) while in Jodhpur, langur population remained unaffected, suggesting that langurs were defended against the drought. Thus artificial provisioning to langurs in Jodhpur area break out the drought (Wait *et al.* 2007b). Ojha and Rajpurohit (2018) also reported that people provide artificial feeding to birds (pigeon, crow, house sparrow etc.) in form of bread, biscuit and cereals due to religious and cultural aspects. The leftover foodstuffs in night consumed by Indian crsted porcupine in Jodhpur city and other part of western Rajasthan. We have reported dependency of Indian palm civet on artificial food provisioning and leftover foods in Parsurammahadev temple region, Aravalli region of Rajasthan. This availability of artificial food has changed species behavior but it has become a major cause of survival and well reproductive success in such areas. Thus, wildlife is benefited with the presence of human around them and human subsidies plays vital role in survival of these species in TD.

The observed floral diversity of the study area includes-Babool (*Acacia nilotica*), Rohira (*Ticomella undulata*), Kumath (*Acacia senegal*), Jaal (*Salvadora persica*), Khejri (*Prosopis cineraria*), Ker (*Capparis decidua*), Pipal (*Ficus religiosa*), Bargad (*Ficus bengalensis*), Neem (*Azadirachta indica*), Ber (*Ziziphus nummularia*), Aak (*Calotropus procera*),Thor (*Euphorbia caducifolia*),Guggal(*Commiphora wightii*), Bawlia (*Vachellia jacquemontii*), Kheemp (*Leptadenia pyrotechnica*), Bui (*Aerva persica*), Phog (*Calligonum polygonoides*), Arna *(Clerodendurm phlomidis),* Grass *(Cymbopogon jwarancusa) etc.*This floral diversity along with agriculture and horticulture crops might be one of the reasons that thrives mammalian species abundance and these animals play important role in sustaining floral diversity by helping in pollination and seed dispersal. Land use pattern of Jodhpur district have total area as per village record is 2256405 hectare, out of which 7032 ha. (0.31%) areas under forest, 122713 ha. (5.43%) permanent pasture and grazing lands and 1410944 ha. (62.53%) area being cultivated. Major crops grown in and around Jodhpur includes Rabi and Khareef crops. Rabi includes Wheat, Barley (cereals), Grams, Pulses, and Rape and Mustard, Taramira and Linseed (Oilseeds) while Khareef includes Paddy, Jowar, Bajra, Maize, Millets (cereals), Moong, Moth, Urad, Chaula and other (pulses), Seesam, Groundnut, Soybean, castor (oilseeds), and Cotton, Sugarcane etc (www.agriculture.rajasthan.gov.in). Grazer species optimally utilize floral food resources while some mammalian species found to be raiders in croplands (*see figure 2*) e.g. Blue Bull and Wild Boars.

The study was conducted in different sub-habitat types of human landscape and species inhabiting such sub-habitats were recorded (see *table-3*). It is clear from the table 3 that the rocky scrub and sandy rocky mixed sub-habitat type shows maximum diversity. These sub-habitat types represent important predator species like Wolf, Jackal, Hyaena, Desert fox, Desert cat etc. while sandy scrub and agricultural areas have major herbivore species and rodent population.

Table 3 : Species observed in different sub- habitat types of human landscape.

S. N.	Type of Sub-Habitat	Observed Mammalian species in study area
1	Rocky scrub	Wolf, jackal, hyaena, desert fox, desert cat, jungle cat, chinkara, black buck, blue bull, wild boars, Hanuman langur porcupine, mongoose, civets, bats and rodents.
2	Sandy scrub	Desert fox, Indian fox, desert cat, chinkara, blue bull, wild boars, mongoose, hedgehog and rodents.
3	Sandy and rocky mixed scrub area	Wolf, jackal, hyaena, desert fox, desert cat,chinkara, black buck, blue bull, wild boars,Hanuman langur,porcupine, mongoose,

		bats, and rodents.
4	Agricultural area	Desert fox, chinkara, black buck, blue bull, wild boars, Hanuman langur, porcupine, desert hare, hedgehog androdents.

Livestock population of Jodhpur according to Rajasthan livestock census (2012) is 3590264. Different livestock population recorded as per Rajasthan livestock census (2012) have mentioned in *table-4*. **Table 4**: Livestock population recorded as per Rajasthan livestock census (2012).

SN	Common Name	Scientific Name	Population
1	Cow	*Bos tarusindicus.*	848343
2	Buffalo	*Bubalus bubalis*	305238
3	Sheep	*Ovis aries.*	731229
4	Goat	*Capra aegagrushircus.*	1681913
5	Camel	*Camelus bactrianus*	16749
6	Donkey	*Equus hemionus*	4176
7	Horses	*Equus ferus*	1616

Table 5. Crop raiding mammalian specie recordedon the basis of Interviews of local communities (N=260).

SN	Sampling site (Village's croplands)	Crop raider species	Crop loss
1	A: Tinwri, Karwad, Manaklao, Bhawad	Blue bull, wild boar, chinkara,porcupine and rodents	5%
2	B: Devaliya, Dangiwas, Ramrawaskalan	Blue bull, wild boar, chinkara, porcupine and rodents	6 %
3	C: GudaBishnoi, Khejarla, Kankani, Luni	Blue bull, wild boar, chinkara, porcupine, jackal and rodents	10%

4	D: Keru, Arna, Barli, Moklawas	Blue bull, wild boar, chinkara, Hanuman langur, porcupine, and rodents	8%

Table 6: Observed predator and predation cases in the study area.

SN	Wild and Domestic(Livestock) species	Observed Predator	Observed species with numbers	Total observed predation cases
A.	**Wild Species**			
1.	Chinkara (*Gazella bennetti*)	Wolf, Feral dogs, Jackal	Wolf (5) Dogs (12) Jackal (1) Fox (0)	18
2.	Black buck (*Antilope cervicapra*)	Wolf, Feral dogs	Wolf (8) Dogs (13) Jackal (0) Fox (0)	21
3.	Blue bull (*Boselaphus tragocamelus*)	Wolf, Feral dogs, Jackal	Wolf (4) Dogs (7) Jackal (0) Fox (0)	11
4.	Wild boar (*Sus scrofa*)	Wolf	Wolf (1) Dogs(0) Jackal (0) Fox (0)	01
5.	Desert Hare (*Lepus tibetanus*)	Wolf, Jackal, Desert fox, Feral dogs	Wolf (7) Dogs (23) Jackal (5) Fox (9)	44
6.	Indian crested porcupine (*Hystrix indica*)	Wolf, Feral dogs,	Wolf (4) Dogs (9) Jackal (0) Fox (0)	13
7.	Gerbils (*Tatera indica*)&Jird (*Meriones spc.*)	Wolf, Jackal, Desert fox, Feral dogs	Wolf (5) Dogs (20) Jackal (21) Fox (26)	72
8.	Mongoose (*Herpestes spc.*)	Wolf, Feral dogs	Wolf (2) Dogs (3) Jackal (0) Fox (0)	05
9.	Hanuman langur (*Semnopithecus entellus*)	Feral dogs	Wolf (0) Dogs (1) Jackal (0) Fox (0)	01
B	**Domestic Species**			
1	Cow (*Bos tarusindicus.*)	Wolf	Wolf (1) Dogs (0) Jackal (0) Fox (0)	01
2	Buffalo (*Bubalus bubalis*)	*No predator*	Wolf (0) Dogs (0) Jackal (0) Fox (0)	00
3	Sheep (*Ovis aries*)	Wolf	Wolf (33) Dogs (0) Jackal (1) Fox (0)	34
4	Goat (*Capra aegagrushircus*)	Wolf	Wolf (12) Dogs (0) Jackal (0) Fox (0)	12
5	Camel (*Camelus bactrianus*)	*No predator*	Wolf (0) Dogs (0) Jackal (0) Fox (0)	00
6	Donkey (*Equus hemionus*)	*No predator*	W(0) D(0) J(0) F(0)	00
7	Horses (*Equus ferus*)	*No predator*	W(0) D(0) J(0) F(0)	00

By studying different croplands area in study (sampling) site (A), site (B), site (C) and site (D) (*see figure 1.*) , The crop raiding by various species were recorded during the day and night. Details of the crop raiding by different mammalian species at various sample sites (A), (B), (C), and (D) in the study area were recorded through direct observations and Interviews with the local community (N = 260) is given in the *table-5*. Thus, there is always exist mutual and harmful interaction between human and wildlife. It is observed that blue bull and wild boar are being the major crop raiders and causes major economic loss to the farmers in these areas where there is predation as in sampling site A and B is comparatively lesser economic loss have been observed mainly due to prey predator interaction which controls these raiding activity. Thus, these interactions are essential to sustain the high mammalian diversity in these areas.

Besides the crop raid the major issue of human wildlife conflict is the livestock depredation by the carnivores. It was found that the major predator of the study area includes *Canis lupus, Canis aureus, Canis familiaris* and *Vulpes vulpespussila*. Total number of the prey and predator cases in the study area are given in the *table 6*. Data gathered from scat analysis, verbal interview and from direct observations during study. From the observed data, it is clear that livestock population and available herbivore prey species are responsible for the survival of top predator the wolf. Other major predator being the feral dogs, which is becoming threat to many prey species. Feral dogs attacks and kill many different mammalian prey species, which has led to drastic population decline of prey species like chinkara, black buck, porcupine etc. During study, we observed that the area where wolves inhabit, feral dog population and their attack case is much lower. Thus, conservation of one major predator species like wolf is important in the study area to run ecosystem smoothly.

Observation and results clearly suggest that the wolf of the study area in human landscape subsidies by the local people in term of livestock depredation specially goat and sheep. Similarly, protection of chinkara and other ungulates by the local community provide enough food to the wolf population of the study area during scarcity of livestock food and during migration.

Figure 2: Pictures A-I showing different mammalian prey species observed amid field study (A- chinkara; B- Blue bull; C- Black buck; D- Indian crested porcupine; E- Hedgehog; F- Wild boar; G- Indian jird; H- Desert hare; I- Common mongoose)

We identified different kind of mortality cases of the mammalian species amid extensive field study. It is observed that mortality was caused by various threats (mentioned in *table 4)* and due to this, lowest occurring species like Wolf, Hyaena, Jackal, Desert fox and other ecological important species is being lost and threatened in this desert ecosystem. Amid study, it is found that major cause of mortality are road accidents, feral dog attacks and habitat loss due to growing industrialization, urbanization, rock mining, soil mining and many other anthropological reasons. By this anthropogenic activities, these species survival in near future is question marked '?'.

Table 7: Threats to mammalian species observed in study area.

SN	Type of Threats	Species affected in study area
1	Road accident	Wolf, Jackal, Desert Fox, Desert Cat, Porcupine, Mongoose, Chinkara, Blue Bull, Wild Boar, Black Buck, Hanuman langur, Civets, Desert Hare, Hedgehog and Rodents.
2	Stuck in fencing	Chinkara, Black Buck, and Blue Bull
3	Predation by feral dog	Desert Fox, Desert Cat, Chinkara, Black Buck, Blue Bull, Hanuman Langur, Porcupine, Desert Hare, and Mongoose
4	Electric shock	Hanuman Langur, Civets, Bats
5	Predation by Wild Carnivore Predator	Chinkara, Blue Bull, Black Buck, Desert Hare, and Rodents
6	Habitat loss	Wolf, Jackal, Hyaena, Desert Cat, Civets and Jungle Cat.
7	Hunting/Poaching/	Chinkara, Black Buck, Desert Hare, Captivity: Hyaena, Jackal and Wolf.
8	Natural calamities	Most all species affacted
9	Diseased and Poisioning	Wolf, Hyaena, Jackal, Hanuman Langur
10	Unsystematic management	Wolf, Hyaena and Jackal

Discussion

By observing and calculating data obtained during extensive field study it is concluded that the study area is species rich in terms of mammalian speciesdiversity, that is directly indicating to sustainingall trophic levels of the food chain in TD regions. Predator species data have also obtained and concluded that the Wolf, Jackal, Fox, Hyaena are major predator animals although there population are very less because of habitat degradation continuously occurring by anthropogenic activity. Rajpurohit *et al.* (2011)reported five predator species in outskirt area of Jodhpur city viz. Indian grey wolf (C*anis lupus*), Stripedhyaena (*Hyaena hyaena*), Golden jackal (*Canis aureus*), Desert fox (*Vulpes vulpes pusilla*) and the Common mongoose (*Herpestes edwardsii*). Ghosh (1996) reported 50 mammalian species in the arid area of western Rajasthan in his work.

Wildlife living in and around human landscape interacts with human beings, which vary in strength from low to high, and frequency from least to general on a range from positive and neutral over to negative. Negative interactions, can be called as human wildlife conflict (Graham *et al.* 2005). Fascinatingly, positive human wildlife interaction has no described term as negative interaction, which reflect the bias towards negative interactions in the writings (Peterson *et al.* 2010). The most straight influence of wildlife on humans is that of attacks which probably for defense, territorial, predatory and for protecting their young (Conover, 2001). Ojha and Rajpurohit (2018) reported first case of wolf attack on human in Jodhpur area of Thar desert. During the period of study, interaction between human and mammalian species were studied. We found that the crop raiding by herbivores and omnivores and livestock predation by carnivores in the study area are the major issues of conflicts.

Species diversity plays very important role in development of ancient human societies, croplands and industrial organizations as while biodiversity is the base upon that human civilization was built (Khan, 1997). Saxena and Prakash, (1992) stated that the livestock in TD is much high that exert depletion of the biological diversity due to over grazing by them. They stated that the ungulates are the major consumers of vegetation, e.g. the blue bull (*Boselaphus tragocamelus*), blackbuck (*Antelope cervicapra*), chinkara (*Gazelle bennetti*) and wild boar (*Sus scrofa*). Other primary consumer includes desert hares (*Lepus nigricollis*), langurs (*Semnopithecus entellus*) and squirrels (*Funambuluspennanti*) with fairly large population sizes.The high numbers of herbivore observed amid study indicates the grazing pressure is increasing which might disturb the ecological food chain of this area. This herbivore species support predator species in this ecosystem and predators regulate the numbers of these grazer's species indicating prey predator relationship in the study area. Wolves have been observed in area with abundant livestock and wild herbivore prey species. Singh and Kumara (2006) reported that the occurrence of wolves lies outside the conserved area and wolves mainly depends on domestic animals for sustenance. Ojha *et al.*, (2019) also observed that wolves in human landscape subsidies by the villagers in terms of devastation specially sheep and goat. They inferred that the protection of chinkara and black buck by the local communities provide enough food for the wolves during shortage of livestock. We observed that predation of wolf was mainly on livestock and wild animals. Many threats have been found to disturb these animals (*table 7*) among which feral dog attacks, road accident and habitat loss being the major threat to mammalian diversity in this study area. Thus, although study area having rich mammalian prey species but these prey species facing severe problems for survival. Among these, prey species viz. wild boar and blue bull's population have been increased tremendously that causing serious problems for the villagers and farmers. For the regulation of these primary consumer species, carnivore predator species should be conserved and their population must be increased so that they can control prey species population to run the ecosystem smoothly. Similarly, we found that the wolf population of the human landscape and community lands are less affected in the drought conditions, compared to the protected area population as observed in other studies (Waite et al., 2007; Chhangani et al., 2018 and Ojha et al 2019)

Besides threats and importance, conservation of this mammalian diversity is as important as conserving wild habitats of the western Rajasthan desert ecosystem. For the conservation, Different type of human subsidies are playing important role. Type of human subsidies by which wild animals are being protected includes- artificial feeding in form of cereals, vegetation, fruits etc, artificial water bodies localy called kheli made for livestock of local villagers also provide water to the wild animal species in extreme summer temperatures.

Thus, conservation of carnivore species is imperative because by conserving them, crop raiders activity can be controlled and grazing pressure can be reduced.

Acknowledgement

Our sincere thanks to Prof. V. K. Singh, vice-chancellor, M.G.S. University, Bikaner, for providing facilities. A sincere thanks to CSIR, New Delhi for providing financial support to Aazad P. Ojha for carry out this research work.We thank animal behavior unit, department of zoology, J.N.V. University, Jodhpur for providing facility to carry out this research work.We thank local people of the study area for providing necessary information and cooperation during intense fieldwork by providing shelter and food.

References :

1. Altmann, J. (1974). Observational study of behavior, sampling methods. *Behaviour*, 49, pp. 227-267.
2. Animal welfare board of India (2020). Mammals schedule species list. Retrieved 31 July, 2020 from http://www.awbi.in/awbi-pdf/wlp.pdf.
3. Conover, M. R. (2001). 'Resolving human-wildlife conflicts: the science of wildlife damage management.' (CRC Press, Florida).
4. Ghosh A.K. (1996). The thar desert ecosystem : In faunal diversity in the Thar desert, Gaps in research, Scipublishers,Jodhpur, 1-18.
5. Gibbs, J. P. (2000) Wetland loss and biodiversity conservation. *Conserv. Biol.*, 14, pp. 314–317.
6. Government of Rajasthan (Agricultural Department) web portal (2020). Jodhpur division. Retrieved 28 April, 2020 from http://www.agriculture.rajasthan.gov.in/content/ agriculture /en/Agriculture-Department-dep/contact-directory/jodhpur-division.html.
7. Government of Rajasthan (Animal Husbandry Department) web portal (2020). Livestock census. Retrieved 30 April, 2020 from http://animalhusbandry.rajasthan.gov.in/ livestock_census .aspx.
8. Graham, K., Beckerman A.P., and Thirgood S. (2005) Human predator-prey conflicts: ecological correlates, prey losses and patterns of management. Biological Conservation 122, pp. 159–171.

9. India Map (2019). Retrieved August 01, 2020 from http://www.surveyofindia.gov.in/pages/ show/86-mapsdata.

10. Indian Council of Agricultural Research (2020). KrishiVigyan Kendra, Jodhpur II: District profile. Retrieved 02 May, 2020, from http://jodhpur2.kvk2.in/district-profile.html.

11. IUCN (2020). Retrieved 30 July, 2020 from www.iucn.org/asia/countries/india.

12. Khan, T. I. (1997). Conservation of biodiversity in western area. The Environmentalist 17, pp. 283-287

13. Malagnoux, M., Sène, E. H. and Atzmon, N., Forests, trees and water in arid lands: a delicate balance. *Unasylva*, 2007, 58, pp. 24–29.

14. Ojha, A. P., Meena, A. K., Sharma, G., & Rajpurohit, L. S. (2017). Human Awareness and Wildlife Conservation in Western Rajasthan. *International Research Journal of Commerce Arts and Science,* 8(9), pp. 170-176.

15. Ojha, A.P. (2018). To study the resilience, ecology and conservation of large mammals in Indian Thar desert. Ph.D. Thesis. Dept. of zoology, J.N.V.U. Jodhpur.

16. Ojha, A. P., & Rajpurohit, L. S. (2018). First case of wolf attack on Human in western Rajasthan, India. *Cheetal,* 55 (1), pp. 45-

17. Ojha, A. P., & Rajpurohit, L. S. (2018). Ecology of Indian crested Porcupine (*Hystrix indica*) in and around Jodhpur, Rajasthan. *Indian forester,* 10, pp. 963-967.

18. Ojha, A. P., Imran, &Chhangani, A. K. (2019).Status of Indian grey wolf (*Canis lupus*) in human landscape of Thar desert, Rajasthan. *Indian forester*, 145 (10), 1009-1012.

19. Peterson, M. N., Birckhead, J. L., Leong, K., Peterson, M. J., and Peterson, T. R. (2010). Rearticulating the myth of human–wildlife conflict. Conservation Letters 3, pp. 74-82

20. Prakash, I. (1994). Mammals of the Thar desert. Scientific Publisher, Jodhpur.

21. Prakash, I (1995). Ecology and Zoogeography of mammals. In R.K. Gupta and I. Prakash (editiors). Environment analysis of Thar desert. English book depot, Dehradun, pp. 448-467.

22. Prakash, I. 1975. The population ecology of the rodents of Rajasthan desert, India. In: *Rodents in desertenvironment* (eds. I.

Prakash and P. K. Ghosh). Dr. W. Junk b.v. Publishers, The Hague, pp. 75-116.

23. Rajpurohit, L. S., Sharma, G., Vijay, P and Ram, C. (2011). Status of five species of predators in Thar Desert, Jodhpur District, Rajasthan (India). Zoo's Print, Vol. 26; pp. 18-20.

24. Saxena, S.K. and Prakash, I. (1992) Rehabilitation of arid grazing lands in the Thar desert. In Ecosystem rehabilitation Vol. 2: ecosystem analysis and synthesis (M.K.Wali, ed.) pp. 37-50. The Netherlands: SPB Academic publications.

25. Singh, M. and Kumara, H. N. (2006). Distribution, status and conservation of Indian gray wolf (*Canis lupus pallipes*) in Karnataka, India. Journal of Zoology, DOI: 10.1111/j.1469-7998.2006.00103.x

26. Smith, T. M., & Smith, R. L. (2012). *Elements of ecology* (8th ed.). Pearson Benjamin Cummings.

27. Waite, T. A, Campbell LG, Chhangani, A. K., Robbins P (2007a) La Nin~a's signature: synchronous decline of the mammal community in a 'protected'area in India. Divers Distrib (in p

28. Waite, T. A, Chhangani, A. K., Campbell, L. G., Rajpurohit, L.S. and Mohnot, S.M. (2007b). Sanctuary in the City: Urban Monkeys Buffered against Catastrophic Die-off during ENSO-related Drought. EcoHealth, 4, pp. 278-286

**[1]Department of zoology,
JNV University, Jodhpur 342005, Rajasthan
[2]Department of zoology,
R.R. government College Alwar 301001, Rajasthan
[3]Deparment of Environment Science,
M.G.S. University, Bikaner 334004, Rajasthan.
Corresponding author*: aazad.ojha@hotmail.com**

5. Aphids : Annual Agricultural Pest in Rajasthan

Dr. Anita Jhajhria

Abstract

Aphids are small, soft-bodied insects that feed on the sap of plants that belong to the family Aphididae. They are significant agricultural pests, causing significant damage to crops worldwide. They are commonly known as plant lice and are found all over the world, feeding on the sap of plants. Aphids are major pests of agricultural crops and can cause significant damage to plants by reducing their growth, vigor, and yield. In Rajasthan, aphids are a major concern for farmers as they can cause significant crop losses. This paper discusses the diversity of annual aphids in Rajasthan, their economic impact, and the strategies for their management.

Keywords : Aphids, Pests, Diversity, Management, and Strategies

Introduction

Rajasthan has a diverse range of agro-climatic conditions, which supports a wide range of plant species. A significant portion of the economy of Rajasthan is agrarian. The agricultural sector of the state accounts for 22.5 percent. The arid state which receives not more than an annual rainfall of 25 mm thrives on agriculture that is done with irrigation systems. Multiple types of rabi and kharif crops are grown in Rajasthan (Fig 1).

This diversity of plants also supports a diverse range of insect species, including aphids. Aphids are small, ranging in size from 1 to 10 millimeters, and can be winged or wingless. They have a characteristic pear-shaped body and are usually green or brown in colour, although some species may be red or black. Aphids have piercing-sucking mouthparts that they use to feed on the sap of plants.Aphids reproduce asexually, with females giving birth to live young ones without the need for fertilization. This allows aphids to reproduce quickly and produce a large population in a short amount of time. Some species of aphids also have a sexual reproduction phase, which allows for greater genetic diversity.

They can migrate great distances, mainly through passive dispersal by winds. Many species are economically important as they infest agricultural and horticultural crops. Several biological traits are associated with aphids, such as thelytokous parthenogenetic viviparity, short generation time, telescopic generations, and polymorphism. These reproductive characteristics allow aphids to quickly colonize ephemeral resources and quickly grow plants and making them ideal enemies of crops. Many species of aphids display complex life cycles with alternation of sexual and asexual generations and host plant alternation.

Viviparous Aphids (subfamily Aphidinae) constitute a monophyletic group within the family with about 3100 extant species worldwide with higher diversity in temperate regions. Their plant-sapsucking way of feeding is unique. Once they fasten their piercing mouthparts to a juicy plant, they tend to stay there and begin to suck the sap. They defecate characteristic sticky sweet honeydew that attracts as food for wasps, butterflies, some moths, and famously, some species of ants which in return protect them from predators.

Valuable contributions in this field have been made by Sreedhar *et al* (2021), Jain *et al* (2020), Khedkar *et al* (2012), Mandal *et al* (2012), Meena *et al* (2013), Pareek and Sen. (1997), Singh and Singh (2019) , Rawat *et al* (2017), Sahoo (2012), Suthar and Meena (2017), Verma (2000), Verma and Nirala (2018), Dara(2019) & Bottrell and Schoenly (2018). The paper also highlights the diversity, and control measures to combat the aphid infestation in crops of Rajasthan.

Diversity of Aphids in Rajasthan : The state is home to several species of aphids that are known to cause significant damage to crops, including *Aphis gossypii, Aphis craccivora, and Myzus persicae* (Figures2, 3, and 4).

Aphis gossypii is a tiny insect, an aphid in the order Hemiptera. The wingless female cotton aphid has an ovoid body about two millimeters long in varying shades of green. The legs are yellow, as are the antennae which are three-quarters of the length of the body. The winged female has a fusiform body. Its head and thorax are black, the abdomen yellowish-green with black lateral spots, and the antennae are longer than those of the apterous female. The nymphs vary in colour, shades of green, tan, and grey.

They often have a dark head, thorax, and wing pads, and the distal portion of the abdomen is usually dark green. The body appears dull because it is dusted with wax secretions. The oval eggs are yellow when first laid but soon turn glossy black. The adults and nymphs of the cotton aphid feed on the underside of leaves or on the growing tips of shoots, sucking juices from the plant.

Aphis Craccivora : The aphid is a polyphagous pest with a worldwide distribution. Legumes are the economically most affected crops. In most populations males are missing and females reproduce by parthenogenesis (anholocyclic life cycle) and by giving birth to live nymphs. The wingless adult is approximately 2 mm long and shiny black while the nymphs are grey dark. The antennae of the adults are white except for the tips, and the legs are dark at the bases, creamy white on most of the tibiae, and blackish at the tips.

Myzus persicae, known as the **green peach aphid**, is a small green aphid belonging to the order Hemiptera. The life cycle of the green peach aphid varies depending on temperature. The average length of life is approximately 23 days. Eggs of this species measure about 0.6 millimeters long and are elliptical in shape. The eggs are initially yellow or green but turn black. The nymphs are initially green, but soon turn yellowish and resemble the viviparous adults. Nymphs that give rise to winged females may be pinkish.

Adult winged aphids have a black head and thorax, and a yellowish-green abdomen with a large dark dorsal patch. They measure approximately 1.8 to 2.1 millimeters in length. The wingless adult aphids are yellowish or greenish in colour.

The adult green peach aphid can be yellowish-green, red, or brown in colour because of morphological differences influenced primarily by the host plants, nutrition, and temperature. The green peach aphid normally reproduces through cyclical parthenogenesis, where there are several generations of apomictic parthenogenesis followed by a single sexual generation.

Fig 1 Mustard farm in Rajasthan (Courtesy Rajasthan Patrika)

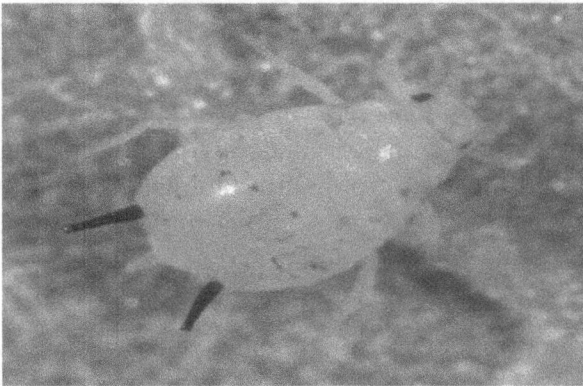

Fig 2 *Aphis gossypii* (Courtesy aphidnet.org)

Fig 3 *Aphis craccivora*(courtesy alchetron.com)

Fig 4 *Myzus persicae* (Courtesy- Safer brand)

Economic Impact of Aphids

They transmit viruses that can cause further damage to crops. In Rajasthan, aphids are a major concern for farmers, particularly in cotton, chili, and mustard crops. Infestations can lead to significant crop losses, which can have a negative impact on the economy of the state.

Management Strategies for Aphids

There are several management strategies that can be used to control aphids in crops. One approach is the use of insecticides, which can be effective in reducing aphid populations. However, the use of insecticides can have negative impacts on the environment and can lead to the development of insecticide resistance in aphids. Therefore, it is important to use insecticides judiciously and to rotate the use of different classes of insecticides.Another approach is the use of biological control agents, to control aphid populations.Cultural practices, such as crop rotation and intercropping, can also be effective in controlling aphids.

Nowadays emphasis is on Integrated Pest management strategy (Fig 5). IPM is a process of holistic evaluation and implementation of pest management strategies in food production systems, landscapes, and urban environments. The goal of IPM is not to eradicate pests entirely but to maintain population levels below economically relevant levels. Effective implementation of IPM programs can reduce costs of management to growers as well as the impact of management on the ecosystem by minimizing the use of pesticides. IPM emphasizes on multifold control measures which are highlighted below:

Types of Control

- Cultural control involves the use of farm management strategies and resistant plant varieties to minimize the impact of certain pests.
- **Biological control** focuses on protecting beneficial species in the field as well as introducing beneficial species in some cases to reduce densities of target pests. Examples include reducing broad-spectrum pesticide use to promote populations of beneficial predators in the field or landscapes or introducing lady beetles to greenhouses to control aphid populations.
- **Mechanical control** is any physical measure taken to trap pest species, exclude them from the area, or eliminate them. Examples include using a grease band on fruit trees to prevent wingless female moths from laying eggs on developing trees in spring, using trap crops to exclude pests from cultivated fields, or discing weeds to eliminate them.
- **Chemical control** is typically a last resort in integrated management systems but can still be used in the context of IPM. The goal of chemical control is to use products that specifically target a pest while also reducing the number of sprays by using periodic sampling and action thresholds.
- **Behavioural control** often involves the use of chemicals but does not involve directly killing the pest species. It is the alteration of pest behavior such as mating, aggregation, or host identification via the use of pheromones and semiochemicals. Pheromones are intraspecific chemical cues used by insects, and semiochemicals are more broadly defined as chemicals that convey signals from one organism to another. Both can be synthetically produced and used to alter the behavior of pest species. An example includes introducing mating disruption pheromones to reduce populations of pest species in the field.

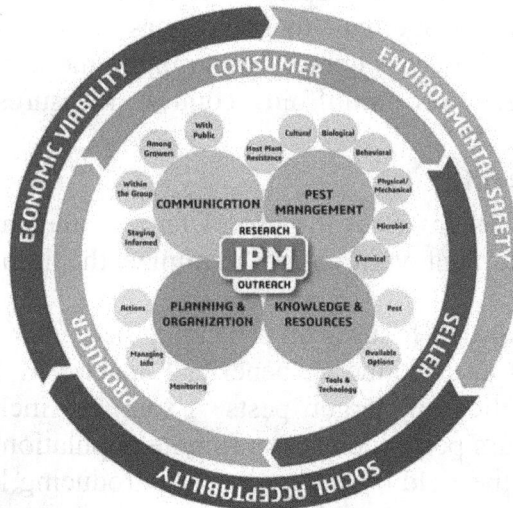

Fig 5 IPM (courtesy academic.oup.com)

Conclusion

Aphids are a significant pest in crops in Rajasthan, causing significant economic losses for farmers. Understanding the diversity of aphids in the state and their management strategies is critical for effective pest control. The use of insecticides, biological control agents, cultural practices, and integrated pest management can be effective in reducing aphid populations and minimizing their impact on crops. By implementing integrated pest management strategies, farmers in Rajasthan can reduce their dependence on insecticides and promote sustainable agriculture practices.

References

1. B. K. Sreedhar, T. K. Hath, S. K. Sahoo and Supriya Okram (2021) Seasonal Incidence of Mustard Aphid *Lipaphis erysimi* (Kalt.) and its Correlation with Weather Factors under Terai Zone of West Bengal *Int.J.Curr.Microbiol.App.Sci* 10(01): 2556-2561
2. Bottrell DG, and Schoenly KG (2018) Integrated pest management for resource-limited farmers: challenges for achieving ecological, social and economic sustainability. *Journal*

of Agricultural Science. 156(3):408–426. doi:10.1017/S0021859618000473.

3. D.K. Jain, R.K. Gangwar , Hemant Swami and H.K. Sumeriya (2020) Bioefficacy of IPM Modules for the Management of Aphid, Lipaphis erysimi Kalt. Infesting Mustard in Rajasthan *International Journal of Current Microbiology and Applied Sciences* Volume 9 Number 6.

4. Dara SK (2019) The New Integrated Pest Management Paradigm for the Modern Age *Journal of Integrated Pest Management*, Volume 10, Issue 1,12, doi.org/10.1093/jipm/pmz010

5. Khedkar AA, Bharpoda TM, Patel MG, Patel CK (2012)Efficacy of different chemical insecticides against mustard aphid, *Lipaphis erysimi* (Kaltenbach) infesting mustard. *International ejournal.*; 2277-9663

6. Mandal D, Bhowmik P, Chatterjee ML (2012) Evaluation of new and conventional insecticides for the management of mustard aphid, *Lipaphis erysimi* Kalt. (Homoptera: Aphididae) on rapeseed (Brassica juncea L.). *The Journal of Plant Protection Sciences.*; 4(2):37-42.

7. Meena H, Singh SP, Nagar R (2013) Evaluation of microbial and bio-products for the management of mustard aphid, *Lipaphis erysimi* (Kalt.). An International Quarterly Journal of Life Science.;8(3):747-750.

8. Pareek, R. K., and P. K. Sen. (1997): Aphids and their natural enemies in major crops of Rajasthan. *Indian Journal of Entomology* 59, no. 2 : 174-183

9. Rajendra Singh and Garima Singh (2019) Species Diversity of Indian Aphids (Hemiptera: Aphididae) *International Journal of Biological Innovations* 1 (1): 23-29

10. Rawat, S. S., S. S. Gurjar, and S. K. Choudhary (2017). Species diversity of aphids in the agroecosystem of arid region of Rajasthan. *Journal of Applied and Natural Science* 9, no. 1 : 25-31.

11. Sahoo, S. K (2012) Incidence and management of mustard aphid (*Lipaphis erysimi* Kaltenbach) in West Bengal, *The Journal of Plant Protection Sciences*, 4(1): 20-26

12. Suthar, R. K., and M. K. Meena (2017): Studies on the diversity of aphids (Aphididae: Hemiptera) infesting different crops in southern Rajasthan. *Annals of Plant Protection Sciences* 25, no. 1: 132-135.
13. Verma and Nirala. (2018) Studies on aphid diversity and population dynamics in mustard ecosystem of Rajasthan. *International Journal of Science and Research* 7, no. 5 : 103-106.
14. Verma K.D (2000). Economically important aphids and their management. In: *IPM System in Agriculture* Vol. 7 (Eds. Upadhyay R.K., Mukerji K.G. and Dubey O.P.), Aditya Books Private Ltd., New Delhi. 143-168.

Associate Professor in Zoology
Shri Kalyan Rajkiya Kanya Mahavidyalaya, Sikar
Rajasthan
email : anita290106@gmail.com

6. Covid-19 and it's Impact on the Economy of The Nation

Sunil Kumar Gupta

Abstract

The Corona Virus termed as Covid-19 is one of the nasty disease from the last year which was emerged from the Wuhan city of China, which have cause a serious impact on the lives of human being not only in China but to the whole world. The World Health Organization (WHO) has declared this disease as a pandemic because it has digested the lives of people in a huge quantity and affected the lives of several crores of people. This pandemic has its impact not only on the lives of human but also affected the economy of the nation whole wide. Due to the spread of Covid-19 virus within and across the country, the government of various nation have announce complete lockdown in all ways i.e. roadways, airways and waterways even railways, in order to break the chain of Covid-19 virus. The lockdown shows a severe impact in every aspect such as education, agriculture, tourism, transport, trade & commerce, etc. The virus has left its scar on both rural and urban areas irrespective of caste, religion, sex, place, time. During the pandemic it has been observed that the migrant workers have suffered most, their bread and butter are based on daily earnings and they barely have savings which assist them to spend during the times of emergency. This research paper aims to explore the impacts of Covid-19 on the economy of the nation to various aspects. The objectives of the researcher is to study the impact of virus on various sectors which have their impact to the nation of the economy and the researcher will consider the secondary data for its study and analyses the certain policies and strategies which adopt by the government to mitigate the spread of Corona virus and to keep the economy of the country in its track.

Keywords : Covid-19, Pandemic, Economy, Government, Lockdown.

Introduction

The year 2020 for the Indian economy was like a black year from everyone's prospective. In the month of January when the first case of Covid-19 recognized in the southern part of India, the government was alert and started to make certain strategies and policies which are to be executed if the case of Covid-19 increases. And as the cases of covid-19 is seen to be adding more and more numbers the government has announced a complete lockdown of the nation first for a period of 21 days and extended further as per the needs. This lockdown had paused the wheels of roadways, railways, airways. This announcement shocked the lower class people i.e. farmers, daily wage earners and specially to the migrant workers, who away from their home for bread and better, becomes jobless overnight. However, the government do not leave the people alone during the time of pandemic and do's everything what is need to be done to keep the people survive at minimum cost. The government not only shows his responsibility towards human being to keep their life alive but also to maintain stability in the economy of the country. The economists and experts viewed that the economy of the country will take a hit from the year 2021 but once again the second wave of Covid-19 appears before the common people in the beginning of the financial year 2021-22. And this time the virus took macabre roof where the number of cases increases to four (4) lakhs plus per day and with the increase in numbers of infected individuals the number of deaths also raised. Once gain the burden and the responsibilities come before the frontline workers to provide selfless service day and night towards the society for humankind and the government too who has to look upon the entire nation by providing precaution and protection to protect the life of common people and in strengthen the economy of the country.

Objectives and Methodology of the Study

The objective of the researcher is to study the impact of Covid-19 on the economy of the nation. To fulfill the above objective and have adequate information for the study, the researcher gives preference to the secondary data. The secondary data has been collected from various sources such as internet, journals, and articles.

Review of Literatures

1. Pak Anton, et al. (2020). In their research paper entitled, "Economic Consequences of the Covid-19 outbreak: the need for epidemic preparedness", emphasize on the impact of Covid-19 on the global economy and financial market. The researchers discuss on the spread of infectious disease and the measures to improve the public health in high risk and low income countries. The global pandemic has its direct impact on the inco me of the individuals due to absenteeism and premature deaths. The researchers suggested that the Corona Virus will not disappear very soon and therefore to protect the lives of common people and the economic prosperity various proactive international actions should be taken to mitigate the spread of Covid-19.

2. Chaudhary, M. et al. (2020). In their paper entitled, "Effect of COVID-19 on Economy in India: Some Reflections for Policy and Programme", emphasizes on assessing the impact of Covid-19 on different sectors. The researcher's mentioned that Covid-19 has taught the policymakers to offer greater momentum to sectors which make better allocation of resources and reduction in income inequalities. The researchers concluded that every crisis provides an opportunity to think again and again for the development of the nation as a whole.

3. Barbate V et al. (2021). In their paper entitled, "COVID-19 and its impact on the India Economy", stated about the short term and long term impact of COVID-19 on the Indian economy. The researchers had adopted decision tree approach for accessing the impact of Covid-19. The researchers found that in the long run the impact of Covid-19 depends on the recovery and the role of the government is very critical amidst Covid-19 pandemic. The researchers suggested to overcome the crisis in the economy the government should adopting two-pronged approach.

4. Garg K. D. et al. (2021). In their paper entitled, "The Impact of COVID-19 Epidemic on Indian Economy Unleashed By machine Learning", aims to explore to what extent a 2020 epidemic i.e. Covid-19 had impacted the economy of India using a machine learning approach. The researchers analyses the data which are collected by using the various models of regression.

5. Agarwal & Singh (2020). In their paper entitled, "Covid-19 and Its Impact on Indian Economy", focus on impact of Corona virus pandemic in the economy of India. The researchers have studied on the different sectors of Indian economy regarding impact of Covid-19 and policy framework of government. The researchers concluded that amidst Covid-19 allowed everyone to rethink, redesign and restructure everything and right decision at the right time will assist to fix the challenges before the government such as economic power and wealth, inequalities, etc.

6. Das & Patnaik (2020). In their research paper entitled, "The Impact of Covid-19 in Indian Economy – An Empirical Study", had mentioned about the impact of Covid-19 in different sectors by analyzing the secondary data with the help of various statistical tools and techniques. The researchers founded that most of the companies are allowing their employees to work from home during the pandemic. Also mentioned that this pandemic has taught the lesson of survival at the minimum cost and the overall cost control in business because the virus has devastated the world in such a way which is beyond imaginable.

7. Sidhu G.S. et al. (2020). In their research paper entitled, **"The Impact of Covid-19 Pandemic on Different Sectors of The Indian Economy – A Descriptive Study",** have emphasizes on the most affected industries due to covid-19 pandemic. The researchers stated that the impact of Covid-19 is unimaginable on the industries and this result in loss of millions of jobs and the only solution to control the infection is vaccination to the population at large. The researchers concluded that digitalization is the key to recover from the illness in quick way and it will be reflect in the long run.

COVID-19 and its Impact in India

The outbreak of global pandemic has affected the nation and the whole world in an enormous way. The Covid-19 has affected the health of the individuals and the lockdown has its impact to the country and brought down the economic and social life standstill. The economic activity of the country has slow down because the manufacturing units are closed and the employees have migrated to their home town in fear of infection. The World Bank estimated earlier that the GDP for the financial year 2021-22 will be 10.1% but on 8th June, 2021 it's forecasted that the GDP will be at 8.3%. The second wave of Covid-19 is unprecedented and it will effect the India's growth rate and further estimated at 7.5% in 2022. The World Bank said that the India's recovery is hampered most then any other country due to the outbreak of Covid-19 since the beginning. The World Bank added that in the year 2019 India registered a growth rate of 4% but in the year 2020 it is contracted by 7.3% and in the near future i.e. in 2023 the GDP of India is expected to grow at 6.5%. The budget of financial year 2021-22 will have a significant policy shift. The government announced that this time the expenditure on the health care system will be doubled than any previous year. To support the economy of the country RBI has announces several measures for the micro, small and medium enterprises and also to other sectors during the time of pandemic, so that their activities should not be hampered to maximum.

❖ **COVID-19 and Health Sector**

The health care system and health services are still in the development stage in India due to improper infrastructure, inadequate facilities, equipments and the limited health care resources are some of the challenges before the government. And if some where such facilities are available then maintenance is the hindrances. The World Health Organization mentioned that though the facilities have been improved to some extent over the last few years but the workforce are not available as per the need and recommended. The outbreak of Covid-19 reveals about the quality and the quantity of the health care system in the country. After the implementation of public policy measures to break the chain of Covid-19, the measures resulted in disruption in the operative functions for all companies including Health Care Sector. The health care sector has also suffered due to certain decline in the demands of health care services either it's a single or multi-specialty or even diagnostics businesses due to nationwide lockdown, which is unanticipated and permanent loss. However, with the outbreak of Corona Virus, India has made a significant advancement in the way of health sector. The government have set up many new hospitals in the midst of Covid-19 and also became aatmanirbhar on most of the health related equipments and facilities. The global pandemic have not only taught about the myriad gaps and challenges in the health care system in India but also highlighted the importance of proper infrastructure and availability of doctors and medical staffs, nurses in adequate number, with adequate facilities for proper care and preventing the transmission of infection to overcome any challenges related to health.

❖ **COVID-19 and Tourism Industry**

After the declaration of Covid-19 as a global pandemic by the World Health Organization, the tourism industry also not left behind from its effects. The tourism industry is regarded to be the backbone of many other businesses such as transport, entertainment, restaurants, retail, etc. and an integral pillar of "Make in India" programme. Tourism is one of the major sources of revenue in terms of foreign exchange, tax collection and also creates employment opportunities at a rapid rate. The contribution of travel and tourism to GDPs is Rs. 15.24 lakh crore in 2017, which is expected to increase to Rs.32.05 lakh crore by 2028. It is also observed that in terms of employment opportunity, India created 6.36 million jobs followed by China and Philippines which is 5.47 and 2.53 million respectively between 2014 and 2019. But the outbreak of Covid-19 has a severe impact on the travel and tourism sector because government imposed restrictions on international travel and also in the country. The World Travel and Tourism Council reported that the Covid-19 is likely to cost almost USD 22 billion and a loss of almost 50 million jobs worldwide. And it's witnessed a significant decline for the year 2020 for India. The sector was struggling to recover from the pain of 2020 in the midst, the second wave of Covid-19 have sight once again. The tourism minister added that vaccination to the entire nation is the only panacea to have positive impact on the tourism industry. The Tourism Ministry innovating new ideology to make understand the geographical spread of the hospitality and for it the ministry launched NIDHI portal and besides that various supportive measures has been taken which will lead India in becoming a global tourism destination. The government makes a target to achieve 2% share in world international tourist.

❖ **COVID-19 and Agricultural Industry**

The primary source of livelihood for the maximum population in India is agricultural. With the outbreak of Covid-19, the government imposed complete lockdown towards the entire nation and these resulted to choice i.e. what consumer's wants and what consumers really needed to survive during the time of pandemic. The Covid-19 changes the pattern of buying and consumptions because the lockdown have snatched the jobs from the many and these reduced the earning capacity of the individuals. Now these individuals are returning back to their home from urban to rural areas and they have no other option other than willing to engage themselves in agricultural sector for livelihood. Due to the primarily decline in the first half of the financial year 2020-21, The Economic Survey estimated that India's GVA will contract by 7.2% for the entire economy of the country for the Financial year 2020-21 but the agricultural sector is the only who shows positive impact of 3.4% at constant prices. This year the rural areas are seen to be mostly affected by Covid-19 disease. And government view that in order to make a positive contribution for agricultural sector to GVA, the prime and major concern is to contain the spread of Corona virus in rural areas by using all possible means. Mr. Ramesh Chand, member of NITI Aayog added that in 2021-22, the agricultural sector will grow by more than 3 percent because the cases of Covid-19 are increasing from the month of May rapidly in the rural areas and during this time no crop is harvested, no crop is sown and from the month of June it seems that the cases are declining and the monsoons also arrives, which will assist to take the agricultural sector at a peak once again.

❖ **COVID-19 and Transport Industry**

The impact of Covid-19 on transport industry has been significant within and across the urban areas. The pandemic has affected the travelling behavior of the individuals resulted in complete dullness towards movement. Transportation not only mean movement of individuals but also various economic activities are related with transportation either directly or indirectly and all these activities are severely affected. After the declaration of Corona virus as a pandemic many government has put restrictions on inter-nation movement and after the announcement of Prime minister regarding the nationwide lockdown in India all the transportation have stopped their movement i.e. roadways, railways, airways, except emergency services are available. This transport industry not only suffered for few days but it last for long because when the process of unlock starts especially the public transportation, the government issue the guidelines for not to carry more than 33% or 50% of passengers. Bal Malkit Singh, who is the chairman-core committee and former president of All India Motor Transport Congress said that due to the spread of Corona Virus and restriction in movement, an around of Rs. 315 crore per day, the transport sector is facing losses. There is a decline in the demand of trucks by 50%. The trucks drivers are already in the financial crisis with the first wave of Covid-19 and the second wave have added some more burden.

❖ **COVID-19 and Manufacturing Industry**

As it is seen that the pandemic is arriving with different version in different year, the expectation and loyalty towards different brands also vary because of inadequate disposable income in the hands of individuals due to lockdown and restrictions on various activities. The India's GDP was contracted by 23.9% for the first quarter of 2020-21 and the share of manufacturing sector falls to 13.8% in 2020-21 first quarters in total Gross Value Added, which was 17.5% in 2019-20 during the same period. The contribution of manufacturing sector to GDP for the year 2020 is 17.4%. The manufacturing sector shows 2% growth in GVA in the year 2020 while in the previous fiscal year it was 7% and the result is only because of the Covid-19 pandemic which slows down the economic activities. However, it is expected that the market size will increase by 5.9% of manufacturing industry in 2021. The manufacturing sector from the year 2006 to 2012, fiscal year shows 9.5% growth every year and the next six (6) year, the growth decline to 7.4% i.e. till 2018. And to boost the manufacturing sector in India, the Government of India launched 'Make in India' program to make India as a world's manufacturing hub and give global recognition to the economy of the country. The government also views that with it 100 million of new jobs can be created by 2022. It is seen that through FDIs, India has received US$ 30 billion in the first half of

2021, which is 15% more in compare to same period last year. To promote a healthy and wealthy environment, the Government of India has launch several schemes and taken various initiatives, for the growth of the manufacturing industry in India. It is reported that by 2025, the India's manufacturing industry has the potential to reach US$ 1 trillion.

Discussion

The outbreak of Covid-19 has pushed not only the economy of India but to the entire world's economy into the state of uncertainty. It's very difficult to measure the panic in the pandemic. The Corona Virus has its impact more or less on each and every sector of the economy and it is totally unimaginable. The manufacturing sector which is also affected due to migration of workers during the pandemic, millions of enterprises include micro, small, medium and large, face an existential threat, which have direct impact on the job of the individuals which in return resulting in losing their livelihoods. The situation is such that the agricultural workers who feed the entire nation, they have nothing and no one to feed them. The health sector is one of the important sectors where government has to give an additional attention by providing maximum facilities to the peoples dwelling in rural, semi-urban and urban areas by establishing health care unit, to overcome such challenges. During the pandemic it is observed that due to lack of equipments and treatment facilities the patients have lost their lives. The government should come forward with various strategies to revive the tourism industry, which is probably the worst hit sector due to Corona Virus. Though the researcher has taken into consideration only few of the prime sectors but the strength of GDP depends on the collective efforts of each and every sectors. The Corona Virus has largely disrupted and has derailed the economy of the nation.

Conclusion

The economy will be in normal as it was only as soon as the governments will success in vaccinating the entire population of the country. The economy was in developing stage in pre-pandemic and now it is totally collapsed and it's a challenge before the government both the central and states to come forward and work with cooperation and co-ordination for the growth of the people and the country. Though the future is uncertain and it is expected that third wave of Covid-19 may come but proper strategy and good policies will assist in tackling such kind of situation. This pandemic will disappear but not early as possible, proactive national and international actions are required not only to protect the economy of the country but also to save the lives of common people. Thus, every crisis teaches us some lesson to think, rethink and again think to developed unique opportunities from the bundle of problems. And this pandemic has left a message to every individuals, the lesson of self reliance and eco-friendly.

References
1. Pak, A., Adegboye, O. A., Adekunle, A. I., Rahman, K., McBryde, E. S., & Eisen, D. P. (2020). Economic consequences of the COVID-19 outbreak: the need for epidemic preparedness. *Frontiers in public health, 8.*
2. Chaudhary, Monika, P. R. Sodani, and Das, S. (2020). Effect of COVID-19 on Economy in India: Some Reflections for Policy and Programme. *Journal of Health Management, 22(2), 169-180.*
3. Barbate, V., Gade, R.N., & Raibagkar, S. S. (2021). COVID-19 and its Impact on the Indian Economy. *Vision, 25*(1), 23-35. – available on: https://www.google.co.in/url?q=https://journals.sagepub.com/doi/full/10.1177/0972262921989126&sa=U&ved=2ahUKEwjov6uo mYjxAhVjIOYKHealBOQQFjAJegQICRAB&usg=AOvVaw0i7 VRLtLBkIuDnrKAai
4. Garg, K.D., Gupta, M., & Kumar, M. (2021). The Impact of COVID-19 Epidemic on Indian Economy Unleashed By Machine Learning. In IOP Conferences Series: Materials Sciences and Engineering (Vol. 1022, No. 1, p. 012085). IOP Publishing – available on: https://www.google.co.in/url?q=https://///iopscience.iop.orgg/artic le/10.1088/1757-899X/1022/1/012085&sa=U&ved=

2ahUKEwjnrOCFoYjxAhUtyzgGHQ_8BuoQFjADegQICBAB&
usg=AOvVaw2zRMXIkbW7BcBck9Wtu2hH

5. Agarwala, S., & Singhb, A. (2020). Covid-19 and its impact on Indian Economy. International Journal of Trade & Commerce-IIARTC, 2. – available on: Https://Www.Researchgate.Net/ Publications/343809191_Covid_19_And_It's_Impact_On_Inian_ Economy

6. Das, K. K., & Patnaik, S. (2020). The Impact of Covid-19 In Indian Economy – An Empirical Study. *International Journal of Electrical Engineering and Technology* (IJEET), 3(11), 194-202. – available on: Https://Papers.Ssrn.Com/Soi3/Papers.Cfm? Abstract_Id=3636058

7. Sidhu, G. S., Rai, J. S., Khaira, K. S., & Kaur, S. (2020). The Impact of Covid-19 Pandemic on Different Sectors of the Indian Economy: A Descriptive Study. *International Journal of Economics and Financial* Issues, 10(5), 113-120. – available on: https://www.econjournals.com/index.php/ijefi/article/view/10461

8. Statista Research Department. (2021). Impact of the Corona virus(COVID-19) on the Indian economy – statistics & facts – available on: https://www.statista.com/topics/6304/covid-19-economic-impact-on-india/#topicHeader_wrapper

9. Business Standard. (2021). Covid impact: World Bank slashes India's FY22 GDP growth forecast to 8.3%. *Press Trust of India.*- available on: https://wap.business-standard.com/article/economy-policy/world-bank-projects-india-s-fy33-gdp-growth-at-8-3-121060801290_1 .html

10. Rekha M. (2020). COVID-19: Health care System in India. *Health Care: Current Reviews* S1:262. – available on: https://www.longdom.org/open-access/covid19-health-care-syatem-in-india-58032.html

11. IBEF (2021). Indian Tourism and Hospitality Industries Analysis - available on: https://www.ibef.org/industry/indian-tourism-and-hospitality-industry-analysis-presentation

12. Monidipa Dey. (2021). Impact of COVID-19 on travel and tourism industry and ways of recovery. Financial Express. – available on: https://financialexpress.com/lifestyle/travel-

tourism/impact-of-covid-19-on-travel-and-tourism-industry-and-ways-of-recovery/2183029/

13. Astha Singh. (2021). Tourism Ministry assures 'positive impact' as India provides vaccines to 140 countries. *RepublicWorld*. https://m.republicworld.com/india-news/general-news/tourism-minister-assures-positive-impact-as-india-provides-vaccines-to-140-countries.html

14. Hussain and Mohapatra. (2021). Impact of COVID-19 second wave on India's agriculture. *Money Control*. – available on: https://www.moneycontrol.com/news/opinion/impact-of-covid-19-second-wave-on-indias-agriculture-6879761.html - accessed on: 14/06/2021.

15. Cariappa, A. A., Acharya, K. K., Adhav, C. A., Sendhil, R., & Ramasundaram, P. (2021). Impact of COVID-19 on the Indian agricultural system: A 10-point strategy for post-pandemic recovery. *Outlook on Agricultural*, 50(1), 26-33. – available on: https://journals.sagepub.com/doi/full/10.1177/0030727021989060

16. PTI. (2021). COVID-19 second wave will not impact India's agri sector: Niti Aayog. *THE HINDU*. – available on: https://www.thehindu.com/news/national/covid-19-second-wave-will-not-impact-indias-agri-sector-niti-aayog/article34743586.ece

17. Agricultural in India: Information About Indian Agricultarl & Its Importance. IBEF. – available on: https://www.ibef.org/industry/agriculture-india.aspx

18. AIMTC. (2021). *Transport sector facing losses of Rs. 315 crore per day due to COVID restrictions: AIMTC*. Business Today. – available on: https://m.businesstoday.in/story/transport-sector-facing-losses-of-rs-315-crore-per-day-due-to-covid-restrictions-aimtc/1/436926.html

19. Paul, B., & Sarkar, S. (2021). The Contagion effects of Covid-19 and Public Transportation System: Conceptualizing the Shifting Paradigm in India. *COVID-19 Pandemic Trajectory in the Developing World*, 231. – available on:ehttps://www.ncbi.nlm.nih.gov/pmc/articles/PMC7981506/#!po=0.485437

20. Arijit Nag. (2021). *Covid Second Wave Will Adversely Impact Manufacturing Sector Again.* Engineering Review. – available on: https://engmag.in/covid-second-wave-will-adversely-impact-manufacturing-sector-again/
21. *MANUFACTURING SECTOR IN INDIA.* IBEF (2021). – avilable on: https://www.ibef.org/industry/manufacturing-sector-india.aspx
22. Vaishali Basu Sharma. (2021). *The Impact of COVID-19 on India's Manufacturing Sector.* THE WIRE. – available on: https://m.thewire.in/article/economy/the-impact-of-covid-19-on-indias-manufacturing-sector

Ph. D. Research Scholar,
Department of Commerce,
Dibrugarh University, Dibrugarh,
Assam
email : sunilg9325@gmail.com

7. Environmental Sustainability and Human Efforts : An Urgent Need to Address Environmental Issues Globally

Dr Seema Yadav

Abstract

The three-pillar notion of (social, economic, and environmental) sustainability is now widely accepted and is typically depicted by three intersecting circles with total sustainability at the centre. Sustainability of the environment requires a multifaceted approach that considers the ecological, social, and economic aspects in order to ensure long-term success. The idea of sustainable development has raised awareness of environmental issues and the value of the functions and services the environment delivers. Sustainability is a management strategy for risks and opportunities in the environmental, social, and economic spheres. The basic goal of sustainability is to reach a point when the extraction, usage, and destruction of the resources of the planet especially by humans who inhabit or utilise it will not go beyond its carrying capacity. Due to their persistence, purpose, and logical expectations in nature, environmental problems necessitate global preventive efforts. The conservation of the environment and the sustainable use of natural resources are issues that are shared by all nations and are a shared global goal. The main field of international regulation and cooperation is environmental protection, which has a worldwide or cross-border scope and necessitates global preventive efforts.

Keywords : Environmental Sustainability, sustainable development, environmental problems, SDGs framework

Introduction

Economic growth and environmental preservation are mutually reliant. Hence, environmental destruction will result from development that disregards its effects on the environment and the ecosystem that supports life. Sustainable development is defined as "meeting the basic requirements of everyone and providing to all the chance to satisfy their ambitions for a better life" in the seminal study Our Common Future, which provided the description above. The ecosystem should be preserved and cared for. It is a location where people can reside and grow their social and economic systems. Also, it is a place where a variety of biodiversity may coexist in a healthy ecosystem (Suryani et al., 2019). A process or situation can be considered sustainable if it can be sustained over the long term. Nature's potential to continue and survive is known as sustainability. (Jimenez, Moorhead, & Wilensky, 2021)Following a 2018 UN report that claimed we have around ten years to dramatically reduce emissions before it will probably be impossible to stabilise global warming, young people all across the world started to "Strike for the Climate." One of the most important problems currently facing humanity is environmental sustainability. The sustainability of our planet's natural resources has come under scrutiny due to rising human populations and a rapid expansion of anthropogenic activity (Arora, 2018). The main objective of sustainability is to get to a point where the extraction, use, and degradation of the planet's resources especially by humans who live on or utilise it will not exceed its (the Earth's) carrying capacity. As "frameworks" for promoting the acquisition of pertinent knowledge, beliefs, attitudes, and skills for sustainable living, organisations, homes, and communities play a crucial role in the sustainability transition (Ofei-Manu & Shimano, 2012). The main focus of international regulation and collaboration, which has a worldwide or cross-border scope, is environmental protection. Global preventive activities are required due to the environmental problems' persistence, intent, and interdisciplinary character (Dogaru, 2013).

Concept of Environmental Sustainability

Globally, there has been a growing focus on sustainability, particularly environmental sustainability (Shen, 2015). Sustaina-bility refers to achieving our goals without affecting the capacity of coming generations to achieve their goals. The capacity to preserve important aspects of the natural environment is known as environmental sustainability. 'Sustain' has been a part of the language for many centuries. 'Sustenare' means "to hold up" or "to support," is a Latin word. Social, environmental, and economic sustainability should all be considered as part of sustainable development (SD), which should then leverage these three factors to help make development sustainable (Goodland, 1995). Today, the concept "sustainable development" is in popularity. Nowadays, many individuals interchangeably refer to sustainability and sustainable development. Finding a simpler phrase to use in place of "sustainable development" may be the driving force behind some people's actions. Because they dislike discussing "development," some people prefer to use the term "sustainability" as a synonym for "sustainable development." There has been a paradigm change in how we think about development. Environmental, economic, and socio-political sustainability can be theoretically divided into three categories that make up the field of sustainable development. Due to the complicated and fragmented historical roots of sustainability, it is necessary to explicitly describe how it is understood before any rigorous operationalization can be done because it is still context-specific and ontologically open (Purvis, Mao, & Robinson, 2019).

Although the idea of sustainability is a relatively recent one, the movement as a whole has origins in social justice, conservationism, internationalism, and other earlier movements with significant legacies. Sustainable development is fundamentally a normative and contestable term, demanding changes in institutional and human behaviour (Wilson, 2003). A sustainability concern is always there whenever there is a strong sense of urgency. This sense of urgency may be connected to an existing situation or to a potential that is known.

In order to achieve permanent prosperity, environmental sustainability takes a holistic strategy that takes into account the ecological, social, and economic components. Environmental, social, and economic risks and possibilities are managed through sustainability. Every time a valuable system, object, process, or attribute is in danger, there is a sustainability concern. In other words, a sustainability issue arises whenever a valuable resource is in danger of not being maintained. In order to minimise environmental issues and meet present-day requirements without jeopardising the ability of future generations to meet their own needs, sustainable development is intended to be promoted. It is important to avoid replicating models without thoroughly examining their theoretical underpinnings and any associated ideologies in order to prevent losing sight of sustainability's fundamentally political aspect (Purvis et al., 2019). The idea of sustainable development has raised society's awareness of environmental issues and helped people understand their significance as well as the functions and services the environment performs (Dogaru, 2013).

Different Dimensions of Environmental Sustainability

These three aspects still serve as the foundation of sustainability today, after forty years of development, with each component focusing on a distinct subset. The environmental component is particularly concerned with energy, water, greenhouse gases, emission, trash, recycling, and packaging (Shen, 2015). The social dimension is more closely linked to public policy, diversity, safety, and anti-corruption efforts as well as investments in local communities, working conditions, human rights, and fair trade (Shen, 2015). Stakeholder value, corporate governance, economic performance, and financial performance are all connected to the economic dimension (Shen, 2015). The definition of environmental sustainability includes sustainable business practises, sustainable scholarly investigation, environmental literacy, ethical and moral responsibility, collaboration between universities and nations, the creation of interdisciplinary curricula, and partnerships with the public sector, non-governmental organisations, and business (Wright, 2002). The sustainable development must be taken into account when establishing the course of action at the level of the entire communitarian process, establishing requirements regarding the information about the long- and short-term goals that are taken care of in all five areas that have an impact on the environment (Dogaru, 2013). In addition to offering a matrix of recommendations for environmental education, he hopes to encourage thought on environmental sustainability in schools. Management will aid in the implementation of educational policies and knowledge development, and the matrix will be utilised as an evaluation tool (Vieira, Campos, Torales, & De, 2016). The sustainable development must be taken into account when establishing the course of action at the level of the entire communitarian process, establishing requirements regarding the information about the long- and short-term goals that are taken care of in all five areas that have an adverse effect on the natural world (Dogaru, 2013).

Environmental Sustainability : An Urgent Need of the Hour

There is no doubt about the necessity of sustainability (Morelli, 2011). UN-MDG 7 encapsulates the significance of environmental sustainability to development. Notwithstanding significant success towards achieving this goal, there is still much work to be done, and new local and global issues threaten the environmental and development advancements made thus far. Although there has been a significant increase in the literature on environmental sustainability, there is little to no experimental evidence to support the central roles that institutions and governance play in the pursuit of environmental sustainability (Adekunle, 2021). The concept of (social, economic, and environmental) sustainability as three interlocking circles with overall sustainability at their centres is now widely accepted (Purvis et al., 2019). One of the main and universal political objectives of the present day is sustainable development (SD). Education must be crucial to creating a sustainable society, as mentioned in Agenda 21 (Bezeljak, Scheuch, & Torkar, 2020). The transition to a more sustainable and environmentally friendly socio-economic paradigm and the fight against climate change both depend critically on environmental education (Velasco-Martínez, Martín-Jaime, Estrada-Vidal, & Tójar-Hurtado, 2020). All nations in the globe have a shared concern with regard to the issues of environmental protection and the sustainable development of natural resources (Dogaru, 2013).

Many people and organisations share the value of sustainability, and they show this value via their policies, day-to-day actions, and behaviours. The objective of environmental sustainability must be attained as soon as humanly possible because it will be an enormous challenge to provide for up to ten billion people in less than two generations without harming the environment on which we all depend (Goodland, 1995). (Mahat, Hashim, Saleh, Nayan, & Norkhaidi, 2019) demonstrated a non-parallel link between students' sustainability knowledge, attitudes, behaviours, and practises.

(Saraiva, de Almeida, Bragança, & Barbosa, 2018) sought to ascertain whether, for the benefit of the students, the ergonomic comfort factor should be incorporated into sustainability assessment methods for educational facilities. Future generations' health and well-being will be gravely compromised if urgent action is not taken today to achieve environmental sustainability. Due to intensive farming's impact on the capacity of the water supply and the fertility of the soil, the food supply will become unstable. The five areas that have an impact on the environment industry, tourism, energy, transport, and agriculture must be taken into account when determining the course of action at the level of the entire communitarian process, establishing requirements regarding the information about the objectives on long and short teen that are cared for (Dogaru, 2013). Environmental sustainability aims to maintain the world's life-support systems in a certain way. The global ecosystem's source capacity offer basic material inputs including food, water, air, and energy, while its sink capabilities digest outputs or waste (Goodland, 1995).

What can be done for Environmental Sustainability : A Multidimensional Approach?

The SDGs framework will need to take into account the connections between environmental problems on a local and global scale, natural resource management, and development. Identifying and addressing a shared agenda to manage shared global environmental hazards and create resilience across all types of countries will be a critical component, taking into account complicated issues including the relationships between different types of governments. One of the terms used most frequently in conversations about climate change is environmental sustainability. The significance of environmental sustainability can significantly influence efforts to combat the climate problem. Sustainability in terms of the environment and the economy is not easy to achieve. This delicate balance between protecting our ecosystem and ensuring a good standard of living is complicated by a variety of factors. There has been little advancement in the fight against climate change and the protection of the ozone layer.

Sustainability is typically driven by complex, unique, and varied incentives. It is implausible to attempt to compile a list of justifications for why so many people, organisations, and communities are striving towards this objective. Environmental Sustainability might benefit or suffer from technology. It is impossible to sustain non-renewable resources. Most environmental services cannot be replaced, and harm to them will have significant irreversible effects. Sulphur and nitrate emissions must be blocked by clean energy technologies and maximal efficacy. The materials used in manufactured goods must be recycled. Massive tree planting must be done to enhance forests (Basiago, 1999).

A comprehensive sustainability programme must include measures to mitigate negative effects and dangers, safeguard the environment from harm, and restore any harm already done. Sustainability would be impossible if human activity continued to deplete or harm essential environmental services that cannot be replaced (Goodland, 1995). Actions for environmental protection should be performed right away since, in the context of human-natural environment ecological dependence, environmental damage results in a decline in the quality of human existence (Suryani et al., 2019). Environmental conservation issues are a difficulty for which there is no single document, but the fusion of current opportunities and increased effectiveness in all spheres of a state's social and economic life would help to address the issue of resources and distribution (Dogaru, 2013).

Ecologists and other biophysical scientists need to assume more accountability for steering the conversation on sustainable development and making sure that initiatives to attain it are quickly put into action (Goodland, 1995). Institutions are increasingly adopting their own policies and implementation strategies, as well as signing national and international sustainability statements for sustainability (Wright, 2002). Encouraging the use of these pedagogies as appropriate for the lecture will probably have the backing of academics who teach in many academic fields. The first step in increasing its occurrence from passing comments in class to suitable and complete engagement with sustainability issues in regard to the subject or field in question is to explain to them that doing so will in some ways constitute teaching sustainability (Christie, Miller, Cooke, & White, 2013). Raising children's awareness of the environment, aptitude for its conservation and administration, as well as their sense of compassion and responsibility, can be a long-term solution (Suryani et al., 2019). Regarding their opinions on education for sustainability and environmental justice, this generation that is most affected by climate change has to be heard directly (Jimenez et al., 2021). Even more essential than the academics' efforts to promote sustainability is the interaction with the community since it will give results significance (Alba-Hidalgo, Benayas del Álamo, & Gutiérrez-Pérez, 2018). Environmental degradation is a result of unsustainable behaviour. Higher education institutions are societal actors in charge of producing future leaders with the knowledge and skills necessary to address societal problems (Menon & Suresh, 2022). The difficulties and problems of promoting responsible consumption, with a focus on the creation of environmental education initiatives to mitigate the effects of climate change (Velasco-Martínez et al., 2020). The requirement for governance-oriented mechanisms necessitates that the various stakeholders in sustainability policies participate in the design of the instruments, prioritising them and, on a technical level, choosing the data to be taken into account (Alba-Hidalgo et al., 2018).

Given the many sustainability factors, such as social, environmental, and economic ones, schools are structures that serve three purposes: educational, social, and cultural. At the educational level, institutions like schools teach children and their families how to respect and protect the environment and conserve energy starting in the very first years of school. They also offer training on many themes and extracurricular activities (Bazzocchi, Ciacci, & Di Naso, 2021). There is no one policy to address the challenge of protection of the environment, but combining existing opportunities and increasing efficiency across all social and economic sectors of states would help to address the issue of resources and distribution. A good deal of interdisciplinarity between (corporate) social responsibility, environmental sustainability, and business ethics is implied by one, which is contained in the responsible management education framework (Petković, Alfirević, & Zlatković Radaković, 2022). Since international legislation and collaboration take on a global or cross-border dimension, environmental sustainability is currently a key topic of focus. Environmental problems require worldwide preventive measures due to their persistence, purpose, and rational expectations in nature.

One of the most crucial pieces of the global climate puzzle is finding a balance between human consumption and natural resource use that respects nature while sustaining our modern way of life. There is a worldwide food crisis, an energy crisis, and an increase in greenhouse gas emissions that will cause a global warming disaster if resource depletion is left unchecked. Sustainable development would result from the promotion of natural resources, conservation, preservation of the ecological system's potential for regeneration, and prevention of the imposition of environmental dangers on future generations. The biophysical environment has constraints that humanity must learn to live with. (Ekins & Zenghelis, 2021) Decision-makers will benefit from an understanding of the processes that spur innovation, alter social norms, and prevent a fixation on carbon- and resource-intensive technologies, infrastructure, and behaviours as they consider how to respond to the increasingly dire warnings of natural scientists about the state of the environment.

Conclusion

The three-pillar theory of sustainability (social, economic, and environmental) is now widely accepted. Environmental sustainability requires a multifaceted approach that considers the ecological, social, and economic aspects in order to attain lasting prosperity. Sustainability is used to manage risks and opportunities in the environmental, social, and economic domains. The primary goal of sustainability is to reach a point when the extraction, use, and degradation of the earth's resources, especially by humans who live on or utilise it, will not go beyond the carrying capacity of the planet. In deciding on a course of action and defining requirements for information about the goals being pursued in each of the five areas that have an impact on the environment, it is necessary to take sustainability into account. The main focus of cooperation and international law is environmental protection, which has a global or transnational scope and necessitates transnational preventive efforts.

References

Adekunle, I. A. (2021). On the search for environmental sustainability in Africa: the role of governance. *Environmental Science and Pollution Research, 28*(12), 14607–14620. https://doi.org/10.1007/s11356-020-11432-5

Alba-Hidalgo, D., Benayas del Álamo, J., & Gutiérrez-Pérez, J. (2018). Towards a Definition of Environmental Sustainability Evaluation in Higher Education. *Higher Education Policy, 31*(4), 1–24. https://doi.org/10.1057/s41307-018-0106-8

Arora, N. K. (2018). Environmental Sustainability—necessary for survival. *Environmental Sustainability, 1*(1), 1–2. https://doi.org/10.1007/s42398-018-0013-3

Basiago, A. D. (1999). Economic, social, and environmental sustainability in development theory and urban planning practice. *Environmentalist, 19*(2), 145–161. https://doi.org/10.1023/A:1006697118620

Bazzocchi, F., Ciacci, C., & Di Naso, V. (2021). Evaluation of environmental and economic sustainability for the building envelope of low-carbon schools. *Sustainability (Switzerland), 13*(4). https://doi.org/10.3390/su13041702

Bezeljak, P., Scheuch, M., & Torkar, G. (2020). Understanding of sustainability and education for sustainable development among pre-service biology teachers. *Sustainability (Switzerland), 12*(17). https://doi.org/10.3390/SU12176892

Christie, B. A., Miller, K. K., Cooke, R., & White, J. G. (2013). Environmental sustainability in higher education: How do academics teach? *Environmental Education Research, 19*(3), 385–414. https://doi.org/10.1080/13504622.2012.698598

Dogaru, L. (2013). The Importance of Environmental Protection and Sustainable Development. *Procedia - Social and Behavioral Sciences, 93*, 1344–1348. https://doi.org/10.1016/j.sbspro.2013.10.041

Ekins, P., & Zenghelis, D. (2021). The costs and benefits of environmental sustainability. *Sustainability Science, 16*(3), 949–965. https://doi.org/10.1007/s11625-021-00910-5

Goodland, R. (1995). The concept of environmental sustainability. *Sustainability, 26,* 1–24. https://doi.org/10.4324/9781315241951-20

Jimenez, J., Moorhead, L., & Wilensky, T. (2021). 'It's my responsibility': perspectives on environmental justice and education for sustainability among international school students in Singapore. *International Studies in Sociology of Education, 30*(1–2). https://doi.org/10.1080/09620214.2020.1856000

Mahat, H., Hashim, M., Saleh, Y., Nayan, N., & Norkhaidi, S. B. (2019). Environmental Sustainability Knowledge, Attitude and Practices among Pre-school Students. In *IOP Conference Series: Earth and Environmental Science* (Vol. 286, pp. 1–11). https://doi.org/10.1088/1755-1315/286/1/012003

Menon, S., & Suresh, M. (2022). Development of assessment framework for environmental sustainability in higher education institutions. *International Journal of Sustainability in Higher Education, 23*(7), 1445–1468. https://doi.org/10.1108/IJSHE-07-2021-0310

Morelli, J. (2011). Environmental Sustainability: A Definition for Environmental Professionals. *Journal of Environmental Sustainability, 1*(1), 1–10. https://doi.org/10.14448/jes.01.0002

Ofei-Manu, P., & Shimano, S. (2012). Sustainable organizations: Evaluating the environmental sustainability of schools and companies in a regional centre of expertise. *International Journal of Environmental, Cultural, Economic and Social Sustainability, 7*(6). https://doi.org/10.18848/1832-2077/cgp/v07i06/55022

Petković, S., Alfirević, N., & Zlatković Radaković, M. (2022). Environmental sustainability and corporate social responsibility of business schools: is there evidence of transdisciplinary effects? *Economic Research-Ekonomska Istrazivanja, 35*(1), 6445–6465. https://doi.org/10.1080/1331677X.2022.2048203

Purvis, B., Mao, Y., & Robinson, D. (2019). Three pillars of sustainability: in search of conceptual origins. *Sustainability Science, 14*(3), 681–695. https://doi.org/10.1007/s11625-018-0627-5

Saraiva, T. S., de Almeida, M., Bragança, L., & Barbosa, M. T.

(2018). Environmental comfort indicators for school buildings in sustainability assessment tools. *Sustainability (Switzerland)*, *10*(1849). https://doi.org/10.3390/su10061849

Shen, D. (2015). Environmental Sustainability and Economic Development: A World View. *Journal of Economics and Sustainable Development*, *6*(6), 60–80.

Suryani, A., Saifulloh, M., Muhibbin, Z., Hanoraga, T., Nurif, M., Trisyanti, U., … Rahmawati, D. (2019). Education for Environmental Sustainability: A Green School Development. *IPTEK Journal of Proceedings Series*, *6*(6), 65–72. Retrieved from http://unesco.unesco.org/images/0010/001056/105607e.p

Velasco-Martínez, L. C., Martín-Jaime, J. J., Estrada-Vidal, L. I., & Tójar-Hurtado, J. C. (2020). Environmental education to change the consumption model and curb climate change. *Sustainability (Switzerland)*, *12*(18). https://doi.org/10.3390/SU12187475

Vieira, S. R., Campos, M. A., Torales, M., & De, J. L. (2016). Proposal for environmental education indicators matrix for assessment of environmental sustainability in school. *Revista Eletrônica Do Mestrado Em Educação Ambiental*, *33*(2), 106–123.

Wilson, E. (2003). *Sustainable Development Frameworks and the issue of climate change.* (S. Buckingham & K. Theobald, Eds.), *Local Environmental Sustainability.* Cambridge, England: Woodhead Publishing Limited. https://doi.org/10.1016/C2013-0-17832-4

Wright, T. S. A. (2002). Definitions and frameworks for environmental sustainability in higher education. *International Journal of Sustainability in Higher Education.* https://doi.org/10.1108/14676370210434679

Assistant Professor,
Department of Education,
The Bhopal School of Social Sciences, Bhopal
M.P.
email : seemayadav1edu@gmail.com

8. Potential Role of Phosphate Solubilizing Bacteria in Augmenting Productivity and Ensuring Sustainable Development

Shilpi Damor*,
Dr.Praveen Goswami
Neeraj Kumar

Due to tremendous population growth, the globe is facing augmented food demand. This is causing excess stress on agricultural production as well as the community. To fulfill this excess yield, application of synthetic phosphate fertilizers to existing soil make up is practiced over rural as well as urban areas. This increased intervention of fertilizers not only causes contamination but also creates severe deteriorating effects like eutrophication, fertility reduction and piling up of toxic elements in soil. There are some soil micro fauna that have the potential to mobilize the insoluble phosphorus so that it can be utilized by plants. These micro organisms enhance crop productivity thus solving the purpose.

Thus, introduction of this Phosphate Solubilizing Microorganisms (PSM) is a futuristic approach to meet the need of the hour without causing any.

Though phosphorus-solubilizing microorganisms can be a key player in improving soil fertility significantly, they are yet to occupy a market superior to chemical fertilizers in large scale agriculture.

Deep insight learning on functional aspects of PSM, their diversity, growth rate, mode of action and appropriate way to use them may help them to achieve a place in our current agricultural systems.

In this chapter, we have discussed the diversity of soil microorganisms that are capable to solubilize phosphorus and so possess the potential to be used as bio fertilizer. The mechanics involved in solubilizing inorganic phosphate and mineralizing organic phosphorus are stated in we have also focused on achieving sustainable agricultural practices by use of PSM, thus making this technology suitable for global application and exploitation.

Introduction

Phosphorus (P) which makes up about 0.2% of a plant's dry weight is second most essential mineral nutrient after nitrogen which limits the crop growth. It directly influences development of plant, its growth and differentiation[1].Various metabolic processes like Photosynthesis, carbohydrate metabolism, energy production, redox-homeostasis, and signaling require this nutrient for their proper functioning.[2], [3]. This makes the phosphorus a nutrient of prime importance and so its deficiency can stifle normal plant growth if it isn't supplied by the soil or in sufficient quantities by fertilizers. As a result, P deficiency can result in considerable agricultural output losses (up to 15%) [4]

Although soil has a lot of phosphorus to be used up by the plants, still of all the content of available phosphorus in soil, the readily available fraction is only 0.1%.The presence of various divalent cations like calcium (Ca), iron (Fe) and aluminum (Al) in soil leads to fixation of available phosphorus, thus creating a deficiency. These cations immobilize phosphorus in the form of soil minerals. Hence, the phosphorus deficiency is created which now becomes the subject of concern. [5]

Chemical fertilizers are introduced into rhizospheric soil to remedy this problem. These fertilizers may cause severe environmental degradation such as groundwater contamination and waterway eutrophication. However, the problem becomes worse when the fertilizer that has been administered becomes immobilized and is no longer available for plant uptake [6].

Therefore it is very urgently required to identify those management practices that are capable of improving fertilization efficiency utilizing already available phosphorus in soil and hence increase crop production as well as reduce the risk of environmental deterioration. The soil micro fauna improvise nutritional consumption of plant and also facilitate various biological activities like solubilization of immobilized soil nutrients[7]

There is certain group of microorganism in the soil and rhizosphere, possessing potential to support plant growth by enhancing the bioavailability of insoluble soil phosphorus [5]. Apart from synthetic way of fertilizers, microbial community can be an effective alternate of releasing phosphorus from total soil phosphorus through solubilization and mineralization[8].This community is referred as phosphate solubilizing microorganisms. [5].

They act on inorganic phosphorus by dissolving them while mineralize organic phosphorus [9, 5].

Therefore inoculation of these microorganisms in soil may prove to be a prominent strategy for improvement of crop yield thereby reducing the use of synthetic fertilizers which may thereby have negative effect [1].

Phosphorus Solubilizing Microorganisms (PSM)

In nature a large group of microbial organisms including bacteria, fungi, actinomycetes, and algae demonstrate phosphorus solubilization and mineralization skill. The group of microbes which tremendously depict the phosphorus solubilization and mineralization property these include Pseudomonas, Agrobacterium and Bacillus spp. Also, fungi , actinomycetes , algae etc.occupy a postion in this communityer reported microbes **include *Rhizobium* [10], *Azotobacter* [11],** *Enterobacter,* *Erwinia* **[12]** *Kushneria* **[5],** *Paenibacillus* **[13],** *Ralstonia,* *Rhodococcus,* *Serratia,* *Bradyrhizobium,* *Salmonella,* *Sinomonas,* **and** *Thiobacillus* **[14,15],**

Among fungal category, that depict similar functional aspects include strains of *Achrothcium, Alternaria, Arthrobotrys, Aspergillus, Cephalosporium, Cladosporium, Curvularia, Cunninghamella, Chaetomium, Fusarium, Glomus, Helminthosporium, Micromonospora, Mortierella, Myrothecium, Oidiodendron, Paecilomyces, Penicillium, Phoma, Pichia fermentans, Populospora, Pythium, Rhizoctonia, Rhizopus, Saccharomyces, Schizosaccharomyces, Schwanniomyces, Sclerotium, Torula, Trichoderma,* **and** *Yarrowia* **[16,11].**Fungi being much defiant then bacteria may prove to be of prime importance in solubilization of inorganic phosphate. Also their capacity to generate increased concentration of organic acids like gluconic, citric, lactic, 2-ketogluconic, oxalic, tartaric and acetic acid [11].

Benefits of Phosphorus Solubilizing Microorganism

Phosphorus which is immobilized in soil can be utilized more properly with the help of these microorganisms which can play a role as bio fertilizers [5].Use of these bio fertilizers can not only be a promising approach by enhancing agricultural yield but also environment friendly approach to increasing food production [7].These microorganisms not only increases phosphorus uptake but also stimulate the efficiency of nitrogen fixation, phytohormone synthesis and some trace elements availability [17]. There have been a lot of field studies and pot experiments which have shown the improved result in terms of plant yield and in terms of phosphorus uptake [18]. These microorganisms also have synergistic effect on growth and development of crop [19].These micro fauna even act as bio control agents by secreting some antifungal compounds like phenolic and flavonoids, thereby wiping out some plant pathogens.

Mechanisms of Inorganic Phosphate Solubilization by PSM

There are a number of mechanism which have been given to explain the working of these microbial fauna.

The most common mechanism is the production of certain organic acids which behave as mineral dissolving compound [20, 11]. These organic acids along with certain cations reduce the pH of the soil to release phosphorus [19]. These are produced by various oxidation pathways in the periplasmic space [21].Production of these organic acids is accompanied by acidification of microbial cell and hence drop in pH of the surrounding this causes Phosphorus iron release by substitution of hydrogen ion for calcium ion. Another mechanism which is commonly seen is release of hydrogen ion to the outer surface in exchange for cation uptake or with the help of hydrogen translocation a TPS [20].It has also been reported that the assimilation of NH4 + in microbial cells involves the release of protons, which leads to the solubilization of phosphorus without the production of organic acids [11].Gluconic acid is the most effective and commonly produced organic acid involved in phosphate solubilization it relates the cation mounts to phosphate does making Phosphorus available [20].

Third mechanism which is involved in the production of in organic acid sulfuric acid nitric acid and carbonic acid and the production of chili eating compounds. To all of the above mechanism it is therefore sad that there is no soul reason for increase in phosphorus solubilization but a multiple factor [22].

Mechanisms of Organic Phosphorus Mineralization

The main mechanism in production of organic acid. Organic matter is the primary source of organic Phosphorus in soil. The total Phosphorus content of soil 30 to 50% can be e from organic phosphorus. This organic Phosphorus occurs in the form of inositol phosphate, phosphor Monu-esters digesters phospholipids nucleic acids for tri esters [20].

Factors Influencing Microbial Phosphate Solubilization

There are certain factors which influence the efficacy of microbial phosphate solubilization. These factors include the availability of various nutrients in the soil, the growth and Functional aspect of the organism. It has been observed that the microorganism solubilize more phosphate in environmentally extreme conditions such as saline, alkaline, highly nutrient deficit soil or soil in extreme hot or cold temperature rather than moderate conditions [11]

There have been various studies on effect temperature on these microbes. In a study it was found that the microbes showed the growth maxima at a temperature range of 20–25°C [23] while there were certain other studies where 28°C was reported as the optimum temperature [24] .

Other factor which influences them is their inter-microbial soil interaction, the level of foliage, ecological parameters, Zonal soil type, plant form, agricultural techniques, usage of land, and the physico-chemical structure of soil such as organic matter [19].

It has also been studied that phosphate is also solubilized more rapidly in warm areas as compared to those in cool and dry climatic areas. The soil which is well aerated allows rapid solubilization as compared to those saturated soil.

Previous usage of land in activities like crop system, livestock rearing or even mixed activities may affect the fertility of soil to a greater extent.

The more abundant biodiversity of phosphate solubilizing microorganisms was observed in soil that underwent crop rotation [2].

Presence of organic matter in soil also favors microbial growth thereby inducing more solubilization. The pH values ranging from 6 to 7.5 works optimally for Phosphorus availability but 800 more than 7.5 limits the availability of phosphorus by fixing it with aluminum iron or calcium [21].

Future Prospects

As more information on PSM and the mechanisms that they employ becomes available, there is every reason to assume that their use as bio fertilizers will become more effective and significant components in the establishment of long-term soil management systems. Consumers of agricultural products are concerned about the items' health, quality, and nutritional worth. As a result, using PSM as bio fertilizers is a viable approach for increasing food production while minimizing health risks and conserving the environment. It is critical that academics continue to learn more about PSM and quickly put their findings into a format that farmers can understand.

Conclusion

The potential of phosphate-solubilizing microorganisms as bio-fertilizers has been demonstrated in this paper. Using soil to mobilize inorganic phosphate and increase its bioavailability for plant usage PSM helps sustainable agriculture by increasing soil fertility and, as a result, crop productivity. PSM as microbial inoculants opens up new possibilities for increased plant productivity. Low-input farming systems and a cleaner environment can both benefit from PSM technology. However, PSB technologies specific to particular locations must be developed, and this information must be transmitted to farmers in a timely manner.

Author Contributions

All authors listed, have made substantial, direct and intellectual contribution to the work, and approved it for publication.

Conflict of Interest Statement

The authors declare that the research was conducted in the absence of any commercial or financial relationships that could be construed as a potential conflict of interest.

References

[1] E. Alori, O. Fawole, and A. Afolayan, "Characterization of arbuscular mycorrhizal spores isolated from southern guinea Savanna of Nigeria," *J. Agric. Sci.*, vol. 4, no. 7, 2012.

[2] G. Azziz *et al.*, "Abundance, diversity and prospecting of culturable phosphate solubilizing bacteria on soils under crop–pasture rotations in a no-tillage regime in Uruguay," *Appl. Soil Ecol.*, vol. 61, pp. 320–326, 2012.

[3] H. Iqbal Tak, F. Ahmad, O. O Babalola, and A. Inam, "Growth, photosynthesis and yield of chickpea as influenced by urban wastewater and different levels of phosphorus," *Int. J. Plant Res.*, vol. 2, no. 2, pp. 6–13, 2012.

[4] V. V. Shenoy and G. M. Kalagudi, "Enhancing plant phosphorus use efficiency for sustainable cropping," *Biotechnol. Adv.*, vol. 23, no. 7–8, pp. 501–513, 2005.

[5] F. Zhu, L. Qu, X. Hong, and X. Sun, "Isolation and characterization of a phosphate-solubilizing halophilic bacterium Kushneria sp. YCWA18 from Daqiao saltern on the coast of yellow sea of China," *Evid. Based. Complement. Alternat. Med.*, vol. 2011, p. 615032, 2011.

[6] J. Kang, A. Amoozegar, D. Hesterberg, and D. L. Osmond, "Phosphorus leaching in a sandy soil as affected by organic and inorganic fertilizer sources," *Geoderma*, vol. 161, no. 3–4, pp. 194–201, 2011.

[7] O. O. Babalola, "Indigenous African agriculture and plant associated microbes: Current practice and future transgenic prospects," *Sci. Res. Essays*, vol. 7, no. 28, 2012.

[8] P. N. Bhattacharyya and D. K. Jha, "Plant growth-promoting rhizobacteria (PGPR): emergence in agriculture," *World J. Microbiol. Biotechnol.*, vol. 28, no. 4, pp. 1327–1350, 2012.

[9] S. B. Sharma, R. Z. Sayyed, M. H. Trivedi, and T. A. Gobi, "Phosphate solubilizing microbes: sustainable approach for managing phosphorus deficiency in agricultural soils," *Springerplus*, vol. 2, no. 1, p. 587, 2013.

[10] F. Tajini, M. Trabelsi, and J.-J. Drevon, "Combined

inoculation with Glomus intraradices and Rhizobium tropici CIAT899 increases phosphorus use efficiency for symbiotic nitrogen fixation in common bean (Phaseolus vulgaris L.)," *Saudi J. Biol. Sci.*, vol. 19, no. 2, pp. 157–163, 2012.

[11] S. Kumar, K. Bauddh, S. C. Barman, and R. P. Singh, "Amendments of microbial biofertilizers and organic substances reduces requirement of urea and DAP with enhanced nutrient availability and productivity of wheat (Triticum aestivum L.)," *Ecol. Eng.*, vol. 71, pp. 432–437, 2014.

[12] U. Chakraborty, B. N. Chakraborty, M. Basnet, and A. P. Chakraborty, "Evaluation of Ochrobactrum anthropi TRS-2 and its talc based formulation for enhancement of growth of tea plants and management of brown root rot disease," *J. Appl. Microbiol.*, vol. 107, no. 2, pp. 625–634, 2009.

[13] L. F. Bidondo, V. Silvani, R. Colombo, M. Pérgola, J. Bompadre, and A. Godeas, "Pre-symbiotic and symbiotic interactions between Glomus intraradices and two Paenibacillus species isolated from AM propagules. In vitro and in vivo assays with soybean (AG043RG) as plant host," *Soil Biol. Biochem.*, vol. 43, no. 9, pp. 1866–1872, 2011.

[14] J. Postma, E. H. Nijhuis, and E. Someus, "Selection of phosphorus solubilizing bacteria with biocontrol potential for growth in phosphorus rich animal bone charcoal," *Appl. Soil Ecol.*, vol. 46, no. 3, pp. 464–469, 2010.

[15] P. David, R. S. Raj, R. Linda, and S. B. Rhema, "Molecular characterization of phosphate solubilizing bacteria (PSB) and plant growth promoting rhizobacteria (PGPR) from pristine soils," *Int. J. Innov. Sci. Eng. Technol*, vol. 1, pp. 317–324, 2014.

[16] R. Srinivasan, M. S. Yandigeri, S. Kashyap, and A. R. Alagawadi, "Effect of salt on survival and P-solubilization potential of phosphate solubilizing microorganisms from salt affected soils," *Saudi J. Biol. Sci.*, vol. 19, no. 4, pp. 427–434, 2012.

[17] P. Wani, M. Khan, and A. Zaidi, "Co-inoculation of nitrogen-fixing and phosphate-solubilizing bacteria to promote growth, yield and nutrient uptake in chickpea," *Acta Agron. Hungar.*, vol. 55, no. 3, pp. 315–323, 2007.

[18] S.-L. Wang, W.-H. Hsu, and T.-W. Liang, "Conversion of squid pen by Pseudomonas aeruginosa K187 fermentation for the production of N-acetyl chitooligosaccharides and biofertilizers," *Carbohydr. Res.*, vol. 345, no. 7, pp. 880–885, 2010.

[19] U. Seshachala and P. Tallapragada, "Phosphate Solubilizers from the Rhizospher of Piper nigrum L. in Karnataka, India," *Chil. J. Agric. Res.*, vol. 72, no. 3, pp. 397–403, 2012.

[20] H. Rodríguez, G. M. Rossolini, T. Gonzalez, J. Li, and B. R. Glick, "Isolation of a gene from Burkholderia cepacia IS-16 encoding a protein that facilitates phosphatase activity," *Curr. Microbiol.*, vol. 40, no. 6, pp. 362–366, 2000.

[21] K. Zhao *et al.*, "Maize rhizosphere in Sichuan, China, hosts plant growth promoting Burkholderia cepacia with phosphate solubilizing and antifungal abilities," *Microbiol. Res.*, vol. 169, no. 1, pp. 76–82, 2014.

[22] K. Y. Kim, G. A. McDonald, and D. Jordan, "Solubilization of hydroxyapatite by Enterobacter agglomerans and cloned Escherichia coli in culture medium," *Biol. Fertil. Soils*, vol. 24, no. 4, pp. 347–352, 1997.

[23] C. White, J. A. Sayer, and G. M. Gadd, "Microbial solubilization and immobilization of toxic metals: key biogeochemical processes for treatment of contamination," *FEMS Microbiol. Rev.*, vol. 20, no. 3–4, pp. 503–516, 1997.

[24] S. C. Kang, G. C. Ha, T. G. Lee, and D. K. Maheshwari, "Solubilization of insoluble inorganic phosphates by a soil inhabiting fungus sp. Ps 102," *Curr. Sci*, vol. 79, pp. 439–442, 2002.

Deptt of Zoology,
Poddar international college, Jaipur

9. Changing Scenario of Literacy Rate after Indepandance in Rural and Urban India

Dr. Surendar Choudhary

Abstract

According to Indian census, literacy is defined as the ability of people to read and write a simple message in any language with some understanding The study examines the trend of urban and rural literacy and gap by residence after independence. The study also analysis the spatial pattern of literacy as well as disparity by residence at district level. The study reveals that after independence in India; a significant increase has recorded in literacy rate in both urban and rural areas. Urban literacy has risen rapidly than rural while 229.63 million illiterates are living in rural area of country which is 81.23 per cent of total illiterates. Gap between urban- rural increased with increase in literacy and recorded 32.33 per cent in 1971 however; after 1971 census, it is decreasing slowly yet it is high. Large part of Jammu & Kashmir, south Punjab, some districts of Haryana, nothern part of Uttar Pradesh, Bihar, Jharkhand, Arunachal Pradesh, almost part of Rajasthan, north part of Gujarat, western and northern district of Madhya Pradesh, southern districts of Odisha and Chhattisgarh, Andhra Pradesh, north-east part of Karnataka as well as border area of Karnataka and Tamil Nadu contain low literacy rate in both urban and rural areas.

Keywords : Trend of Literacy and Gap by Residence, Spatial Pattern

Introduction

It is not mandatory that to be treated as a literate, a person should have received any formal education or acquired any minimum educational standard. Literacy status can be acquired through adult literacy classes or by attending any non-formal education system. Persons who are unfortunately blind and read in Braille are also treated as literates. From 1991 census, children below seven years are ignored when working out literacy rate in the country and the population aged seven years and above only would be classified as

95

literate or illiterate. The proportion of literate persons in a population is known as literacy level and the process of dissemination of literacy among the people in a society known as literacy transition. Literacy is related to all type of development which prepares the individual for full participation in a rapidly changing social and economic order.

An overall progress in literacy is necessary in a country; equally important is its distributional spread in all its areas – towns and villages, social classes and the two sexes (Gosal, 1979) but India is suffering with low literacy rate as well as high disparity by residence.

Study Area

It is an all India Study. India is located in the northern and eastern hemispheres. It is extended from 6^0 45' north to 37^0 6' north latitudes and 68^0 7' east to 97^0 25' east longitudes. It has 28 states, 7 union territories and 640 districts at the time of census enumeration (2011).

Objectives of the Study

To ex line the trend of urban and rural literacy rates (1951-2011).
To re sent spatial pattern of literacy at district level.
To idenify disparity by residence in literacy at district level.

Data and Methodology

In this study, data have collected from Primary Census Abstract published by office of the Registrar General & Census Commissioner, India as well as Selected Educational Statistics, Ministry of Human Resource Development, Government of India.

Methodology is central to any research work which helps in scientific description and explanations of reality. Absolute figures are converted into percentages as well as ratios and these percentages and ratios are processed for necessary cartographic representations and interpretation. Requisite maps have been drawn with the help of Arc GIS software. Sopher's Disparity Index (1980) modified by Kundu and Rao (1985) as given below, has been used to compute disparity by residence in literacy at district level.

Role of Sustainable Development in Environmental Conservation

Ds = Log(x2/x1) + Log (200-x1/200-x2) Here,
Ds = Urban-Rural Disparity Index X2 = Urban Literacy Rate
X1 = Rural Literacy Rate

Table 1

Urban and Rural Literacy Rate in India			
(in per cent)			
Year	Urban Literacy Rate	Rural Literacy Rate	Gap between Urban-Rural Literacy Rate	Ratio of Urban-Rural Literacy Rate
1951	34.59	12.10	22.49	2.86 : 1
1961	54.40	22.50	31.90	2.42 : 1
1971	60.22	27.89	32.33	2.16 : 1
1981	67.23	36.01	31.22	1.87 : 1
1991	73.08	44.69	28.39	1.64 : 1
2001	79.92	58.74	21.18	1.36 : 1
2011	84.11	67.77	16.34	1.24 : 1

Source : Adopted and computed from:
• Selected Educational Statistics (1999-2000), Ministry of Human Resource Development, Government of India.
• Primary Census Abstract, Census of India, 2001.
• Primary Census Abstract, Census of India, 2011.

Note : Literacy rates for 1951 census to 1971 census relate to population aged five year and above while the rates for the 1981 census to 2011 census, relate to the population aged seven year and above.

Urban Literacy Rate
There were 49.01 million illiterates in urban area of country at the time of 1991 census enumeration which was 14.90 per cent of total illiterates. The urban illiterates increased 4.06 million after 1991 and recorded

53.07 million in 2011 census which is 18.77 per cent of total illiterates. Urban literacy rate in India is increased rapidly. According to 1951 census; it was 34.59 per cent which increased up to 67.23 per cent in 1981. During 2001 census it was 79.92 per cent and now in 2011 census; it has recorded 84.11 per cent. Occupational necessity, better educational facilities, socially and economically capability to get education, less prejudices against female's mobility and education, better health condition, better situation of law and order, migration of educated rural people to urban areas are the major causes of high literacy in urban area. When we examine state wise; the highest urban literacy is found in Mizoram (97.63 per cent) followed by Kerala (95.11 per cent), Tripura (93.47 per cent), Himachal Pradesh (91.10 per cent) and Meghalaya (90.79 per cent). All Union Territories contain literacy rates above 86 per cent. On the other hand, lowest literacy rate is found in Uttar Pradesh (75.14 per cent) followed by Bihar (76.86 per cent), Jammu & Kashmir (77.12 per cent), Rajasthan (79.68 per cent) and Andhra Pradesh (80.09 per cent). When we analysis district level, it varies from 56 per cent in Rampur district of Madhya Pradesh to 98.27 per cent in Aizawl district of Mizoram. Figure 2 shows that 344 districts out of 637 contain low literacy from the national average. Regional variation also exists.

Table 2

Urban and Rural Literacy Rate (2011) (in per cent)			
State/Union Territory	Urban Literacy Rate	Rural Literacy Rate	Gap by Residence in Literacy Rate
Mizoram	97.63	84.10	13.53
Kerala	95.11	92.98	2.12
Tripura	93.47	84.90	8.57
Himachal Pradesh	91.10	81.85	9.25
Meghalaya	90.79	69.92	20.87
Goa	89.95	86.65	3.30
Nagaland	89.62	75.35	14.28
Sikkim	88.71	78.95	9.76
Maharashtra	88.69	77.01	11.68
Assam	88.47	69.34	19.13
Tamil Nadu	87.04	73.54	13.50

Gujarat	86.31	71.71	14.60
Karnataka	85.78	68.73	17.04
Odisha	85.75	70.22	15.53
Manipur	85.38	73.40	11.98
West Bengal	84.78	72.13	12.65
Uttarakhand	84.45	76.31	8.14
Chhattisgarh	84.05	65.99	18.06
Punjab	83.18	71.42	11.76
Haryana	83.14	71.42	11.73
Arunachal Pradesh	82.93	59.94	22.99
Madhya Pradesh	82.85	63.94	18.91
Jharkhand	82.26	61.11	21.14
Andhra Pradesh	80.09	60.45	19.64
Rajasthan	79.68	61.44	18.24
Jammu & Kashmir	77.12	63.18	13.94
Bihar	76.86	59.78	17.08
Uttar Pradesh	75.14	65.46	9.68
Union Territories			
Lakshadweep	91.92	91.58	0.34
Andaman & Nicobar Islands	90.10	84.50	5.60
Dadra & Nagar Haveli	89.79	64.12	25.66
Daman & Diu	88.96	81.36	7.59
Puducherry	88.49	80.10	8.40
NCT of Delhi	86.32	81.86	4.46
Chandigarh	86.19	80.75	5.45
India	**84.11**	**67.77**	**16.34**

Source : Calculated from- Primary Census Abstract, Census of India, 2011.

Note : Population in age group 0-6 is ignored.

When we examine state wise; it is found highest in Kerala (92.98 per cent) followed by Goa (86.65 per cent), Tripura (84.90 per cent), Mizoram (84.10 per cent) and Himachal Pradesh (81.85 per cent). Dadra & Nagar Haveli contains low literacy rate (64.12 per cent) while rest union territories contain literacy rates above 80 per cent. On the other hand, lowest literacy rate is found in Bihar (59.78 per cent) followed by Arunachal Pradesh (59.94 per cent), Andhra Pradesh (60.45 per cent), Jharkhand (61.11 per cent) and Rajasthan (61.44 per cent).

Remarkable increase has recorded by some states and union territories during the last decade such as Bihar (15.86 per cent) followed by Jharkhand (15.37 per cent), Tripura (15.18 per cent), Dadra & Nagar Haveli (14.78 per cent), Meghalaya (13.63 per cent), Jammu & Kashmir (13.40 per cent), Uttar Pradesh (12.93 per cent), Nagaland (12.55 per cent), Sikkim (12.12 per cent) and Arunachal Pradesh (12.11 per cent) while at national level it is remaining 9.02 per cent during same decade.

When we analysis district level; literacy rate varies from 32.08 per cent in Alirajpur district of Madhya Pradesh to 97.59 per cent in Serchhip district of Mizoram. Figure 3 shows that districts which are located in western, southern and north-eastern part of country as well as socio-economically developed small states such as Himachal Pradesh, Uttrakhand and Haryana contain high literacy rate due to coastal location, high degree of urbanization, more diversified economy, modern agricultural system, considerable proportion of Christian population, early start of modern education under state patronage, greater allocation of funds for the development of education.

Rural Literacy Rate

When we see the status of illiterates; we found that there were 279.82 million illiterates in rural area of country at the time of 1991 census enumeration which was 85.10 per cent of total illiterates. The rural illiterates decreased 50.19 million after 1991 and recorded 229.63 million in 2011 census which is 81.23 per cent of total illiterates Rural literacy rate has increased slowly. According to 1951 census; it was only 12.10 per cent which increased up to 36.01 per cent in 1981 and now in 2011 census; it has recorded 67.77 per cent.On the other hand; low literacy rates are found in Jammu & Kashmir, Uttar Pradesh, Bihar, Arunachal Pradesh, Rajasthan, Madhya Pradesh, Jharkhand, southern districts of Chhattisgarh and

Odisha as well as Andhra Pradesh due to subsistence economy, low role of private sector, history of native rule, prejudice against females, high proportion of peoples which are backward (Muslim, scheduled castes and scheduled tribes). However; intra-state variation also exists in these states.

Urban-Rural Disparity in Literacy

Urban-rural disparity in literacy is existing continue. In 1951; the gap between urban-rural literacy rates was 22.49 per cent at national level which increased with increase in literacy and recorded 32.33 per cent in 1971 however; after 1971 census, it is decreasing slowly. During 2001 census, it recorded 21.18 per cent and now in 2011 census, it is 16.34 per cent which is high.

Here, urban-rural disparity in literacy has also calculated by Sopher's Disparity Index (1980) modified by Kundu and Rao (1985). Score of disparity index is found 0.15 at national level. When we examine state wise; the highest score of disparity index is found in Arunachal Pradesh (0.22) followed by Jharkhand (0.20), Meghalaya and Andhra Pradesh (0.19), Madhya Pradesh (0.18) and Assam (0.17). On the other hand; Kerala (0.02), Goa (0.03), Uttarakhand (0.07), Tripura and Himachal Pradesh (0.08) as well as Sikkim and Uttar Pradesh (0.09) contain low disparity.

Among the union territories; Dadra & Nagar Haveli contains highest disparity (0.24) while rest union territories contain low disparity.

Conclusion

After independence in India; a significant increase has recorded in literacy rate in both urban and rural areas. Urban literacy has risen rapidly than rural while 229.63 million illiterates are living in rural area of country which is 81.23 per cent of total illiterates.

Gap between urban-rural increased with increase in literacy and recorded 32.33 per cent in 1971 however; after 1971 census, it is decreasing slowly yet it is high.

Large part of Jammu & Kashmir, south Punjab, some districts of Haryana, nothern part of Uttar Pradesh, Bihar, Jharkhand, Arunachal Pradesh, almost part of Rajasthan, north part of Gujarat, western and northern districts of Madhya Pradesh, southern districts of Odisha and Chhattisgarh, Andhra Pradesh, north-east part of Karnataka as well as border area of Karnataka and Tamil Nadu contain low literacy rate in both urban and rural areas. Patriarchal society and low status of female, teaching other than mother tongue, minor role of private sector, engagement the school age children in economic activities, little functional value of education for deprived section of society, less diversified economy, unequal distribution of resources, poverty, low health condition, backward agriculture system, low level of infrastructure facilities, low level of urbanization and industrialization, terror and naxalite activities are the major causes of low literacy in these areas.

References

1. Gosal, G.S. (1979). Spatial Perspective on Literacy in India. Population Geography, 1, 41-67.
2. Ministry of Human Resource Development. Selected Educational Statistics.
3. Office of the Registrar General & Census Commissioner, India. (2001). Primary Census Abstract. Retrieved from http://censusindia.gov.in/DigitalLibrary/TablesSeries2001.aspx
4. Office of the Registrar General & Census Commissioner, India. (2011). Primary Census Abstract. Retrieved from http://www.censusindia.gov.in/2011census/population_enumeration.htm

Assistant Professor-Geography
Sndb Govt Pg College, Nohar, Hanumangarh,
email : Surenchoudharyo4@Gmail,

10. Synthesis, Characterization and Antibacterial studies of Transition Metal Complexes with Containing Nitrogenase base of DNA By Green Approach

Dr. Raja Ram

Abstract

This study explain the synthesis, spectral and anti microbial study of the complexes of Transition metals with pyrimidine derivative ligands. In this chapter I have discussed on Mn(II) transition metal. The complexes have been characterized on the basis of elemental analysis, IR, UV and magnetic susceptibility studies. Antibacterial activities of these ligands and complexes have also been reported on *S. aureus* and *E.coli* microorganisms. Antibacterial investigations carried out by disc diffusion method. The diffuse reflectance spectrums of the complexes show bands in the region 17636 cm^{-1} to 26881cm^{-1}, assignable to $^6A_{1g} \rightarrow {}^4T_{2g}$, $^6A_{1g} \rightarrow {}^4E_g$, $^4A_{1g}$ (4G) transitions. These are also typical of tetrahedral environment around the Manganese. The magnetic moment (5.79-5.92 BM) of the complex indicates high tetrahedral environment. The green method of synthesis of these complexes carried out by green microwave bioreactor (GMBR). This method is easily, appropriate and eco-friendly.

Keywords : Microwave, amide, 3-d metals Antibacterial, Tetrahedral

Introduction

Manganese transition metal is more necessary for production iron and steel by virtue of its sulfur-fixing, deoxidizing alloying properties (1). This metal has been broadly uses in alloys of aluminium metal and key component of low-cost stainless steel formation. MnO_2 is used in dry cells and as a catalyst. $KMnO_4$ is generally used as a potent oxidizer and as a typical medicine (disinfectant). Manganese oxide is a brown pigment that can be used to make paint and is a component of natural umber. Manganese phosphate is used for rust and corrosion prevention on steel. Manganese will be mostly replaced with lithium battery technology in manufacture of disposable battery, standard and alkaline cells (2-3). Manganese particles usually settle to earth within some days. Humans enhance manganese concentrations in the air by industrial activities and through burning fossil fuels. Manganese that derives from human sources can also enter on surface water, ground water and sewage water. Through the application of manganese pesticides, manganese enters in soil (4-5). Manganese plays an important role for plants growth. Deficiency of manganese ions causes disturbances in plant mechanism. Many herbs also contain manganese, burdock root, fennel dandelion, fenugreek, ginseng, horsetail, lemongrass, seed,parsley, peppermint, chamomile, wild yam and raspberry (6). In mammalian cells, manganese causes DNA damages and chromosome aberrations. Large amount of manganese affect fertility in mammals and are toxic to the embryo and foetus (7-8). Manganese has been shown to cross the blood brain barrier and a limited amount of manganese is also able to cross the placenta during pregnancy, enabling it to reach a developing fetus (9-10). Manganese deficiency in the foetus may also causes malformation of the inner ear, ataxia and bone malformation. Lack of co-ordination head retraction, tremor, loss of righting reflexes, hyper irritability, faulty cartilage and bone matrix formation, heart problems and learning difficulties also occur (11). Metal or metalloid of amide are compounds which contain one or more (–$CONH_2$) ligand groups or a simple derivative [such as –CONHR, -$CONR_2$, where R = methyl, phenyl, acetyl etc.) attached to metal. (12-18).

Experimetal

Apparatus

(i) EC Double Beam UV-VIS Spectrophotometer (UV 5704SS), with quartz cell of 10 mm light path was used for Electronic spectral measurement at GCRC (Green Chemistry Research Center) Govt. Dungar College (NAAC A-Grade) Bikaner, (Raj.).

(ii) IR spectra were recorded on Bruker Optic Model Alpha (FT-IR) (Zn-Se Optics, ATR) (4000-500 cm-1) using KBr disc at SIL,

P.G. Dept. of chemistry, Govt. Dungar College (NAAC-A-Grade) Bikaner, Rajasthan.

(iii) Microwave synthesis was carried out in domestic microwave oven and GMBR (Green Microwave Biochemical Reactor) at GCRC, P.G. Dept. of Chemistry, Govt. Dungar College (NAAC-A- Grade) Bikaner, Rajasthan.

(iv) All biological activities have been carried out with horizontal laminar, BIFR, Bikaner.

2.2 Materials and Method

For the synthesis of Mn(II) complexes with amide group containing ligands, a solution of $MnCl_2$ (1mmole in 30 mL ethyl alcohol) has been taken in a 250 ml round bottom flask, in this solution respective amide ligand (i.e. $(N6H2MC4PB)_2Cl_2$, $(N6H2MC4PB)_2Cl_2$, $(N26DH4PB)_2Cl_2$, $(N26DH4PA)_2Cl_2$ (0.003 mole) was added slowly with constant stirring. The reaction mixture was placed on a magnetic stirrer with constant stirring for more than 6-7 hrs at room temperature.

In the microwave synthesis, the reaction mixture was irradiated in a microwave reactor (GMBR) for 2-5 minutes. The solid precipitate obtained in both the methods was separated and crystallized. Crystals were purified and recrystalized with ethyl alcohol and dried under vacuum.

Results and Discussion

The complexes of Mn (II) with all the amide group containing ligands are stable at room temperatures over a long period of time. The manganese complexes under investigations were white (brown) coloured powder; these complexes were, partially soluble in DMSO and insoluble in all other solvents. The elemental and metal estimations give satisfactory results. The physical and analytical data of complexes are given in Table 1

(i). Vibrational Spectra

Vibrational spectra were recorded in KBr pellets and polyethylene film in mid and far IR regions and some diagnostic bands are presented in Table 3.

The IR bands due to amide v (N-H) mode observed at 3163-3382 cm-1 for the free amide group containing ligands are shifted to higher frequencies indicating non-participation of nitrogen atom of amide group in coordination. Amide 1 bands due to v (C=O) shift negatively opposite to that of v (N-H) in the complexes suggesting carbonyl oxygen coordination (19). In complexes it is represented that pyrimidinyl nitrogen participates in bonding, which has been confirmed by the 16-100 cm^{-1} negative shifting of pyrimidinyl ring peak in complexes to the comparison of ligands. (Figure 5 to 8). These observations have ambiguous and support   the   final structural   conclusions   of   the   complexes   and   the mode of bonding in them.(Fig. 9-12)

ii). Magnetic Susceptibility Measurements

Complexes of bivalent manganese are known in both high spin (S=5/2) and low spin (S = 1/2) states. Because of the additional stability of the half filled d-orbitals Mn (II) generally forms high spin complexes which have an orbitally degenerate 6S ground state term and the spin only magnetic moment of 5.9 ± 0.1 BM is expected which will be independent of the temperature and of stereochemistry (20). The magnetic susceptibility measurements have been carried out in the polycrystalline state at room temperature and the results are given in Table 2. All the manganese (II) complexes have magnetic moment values in the range 5.70-5.92 BM indicating the presence of five unpaired electrons and hence these are high spin complexes with tetrahedral coordinate manganese (21).

(iii). Electronic Spectra

The electronic spectra of the manganese complexes with amide group containing ligands show weak absorption in the visible region. This is presented in Table 2 and in Fig.1 to 4.

The observed spectra(of the manganese (II) complexes with the ligands exhibit bands in the region 17636 cm-1 and 28011 cm-1 assignable to

$$^{6}A_{1g} \rightarrow ^{4}T_{2G} \text{ and } ^{6}A_{1g} \rightarrow ^{4}E_{g}, ^{4}A_{1g} (4G)$$

The electronic spectral transitions of Mn complexes with the pyrimidine derivative   ligands are typical of tetrahedral (Td) environment around the Mn (22).

Thermal Studies

The complexes of Mn (II) with the amide group containing ligands show first order kinetics in their thermal decomposition reaction. This is based on a straight line plot of Coats and Redfern (for n = 1). Activation energy has been carried out by the linearization method of Goats and Redfern. The thermal studies give the description about the thermal stability of the complexes. It has been observed that no decomposition takes place at room temperature and complexes are fairly stable well above the room temperature. The initial decomposition started above 500K.

Conclusions

On the basis of vibration spectra, the amide group containing ligands show bidentate behavior in respect of Mn(II) complexes by coordinating through carbonyl oxygen of amide groups and nitrogen of pyrimidine ring. Thus, Mn (II) adopts tetrahedral geometry in the complexes with bioactive amide ligands. On the basis of these studies the tentative structures have been proposed for the complexes and which are given in Fig. 9 to 12 for Mn(II) complexes. The complexes synthesized by novel green method are at par with conventional synthesis and in many cases yield was found to be better than conventional synthesis.

Acknowledgements

Author (RR) is thankful to all members of GCRC.

References.

1. Burns RE, Helgoland Marine Research, 33 (1-4) (1980) 433.
2. Sistrunk Shannon C, Ross Matthew K & Filipov Nikolay, Environ. Toxicol Pharmacol., 23 (3) (2007) 286.
3. Faglin Zhang, Xu Zhaofa, Gao Jian Xu Bin & Deng Yu, Environ. Toxicol Pharmacol., 26 (2) (2008) 232.
4. Vandenabeele J, Vande Woestyne M, Houwen F, Germonpre R, Vandesande D & Verstraete W, Microbial Ecology, 29(1) (1995)83.
5. Granina LZ & Callender E, Hydrobiologia, 568 (2006) 41.

6. Pae Chi-Un, Yoon Su-Jung, Patkar Ashwin, Kim Jung- Lin, Jun Tae- Youn, Lee Chul & Paik In-Ho, Progress in Neuro-Psychopharmacology and Biological Psychiatry 30(7) (2006) 1326.
7. Poranen Minna M, Salgado Paula S, Koivunen Minni RL,Wright Sam, Bamford Dennis H, Satuart David I & Grimes Jonathan M, Nucleic Acids Research, 36 (20) (2008) 6633.
8. Papp-Wallace Kristztina M, Moomaw Andrea S & Maguire Michael E, Microbiology Monograph, 6 (2007) 235.
9. Gerber GB, Leonard A & Hantson P, Critical Review in Oncology/Hematology, 42 (1) (2002) 25.
10. Komura J & Sakamoto M, Environ. Res; 57 (1) (1992) 34.
11. Kitao Mitsutoshi, Lei Thomas T & Koite Takayoshi, Physiologia Platarum, 101 (2) (2006) 249.
12. Garg B.S. , Bhojak N., Sharma R.K., Bist J.S. and Mittal S., 1999. Separation and preconcentration of metal ions and their estimation in vitamin, steel and milk sample using o-vanillin-immobilized silica gel. Talanta.48, 1, 49 55.
13. Bhojak N., Gudasaria D. D., Khiwani N. & Jain R., (2007). "Microwave Assisted Synthesis Spectral and Antibacterial Investigations on Complexes of Mn (II) With Amide Containing Ligands." E-Journal of Chemistry, 4(2), 232-237.
14. Garg B. S., Bhojak N., Nandan D. (2005). "Micellar spectrofluorimetric determination of lead (II) in natural water, waste water and egg samples with N-(2'-pyridyl)- 2-hydroxybenzamide".Ind. J. Chem., 44A, 1504.
15. Raja Ram, Verma K.K., Solanki K.and Bhojak N. (2015). Microwave assisted synthesis, spectral and antibacterial investigations on complexes of Co (II) with amide containing ligands. International Journal of New Technologies in Science and Engineering. 2(6), 92-100.
16. Verma K. K., Soni Gupta P., Solanki K.and Bhojak N. (2015). "Microwave Assisted Synthesis, Characterisation and Anti microbial activities of few Cobalt (II) Thiosemicarbazones Complexes. World Journal of pharmacy and pharmaceutical sciences." 4(11), 1673-1683.

17. Raja Ram, Verma K. K., Bhandari H. S. and Bhojak N. (2015). "Microwave assisted synthesis, spectral and antibacterial investigations on complexes of Ni (II) with amide group containing ligands." IARJSET, 2(11), 40-43.
18. Singh B. and Bhojak N. (2008). "Microwave assisted synthesis, spectral and antibacterial investigations on complexes of Mn (II) with amide containing ligands." RJC,1(1), 105-109,
19. Garg BS, Kumar V & Reddy MJ, Transition Met. Chem., 18 (1993) 364.
20. 38Figgis BN & Lewis J, Progress in Inorganic Chemistry, (1964) 37.
21. 39Singh R, Sharma K & Fahmi N, Transition Met. Chem., 24 (1999)562.
22. 40Paul RC, Chopra RS, Bhambri RK & Singh G, J. Inorg. Nucl. Chem., 36 (1974) 3703.

Table- 1
Physico-chemical Data of Mn (II) Metal Complexes
(C.M.= Conventional method, M.M.= Microwave method)

S.N.	Complexes	Colour	m.p. (°C)	Reaction period		Yield %		Elemental analysis Calculated(Found)%		
				C.M. hrs.	M.M. min.	C.M.	M.M.	C	H	N
1	[Mn-(N6H2MC4PB)₂]Cl₂,	Off white	304	6.5	2.00	45	55	42.58 (42.50)	2.90 (2.85)	13.54 (13.50)
2	[Mn-(N6H2MC4PB)₂]Cl₂,	Light buff	310	6.5	2.30	40	45	33.88 (33.80)	3.29 (3.24)	19.76 (1968)
3	[Mn-(N26DH4PB)₂]Cl₂,	Orange	288	7	2.00	45	55	44.89 (44.80)	3.06 (3.00)	14.28 (14.20)
4	[Mn-(N26DH4PA)₂]Cl₂	Orange	295	6.5	2.00	45	55	31.03 (30.95)	3.01 (2.96)	18.10 (18.00)

Table-2
Magnetic moments and electronic Spectral data of ligand and Mn(II) metal complex

S. N.	Ligand and Complex	R_f value	μ_{eff} (BM)	Electronic Spectral Bands λ_{max} (cm^{-1})	Tentative assignments	Expected Geometry
1	[Mn-(N6H2MC4PB)2]Cl2	(0.711)h	5.88	18903,20120,21691,24038, 24570,27322,	$^6A_{1g}\rightarrow{}^4T_{2G}$ $^6A_{1g}\rightarrow{}^4E_g$, $^4A_{1g}$ (4G)	Tetrahedral
2	[Mn-(N6H2MC4PA)2]Cl2	(0.818)g	5.78	18939,20161,21621,22624, 24570,26917,	$^6A_{1g}\rightarrow{}^4T_{2G}$ $^6A_{1g}\rightarrow{}^4E_g$, $^4A_{1g}$ (4G)	Tetrahedral
3	[Mn-(N26DH4PB)2]Cl2	(0.792)h	5.70	18832,19230,24691,26990	$^6A_{1g}\rightarrow{}^4T_{2G}$ $^6A_{1g}\rightarrow{}^4E_g$, $^4A_{1g}$ (4G)	Tetrahedral
4	[Mn-(N26DH4PA)2]Cl2	(0.875)g	5.82	19083,21645,23952,24630, 26075	$^6A_{1g}\rightarrow{}^4T_{2G}$ $^6A_{1g}\rightarrow{}^4E_g$, $^4A_{1g}$ (4G)	Tetrahedral

a = ethyl acetate: carbon tetrachloride (2:8), b = ethyl acetate: carbon tetrachloride (4:6), d = ethyl acetate: carbon tetrachloride (6:4), e= ethyl acetate: acetone (5:5), f = acetone: carbon tetrachloride (5:5), g= acetone: carbon tetrachloride (6:4)

Table- 3
IR Vibrational frequencies of Mn(II) transition metal complexes

S.N.	Complexes	v_{N-H} (amide)	$(v_{C=O})_a$	$(v_{C-N+\delta N-H})^b$	$(v_{N-H+\delta C-N})^c$	Pyrimidin yl	v_{M-N}	v_{M-O}	v_{M-cl}
1	N6H2MC4PB	3163	1706	1421	1284	1685			
	[Mn-(N6H2MC4PB)2Cl2]	3172	1685	1532	1404	1624	504	538	----
2	N6H2MC4PA	3175	1715	1340	1242	1683			
	[Mn-(N6H2MC4PA)2Cl2]	3186	1648	1442	1382	1604	472	535	----
3	N26DH4PB	3353	1714	1422	1282	1582			
	[Mn-(N26DH4PB)2Cl2	3445	1623	1457	1362	1558	434	476	----
4	N26DH4PA	3196	1716	1284	1249	1416			
	[Mn-(N26DH4PA)2Cl2	3420	1702	1354	1292	1400	468	543	----

Fig. 1-4
Transition Spectra of Mn(II) Complexes

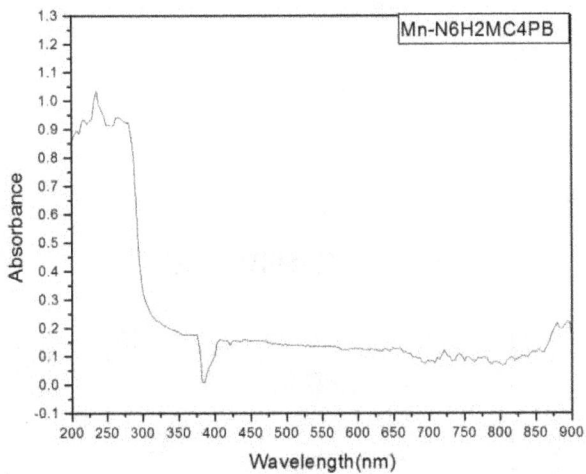

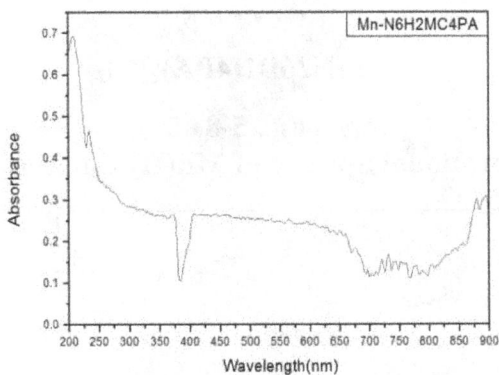

[Mn-(N6H2MC4PB)$_2$]Cl$_2$

[Mn-(N6H2MC4PA)2]Cl$_2$

[Mn-(N26DH4PB)₂]Cl₂

[Mn-(N26DH4PA)₂]Cl₂

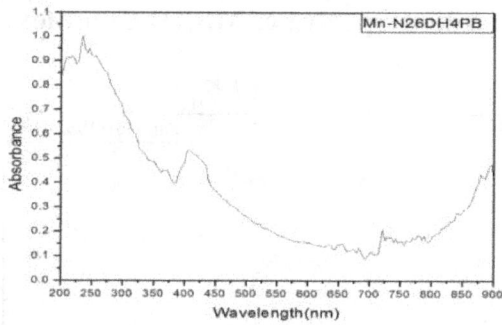

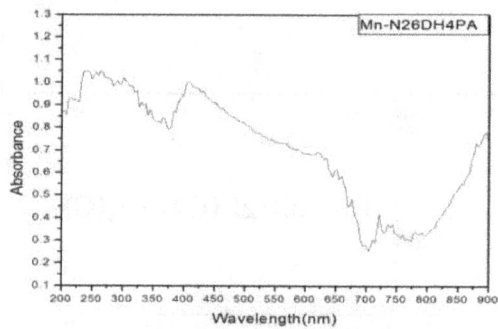

Fig. 5-8
Vibrational Spectra of Mn(II) Complexes

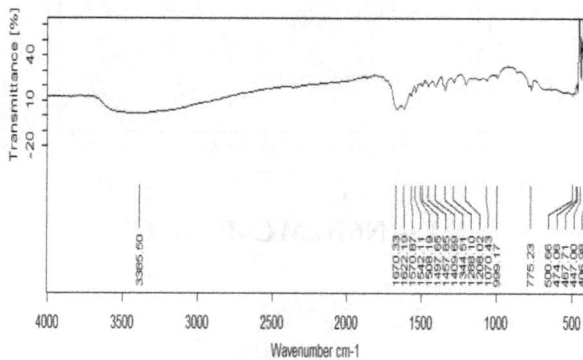

[Mn-(N6H2MC4PB)₂]Cl₂

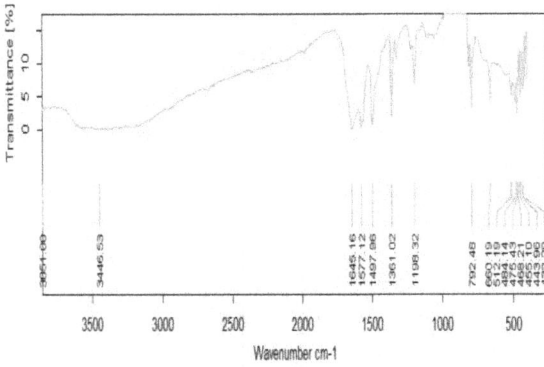

[Mn-(N6H2MC4PB)₂]Cl₂

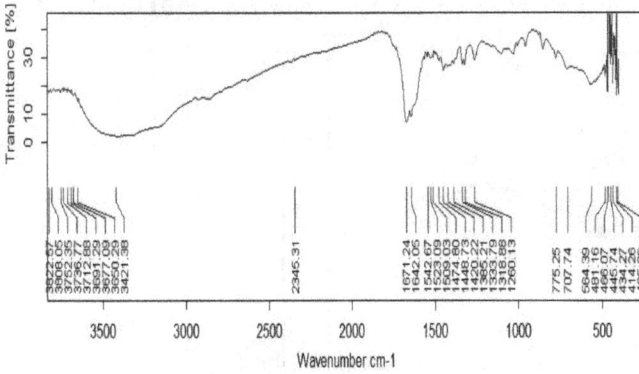

[Mn-(N26DH4PB)₂]Cl₂

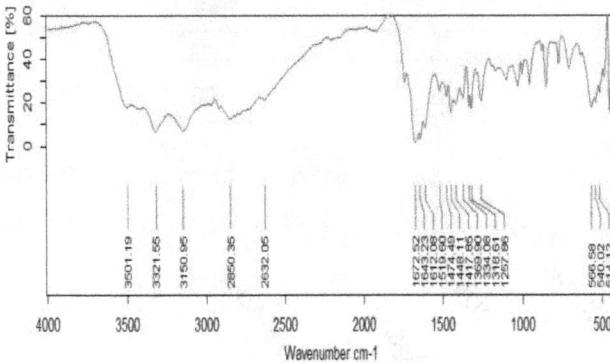

[Mn-(N26DH4PA)₂]Cl₂

113

Fig. 9-12
Tentative structure of complexes

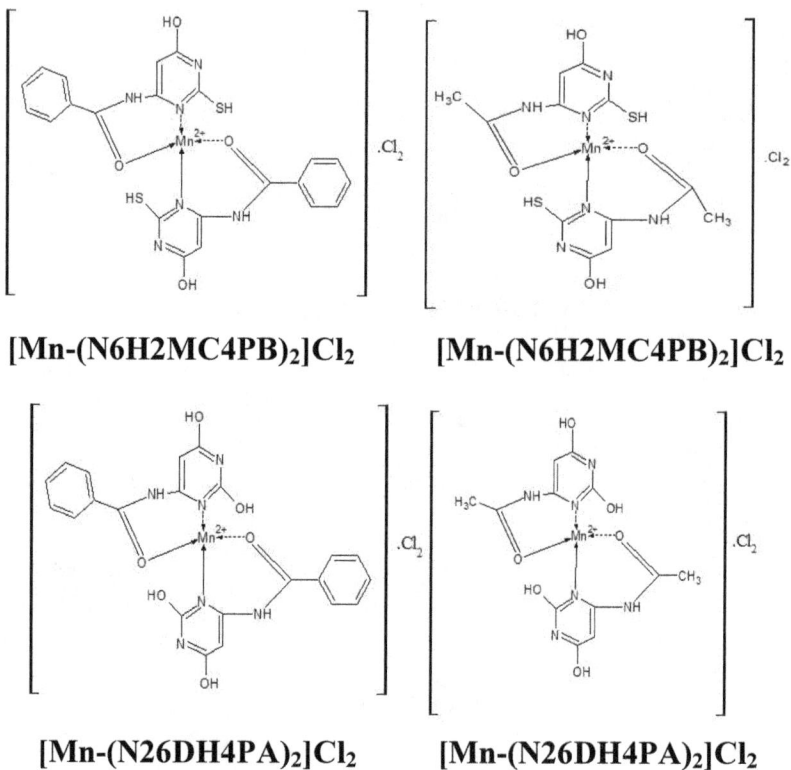

[Mn-(N6H2MC4PB)₂]Cl₂

[Mn-(N6H2MC4PB)₂]Cl₂

[Mn-(N26DH4PA)₂]Cl₂

[Mn-(N26DH4PA)₂]Cl₂

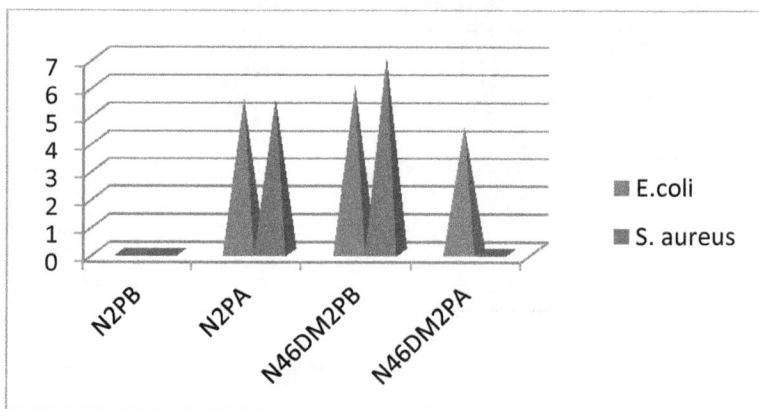

Fig.13. Biological activity of amide Ligands.

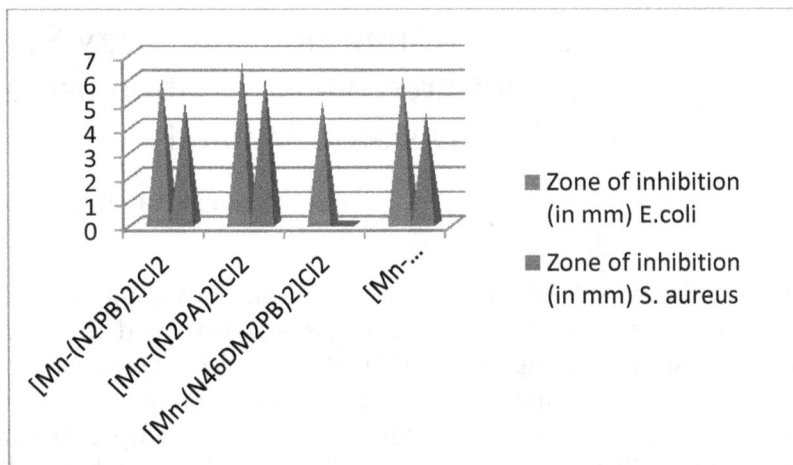

Fig.14. Biological activity of metal complexes containing amide Ligands.

Green Chemistry Research Centre (GCRC),
Department of Chemistry,
Govt. Dungar (NAAC GRADE- 'A'), Bikaner
M.G.S. University, Bikaner-India
email : r.r.khararia@gmail.com

11. An Application of Intuitionistic Fuzzy Set Theory in Student Career Determination using Euclidean Distance Method

Dr. Prakash Rajaram Chavan

Abstract

Intuitionist fuzzy set (IFS) is very useful in providing a flexible model to elaborate uncertainty and vagueness involved in multiple criteria decision making (MCDM) theory. We show a novel application of intuitionist fuzzy set in a more challenging area of decision making (i.e. student career choice). An example of career determination will be presented, assuming there is a database (i.e. a description of a set of subjects, and a set of careers. We will describe the state of students knowing the results of their performance. The problem description uses the concept of IFS that makes it possible to render two important facts. In this paper, we reviewed the concept of IFS and proposed its application in career determination using normalized Euclidean distance method to measure the distance between each student and each career respectively. Solution is obtained by looking for the smallest distance between each student and each career.

Keywords: Fuzzy sets, intuitionist fuzzy sets, career choice, career determination

Introduction

Fuzzy sets (FS) introduced by (Zadeh, 1965) has showed meaningful applications in many fields of study. The idea of fuzzy set is welcome because it handles uncertainty and vagueness which Centurion set could not address. In fuzzy set theory, the membership of an element to a fuzzy set is a single value between zero and one. However in reality, it may not always be true that the degree of non-membership of an element in a fuzzy set is equal to 1 minus the membership degree because there may be some hesitation degree. Therefore, a generalization of fuzzy sets was proposed by (Atanassov, 1983, 1986) as intuitionist fuzzy sets (IFS) which incorporate the degree of hesitation called hesitation margin (and is defined as 1 minus the sum of membership and non-membership degrees respectively). The notion of defining intuitionistic fuzzy set as generalized fuzzy set is quite interesting and useful in many application areas. The knowledge and Semantic representation of intuitionistic fuzzy set become more meaningful, resourceful and applicable since it includes the degree of belongingness, degree of non-belongingness and the hesitation margin (Atanassov, 1994, 1999). Szmidt and Kacprzyk (2001) showed that intuitionistic fuzzy sets are pretty useful in situations when description of a problem by a linguistic variable given in terms of a membership function only seems too rough. Due to the flexibility of IFS in handling uncertainty, they are tool for a more human consistent reasoning under imperfectly defined facts and imprecise knowledge (Szmidt and Kacprzyk, 2004).

De et al (2001) gave an intuitionistic fuzzy sets approach in medical diagnosis using three steps such as; determination of symptoms, formulation of medical knowledge based on intuitionistic fuzzy relations, and determination of diagnosis on the basis of composition of intuitionistic fuzzy relations. Intuitionistic fuzzy set is a tool in modelling real life problems like sale analysis, new product marketing, financial services, negotiation process, psychological investigations etc. since there is a fair chance of the existence of a non-null hesitation part at each moment of evaluation of an unknown object (Szmidt and Kacprzyk, 1997, 2001). Atanassov (1999, 2012) carried out rigorous research based on the theory and applications of intuitionistic fuzzy sets. Many applications of IFS are carried out using distance measures approach. Distance measure between intuitionistic fuzzy sets is an important concept in fuzzy mathematics because of its wide applications in real world, such as pattern recognition, machine learning, decision making and market prediction. Many distance measures between intuitionistic fuzzy sets have been proposed and researched in recent years (Szmidt and Kacprzyk, 1997, 2000 and Wang and Xin, 2005) and used by (Szmidt and Kacprzyk, 2001, 2004) in medical diagnosis.

We show a novel application of intuitionistic fuzzy set in a more challenging area of decision making (i.e. career choice). An example of career determination will be presented, assuming there is a database (i.e. a description of a set of subjects S, and a set of careers C). We will describe the state of students knowing the results of their performance. The problem description uses the concept of IFS

117

that makes it possible to render two important facts. First, values of each subject performance changes for each student. Second, in a career determination database describing career for different students, it should be taken into account that for different students aiming for the same career, values of the same subject performance can be different. We use the normalized Euclidean distance method given in (Szmidt and Kacprzyk, 1997, 2000, 2014) to measure the distance between each student and each career. The smallest obtained value, points out a proper career determination based on academic performance.

2. Concept of Intuitionistic Fuzzy Sets

Definition 1 (Zadeh, 1965) : Let X be a nonempty set. A fuzzy set A drawn from X is defined as $A = \{(x, \mu_A(x)): x \in X\}$, where $\mu_A(x)$: $X \longrightarrow [0,1]$ is the membership function of the fuzzy set A. Fuzzy set is a collection of objects with graded membership i.e. having degrees of membership.

Definition 2 (Atanassov, 1999) : Let X be a nonempty set. An intuitionistic fuzzy set A in X is an object having the form $A = \{(x, \mu_A(x), \nu_A(x)): x \in X\}$, where the functions $\mu_A(x), \nu_A(x): X \longrightarrow [0,1]$ define respectively, the degree of membership and degree of non-membership of the element $x \in X$ to the set A which is a subset of X, and for every element $x \in X, 0 \leq \mu_A(x) + \nu_A(x) \leq 1$. Furthermore, we have $\pi_A(x) = 1 - \mu_A(x) - \nu_A(x)$ called the intuitionistic fuzzy set index or hesitation margin of x in A. $\pi_A(x)$ is the degree of indeterminacy of $x \in X$ to the IFS A and $\pi_A(x) \in [0,1]$ i.e., $\pi_A(x): X \longrightarrow [0,1]$ and $0 \leq \pi_A \leq 1$ for every $x \in X$. $\pi_A(x)$ expresses the lack of knowledge of whether x belongs to IFS A or not.

For example, let A be an intuitionistic fuzzy set with $\mu_A(x) = 0.5$ and $\nu_A(x) = 0.3 \Rightarrow \pi_A(x) = 1 - (0.5 + 0.3) = 0.2$. It can be interpreted as "the degree that the object x belongs to IFS A is 0.5, the degree that the object x does not belong to IFS A is 0.3 and the degree of hesitancy is 0.2".

3. Basic Relations and Operations on Intuitionistic Fuzzy Sets

1. [inclusion] $A \subseteq B \leftrightarrow \mu_A(x) \leq \mu_B(x) \text{ and } \nu_A(x) \geq \nu_B(x) \ \forall x \in X$
2. [equality] $A = B \leftrightarrow \mu_A(x) = \mu_B(x) \text{ and } \nu_A(x) = \nu_B(x) \ \forall x \in X$
3. [complement] $A^c = \{(x, \nu_A(x), \mu_A(x)): x \in X\}$
4. [union]
   $A \cup B = \{(x, max(\mu_A(x), \mu_B(x)), min(\nu_A(x), \nu_B(x))): x \in X\}$
5. [intersection]
   $A \cap B = \{(x, min(\mu_A(x), \mu_B(x)), max(\nu_A(x), \nu_B(x))): x \in X\}$
6. [addition] $A \oplus B = \{(x, \mu_A(x) + \mu_B(x) - \mu_A(x)\mu_B(x), \nu_A(x)\nu_B(x)): x \in X\}$
7. [multiplication] $A \otimes B = \{(x, \mu_A(x)\mu_B(x), \nu_A(x) + \nu_B(x) - \nu_A(x)\nu_B(x)): x \in X\}$

8. [difference] $A - B = \{x, \min($
$\mu_A(x), v_B(x)), \max(v_A(x), \mu_B(x))\rangle: x \in X\}$

9. [symmetric difference]
$A\Delta B = \{\langle x, \max[\min(\mu_A, v_B), \min(\mu_B, v_A)], \min[$
$\max(v_A, \mu_B), \max(v_B, \mu_A)]\rangle: x \in X\}$

10. [Cartesian product] $A \times B = \{\langle \mu_A(x)\mu_B(x), v_A(x)v_B(x)\rangle: x \in X\}$.

Theorem 1: Let A and B be two IFS in a nonempty set X, then; (i) $A - B = A \cap B^c$

(ii) $A - B = B - A$ iff $A = B$ (iii) $A - B = B^c - A^c$.

   Proof: (i) Let $A = \{\langle \mu_A(x), v_A(x)\rangle x \in X\}$ and $B = \{\langle x, \mu_B(x),$ $v_B(x)\rangle x \in X\}$ for $A, B \in X$, then $A - B = \{x, \min($ $\mu_A(x), v_B(x)), \max(v_A(x), \mu_B(x))\rangle x \in X\}$. But $B^c = \{\langle x, v_B(x), \mu_B(x)\rangle x \in X\}, \Rightarrow$ $A \cap B^c = \{x, \min(\mu_A(x), v_B(x)), \max(v_A(x), \mu_B(x))\rangle x \in X\}$ since $A \cap B = \{x, \min(\mu_A(x), \mu_B(x)), \max(v_A(x), v_B(x))\rangle x \in X\}$. The result follows.

   (ii) $A - B = \{x, \min(\mu_A(x), v_B(x)), \max(v_A(x), \mu_B(x))\rangle x \in X\}$. If $A = B \Rightarrow \mu_A(x) = \mu_B(x)$ and $v_A(x) = v_B(x) \ \forall \ x \in X$. From this, it is certain that $B - A = A - B$ and the result follows.

   (iii) $A - B = \{x, \min(\mu_A(x), v_B(x)), \max(v_A(x), \mu_B(x))\rangle x \in X\}$. Given that, $A^c = \{\langle x, v_A(x), \mu_A(x)\rangle x \in X\}$ and $B^c = \{\langle x, v_B(x), \mu_B(x)\rangle x \in X\}$, it implies that, $B^c - A^c = \{x, \min($ $v_B(x), \mu_A(x)), \max(\mu_B(x), v_A(x))\rangle x \in X\}$ and the result is straightforward.

   Corollary 1: Whenever $A = B$, $A\Delta B = B\Delta A \ \forall \ A, B \in X$.

   Proof is straightforward from the proof of theorem 1 (ii).

   Theorem 2: Let A and B be two IFS in a nonempty set X, then;
(i)$A - A = \Phi$ (ii) $A - \Phi = A$ (iii) $A - B \subseteq A$ (iv) $A - B = \Phi$ iff $A = B$ (v) $A - B = A$ iff $B = \Phi$ (vi) $A - B = A$ iff $A \cap B = \Phi$

   It is easy to prove the above results.

   Theorem 3: For IFS A, B, C in X and $A \subseteq B \subseteq C$, then we have; (i) $B - A \subseteq C - A$ (ii)$B\Delta A \subseteq C\Delta A$.

   Proof: (i) Given that $A, B, C \in X$ and $A \subseteq B \subseteq C \Rightarrow$ "$\subseteq$" is transitive
$A \subseteq B$ and $\subseteq C$ $A \subseteq C \Rightarrow$ i.e.
$\mu_A(x) \leq \mu_B(x) \leq \mu_C(x)$ and $v_A(x) \geq v_B(x) \geq v_C(x) \ \forall \ x \in X$. Since A is

the smallest of B and C, subtracting A from both side of $B \subseteq C$ means nothing, i.e. $\Rightarrow B - A \subseteq C - A$. The result follows.

Since "Δ" is the extension of "$-$", the result of (ii) follows.

Corollary 2: From the basic operations, we deduced the following relations:

1. $A \times B = B \times A$
2. $(A \times B) \times C = A \times (B \times C)$
3. $A \times (B \cup C) = (A \times B) \cup (A \times C)$
4. $A \times (B \cap C) = (A \times B) \cap (A \times C)$
5. $A \times (B \oplus C) = (A \times B) \oplus (A \times C)$
6. $A \times (B \otimes C) = (A \times B) \otimes (A \times C)$

4. Algebra Laws in Intuitionistic Fuzzy Sets

Let A, B and C be IFS in X, then the following algebra follow:

1 Complementary Law: $(A^c)^c = A$

2 Idempotent Laws: $(i) A \cup A = A$ $(ii) A \cap A = A$

3 Commutative Laws: (i) $A \cup B = B \cup A$ (ii) $A \cap B = B \cap A$ $(iii) A \oplus B = B \oplus A$ (iv) $A \otimes B = B \otimes A$

4 Associative Laws:

$(i)(A \cup B) \cup C = A \cup (B \cup C)$ (ii) $(A \cap B) \cap C = A \cap (B \cap C)$ (iii) $A \oplus (B \oplus C) = (A \oplus B) \oplus C$ (iv) $A \otimes (B \otimes C) = (A \otimes B) \otimes C$

5 Distributive Laws:

$(i) A \cup (B \cap C) = (A \cup B) \cap (A \cup C)$ $(ii) A \cap (B \cup C) = (A \cap B) \cup (A \cap C)$

(iii) $A \oplus (B \cup C) = (A \oplus B) \cup (A \oplus C)$ (iv) $A \oplus (B \cap C) = (A \oplus B) \cap (A \oplus C)$

(v) $A \otimes (B \cup C) = (A \otimes B) \cup (A \otimes C)$ (vi) $A \otimes (B \cap C) = (A \otimes B) \cap (A \otimes C)$

6 De Morgan's laws:

(i) $(A \cup B)^c = A^c \cap B^c$ (ii) $(A \cap B)^c = A^c \cup B^c$ (iii) $(A \oplus B)^c = A^c \otimes B^c$ (iv) $(A \otimes B)^c = A^c \oplus B^c$

7 Absorption Laws: $(i) A \cap (A \cup B) = A$ $(ii) A \cup (A \cap B) = A$

8 (i) $\Phi^c = X$ (ii) $X^c = \Phi$ (iii) $A \cup \Phi = A$ (iv) $A \cap \Phi = \Phi$ $(v) A \cap A^c = \Phi$

9 $(i) A \cup X = X$ $(ii) A \cup A^c = X$ $(iii) A \cap X = A$

Note: Distributive Laws hold for both right and left hands. The proofs follow from the basic operations.

Theorem 4: Let A, B, C be IFS in X and $B \subseteq C$, then we have; (i) $A \oplus B \subseteq A \oplus C$ (ii) $A \otimes B \subseteq A \otimes C$ (iii) $A \cup B \subseteq A \cup C$ (iv) $A \cap B \subseteq A \cap C$.

Proof: (i) Given that $A, B, C \in X$ and $B \subseteq C$, it means $\mu_B(x) \leq \mu_C(x)$ and $v_B(x) \geq v_C(x)$ for every $x \in X$. If another IFS $A \in X$ is added to $B \subseteq C$, it is certain that, $A \oplus B \subseteq A \oplus C$ and the result follows.

Results of (ii) – (iv) follow from the proof of (i)

Theorem 5: Let A and B be IFS in X, then (i) $A \cap B = A$ or $A \cap B = B$, (ii) $A \cup B = A$ or $A \cup B = B$ iff $A = B$.

Proof: (i) For $A, B, C \in X$, it implies that $A \cap B \in X$. If $A = B \Rightarrow \mu_A(x) = \mu_B(x)$ and $v_A(x) = v_B(x)$ $\forall x \in X$. Since $A = B$, from idempotent laws, $A \cap B = A$ or $A \cap B = B$. The result follows. Result of (ii) follows from (i).

Definition 3 (Szmidt and Kacprzyk, 2014): The normalized Euclidean distance d_{n-H} (A, B) between two IFS A and B is defined as d_{n-H}

$$(A, B) = (\tfrac{1}{2n} \textstyle\sum_{i=1}^{n} [\, (\mu_A(x_i) - \mu_B(x_i))^2 + (v_A(x_i) - v_B(x_i))^2 + (\pi_A(x_i) - \pi_B(x_i))^2])^{\frac{1}{2}}$$

, $X = \{x_1, x_2, \dots, x_n\}$ for $i = 1, 2, \dots, n$.

5. Application 0f Intuitionistic Fuzzy Sets in Student Career Determination

The essence of providing adequate information to students for proper career choice cannot be overemphasized. This is paramount because thenumerous problems of lack of proper career guide faced by students are of great consequence on their career choice and efficiency. Therefore, it is expedient that students be given sufficient information on career determination or choice to enhance adequate planning, preparation and proficiency. Among the career determining factors such as academic performance, interest, personality make-up etc.; the first mentioned seems to be overriding. We use intuitionist fuzzy sets as tool since it incorporate the membership degree (i.e. the marks of the questions answered by the student), the non-membership degree (i.e. the marks of the questions the student failed) and the hesitation degree (which is the mark allocated to the questionsthe student do not attempt).

Let $S = \{s_1, s_2, s_3, s_4\}$ be the set of students, $C = \{$ medicine, pharmacy, B.Sc, Bio-tech$\}$ be the set of careers and $Su = \{$English Language, Mathematics, Biology, Physics, Chemistry$\}$

be the set of subjects related to the careers. We assume the above students sit for examinations (i.e. over 100 marks total) on the above mentioned subjects to determine their career placements and choices. The table below shows careers and related subjects requirements.

Table 1 Careers vs Subjects

	English Language	Mathematics	Biology	Physics	Chemistry
Medicineedicine	(0.8,0.1,0.1)	(0.7,0.2,0.1)	(0.9,0.0,0.1)	(0.6,0.3,0.1)	(0.8,0.1,0.1)
pharmacy	(0.9,0.1,0.0)	(0.8,0.1,0.1)	(0.8,0.1,0.1)	(0.5,0.3,0.2)	(0.7,0.2,0.1)
B. Sc.	(0.5,0.3,0.2)	(0.5,0.2,0.3)	(0.9,0.0,0.1)	(0.5,0.4,0.1)	(0.7,0.1,0.2)
Biotechnology	(0.7,0.2,0.1)	(0.5,0.4,0.1)	(0.9,0.1,0.0)	(0.6,0.3,01)	(0.8,0.0,0.2)

Each performance is described by three numbers i.e. membership μ, non-membership ν and hesitation margin π. After the various examinations, the students obtained the following marks as shown in the table below.

Table 2 Students vs Subjects

	English Language	Mathematics	Biology	Physics	Chemistry
S_1	(0.6,0.3,0.1)	(0.5,0.4,0.1)	(0.6,0.2,0.2)	(0.5,0.3,0.2)	(0.5,0.5,0.0)
S_2	(0.5,0.3,0.2)	(0.6,0.2,0.2)	(0.5,0.3,0.2)	(0.4,0.5,0.1)	(0.7,0.2,0.1)
S_3	(0.7,0.1,0.2)	(0.6,0.3,0.1)	(0.7,0.1,0.2)	(0.5,0.4,0.1)	(0.4,0.5,0.1)
S_4	(0.6,0.4,0.0)	(0.8,0.1,0.1)	(0.6,0.0,0.4)	(0.6,0.3,0.1)	(0.5,0.3,0.2)

Using Def. 3 above to calculate the distance between each student and each career with reference to the subjects, we get the table below.

Table 3 Students vs Careers

	medicine	pharmacy	B.Sc.	Bio-Technology
S_1	0.1006	0.0897	0.0904	0.0805
S_2	0.0738	0.0856	0.0591	0.0954
S_3	0.0781	0.0805	0.0811	0.0857
S_4	0.0831	0.0749	0.0928	0.1014

From the above table, the shortest distance gives the proper career determination. S_1 is to read Biotechnology (Biologist), S_2 is to read B.Sc. (Bachelor of Science), S_3 is to read medicine (doctor), and S_4 is to read pharmacy (pharmacist).

Conclusion

This novel application of intuitionist fuzzy sets in career determination is of great significance because it provides accurate and proper career choice based on academic performance. Career choice is a delicate decision making problem since it has a reverberatory effect on efficiency and competency if not properly handled. In the proposed application, we used normalized Euclidean distance to calculate the distance of each student from each career in respect to the subjects, to obtained results.

References :

1. K.T. Atanassov, New operations defined over intuitionistic fuzzy sets, Fuzzy Sets and Systems Vol. 61, 2 (1994) 137-142.
2. K.T. Atanassov, Intuitionistic fuzzy sets: theory and application, Springer (1999).
3. K.T. Atanassov, On Intuitionistic fuzzy sets, Springer (2012).
4. S. K. De, R. Biswas, A.R. Roy, An application of intuitionistic fuzzy sets in medical diagnostic, Fuzzy sets and systems 117 (2) (2001) 209-213.
5. T. K. Shinoj, J. J. Sunil, Intuitionistic Fuzzy multisets and its application in medical diagnosis, International journal of mathematical and computational sciences 6(2012)34-38.
6. E. Szmidt, J. Kacprzyk, On measuring distances between intuitionistic fuzzy Sets, Notes on IFS 3 (4) (1997) 1-3.
7. E. Szmidt, J. Kacprzyk, Distances between intuitionistic fuzzy Sets, Fuzzy Sets and Systems 114 (3) (2000) 505-518.
8. E. Szmidt, J. Kacprzyk, Intuitionistic fuzzy sets in some medical applications, Note on IFS 7 (4) (2001) 58-64.
9. E. Szmidt, J. Kacprzyk, Medical diagnostic reasoning using a similaritymeasure for intuitionistic fuzzy sets, Note on IFS 10 (4) (2004) 61-69.

10. E. Szmidt, Distances and similarities in intuitionistic fuzzy sets, Springer (2014).
11. W. Wang, X. Xin, Distance measure between intuitionistic fuzzy sets. Pattern Recognition Letters 26 (2005) 2063-2069. L.A. Zadeh, Fuzzy sets, Information and Control 8 (1965) 338-353.

Head &Assistant Professor
Department of Statistics
Smt. Kasturbai Walchand College (Arts & Science), Sangli,
Affiliated to Shivaji University, Kolhapur, Maharashtra
email : Prchava83@gmail.com

12. A Review Probe on Copper Toxicity

T.Ranjani

Abstract

The essentiality of copper for humans and animals has been recognized for nearly a century. Dietary reference intakes for copper were established almost a decade ago. Based on a lack of experimental data, Adequate Intake levels for copper have been established for infants 0–6 mo of age (200 µg/d) and for those between 7 and 12 mo (220 µg/d). This review probe helps to identify and rectify the toxicity of coper by diet.

Introduction

Copper is the 26th element in abundance in the crust of the earth and is the 29th element in the periodic table with 2 stable and 9 radioactive isotopes. Due to its high redox potential, excess copper is toxic. The essentiality of copper for humans and animals has been recognized for nearly a century. The essentiality of copper for animals and humans has been known for nearly a century. Needed in only trace amounts, the human body contains slightly >100 mg, although measurements are scarce. Only kidney and liver exceed the concentration of copper in brain (~5 µg/g), with heart being close behind.

Diet Recommendations

Dietary reference intakes for copper were established almost a decade ago. Based on a lack of experimental data, Adequate Intake levels for copper have been established for infants 0–6 mo of age (200 µg/d) and for those between 7 and 12 mo (220 µg/d). The RDA increases throughout childhood and adolescence (all in µg/d: 1–3 y old, 340; 4–8 y, 440; 9–13 y, 700; 19–50+ y, 900). Copper needs increase in pregnancy (1000 µg/d) and lactation (1300 µg/d). Upper tolerable intake levels have also been established for copper, varying from 1000 µg/d at 1–3 y old to 10,000 µg/d in adults. Interestingly, copper recommendations for adults in the UK, the European Community, and Australia/New Zealand range from 1.1 to 1.2 mg/d, suggesting that the U.S. and Canadian RDA values for adults may be low.

Food Sources

Copper absorption, at 55–75%, is considerably higher than for that of other trace elements; absorption occurs mainly in the upper small intestine. The copper concentration of foods is an important characteristic determining nutritional usefulness. In order of increasing concentration on a weight basis, fats and oils, dairy products, sugar, tuna, and lettuce are low in copper (all <0.4 µg/g); legumes, mushrooms, chocolate, nuts and seeds, and liver are high in copper (all >2.4 µg/g). Although not high in copper, bread, potatoes, and tomatoes are consumed in sufficiently large amounts by U.S. adults to substantially contribute to copper intake. Copper and magnesium are highly correlated in U.S. diets and food groups high in folate tend to be high in copper.

Toxicity

Copper toxicity risks are higher for neonates and infants given an immature biliary excretion system and enhanced intestinal absorption. Copper loading is observed clinically today in the setting of Wilson's disease and other disorders in which biliary copper excretion is impaired, such as biliary cirrhosis and biliary atresia. Copper toxicity is rather rare in humans and animals, because mammals have evolved precise homeostatic control of copper due to the high reactivity of the free metal. Free copper in cells and in the body is extremely low; copper almost always exists in biological systems bound to proteins. Ingestion of high copper levels may, however, override the innate Advancheckpoints designed to regulate overall body copper levels, including, but not limited to, enhanced intestinal absorption in the absence of a physiological demand for copper. Due to possible adverse consequences of high copper ingestion, an upper tolerable intake level of 10 mg/d has been established.

Acute Toxicity

Case Reports and Population-Based Studies

Human cases of acute copper toxicosis are presented in this section. The cases are cited in reports by the NRC (1977), EPA (1987), the U.S. Agency for Toxic Substances and Disease Registry (ATSDR 1990), and the World Health Organization's International Programme of Chemical Safety (IPCS 1998).

Most human data on high-dose acute poisoning are based on cases of suicidal intent with the ingestion of copper compounds or accidental consumption of copper-contaminated foods and beverages. In such cases, it is difficult to estimate the quantity of copper consumed, whether it was in solid form, aqueous suspension, or solution. It is also difficult to control for potential confounding factors, such as microbial agents and their toxins. Following acute ingestion of copper salts (e.g., copper sulfate) in amounts that exceed approximately 1 g, systemic effects are generally observed.

Chronic Copper Toxicity

copper-loaded metallothionein (MT) into lysosomes, where it is incompletely degraded and polymerized to an insoluble material containing reactive copper (Koizumi et al. 1998). This copper, together with iron, has been postulated to catalyze Fenton-type reactions and lysosomal lipid peroxidation, leading to hepatocyte necrosis (Ma et al. 1997; Koizumi et al. 1998; Klein et al. 1998). Subsequent to phagocytosis by Kupffer cells, the reactive copper might amplify liver damage either directly or through stimulation of those cells (Klein et al. 1998). There is no general consensus regarding the role of MT in lipid peroxidation as the primary mechanism mediating copper toxicity. In vitro studies suggest that other thiolrich cellular proteins might represent the primary site of copper-induced injury (Sokol et al. 1989). In that model, disturbances in the normal function of glutathione (GSH) in complexing copper soon after its uptake into the cell and the subsequent transfer of the complexed metal to MT where it is normally stored are cited as a potential mechanism of copper toxicosis

Literature Cited

1. Copper Dietary reference intakes for vitamin A vitamin K, arsenic, boron, chromium, copper, iodine, iron, manganese, molybdenum, nickel, silicon, vanadium, and zinc. Washington, DC: The National Academies Press;2001. P. 224–57.
2. Copper, JameCollins and Leslie M. Klevay, Advanced Nutrition

3. Koizumi, M., J. Fujii, K. Suzuki, T. Inoue, T. Inoue, J.M. Gutteridge and N. Taniguchi. 1998. A marked increase in free copper levels in the plasma and liver of LEC rats: an animal model for Wilson disease and liver cancer. Free Radic. Res. 28(5):441–450.
4. Kumar N. Copper deficiency myelopathy (human swayback). Mayo Clin Proc. 2006;81:1371–84 [PubMed] [Google Scholar]
5. Kelkar P, Chang S, Muley SA. Response to oral supplementation in copper deficiency myeloneuropathy. J Clin Neuromuscul Dis. 2008;10:1–3
6. Klein W.J., E.N. Metz and A.R. Price. 1972. Acute copper intoxication. A hazard of hemodialysis. Arch. Intern. Med. 129(4):578–582.
7. Ma, Y., D. Zhang, T. Kawabata, T. Kiriu, S. Toyokumi, K. Uchida and S. Okada. 1997. Copper and iron-induced oxidative damage in non-tumor bearing LEC rats. Pathol. Int. 47(4):203–208.

Assistant Professor,
Department of Nutrition and Dietetics,
K. S. R. College of Arts and Science for Women, Nammakal
email : ranjanithirumalairaaja20@gmail.com

13. Current Scenario of Wild Fires in India- A Review

Vinod Kumari

Abstract

A Wild Fire is an uncontrolled fire that occurs in vegetation found in wildlands. It is often observed during summers. Sometimes, these fires are getting worse and spread to bigger areas. Wild fires that burn near communities can become dangerous and even deadly if they grow out of control. In India, Dry deciduous forests experience severe fires. Every year, fires of various size and ferocity spread across wide areas of woodlands. Wild fires generate significant economic losses as well as environmental, recreational, and fatal devastation. Longer fire seasons are observed in past few years in India, which are the result of extreme meteorological conditions, such as higher temperatures and more droughts. It is major environmental issue which have emerged due to climate change. The present paper deals with types of wild fires, India forest cover and wild fires threat, forest fire incidences, FSI fire monitoring system, FSI'S 2021 report, challenges in future.

Keywords : Wild fire, Natural resources, Biodiversity, Climate change, Implications.

Introduction

Wildfires are fires that rage out of control, destroying everything in their path—plants, animals, grasslands, and bushes. It is also known as a vegetation, bush, or forest fire. It consumes the natural fuels and its spreads depend on environmental conditions. Millions of hectares of forest, woodlands, and other vegetation are burned by wildfires every year, resulting in the deaths of numerous people and animals as well as significant economic losses due to the resources lost and the expense of suppression. Additionally, there are effects on society and the environment, such as harm from smoke to human health, loss of biodiversity, production of greenhouse gases, destruction of infrastructure and recreational assets (F.A.O., 2007). The incidence of forest fires has drastically risen as a result of increasing human interaction with the natural forest environment.

India's forests are regularly set on fire in one area or another. The season for forest fires varies across the nation. The fire season varies from region to region depending on the vegetation type, climate, and several other factors. Although the country's prime forest fire season ranges from February to June, some forests are vulnerable to fires all year long. In India, dry deciduous forests are more vulnerable to major fires than evergreen, semi-evergreen, and highland temperate forests (I.S.F.R., 2015).

Types of Wild Fires

Forest fires are of three types- Crown Fires, Surface Fires and Ground Fires. Crown fires consume trees from the base of the tree to the crown. These fires are the most dangerous and ferocious. Only surface trash and duff are burned in surface fires. These flames are the simplest to extinguish and do the least harm to the forest. Deep clumps of humus, peat, and other similar dead plants that have dried out sufficiently to ignite can catch fire, causing ground fires (also known as underground or subsurface fires). Although they burn slowly, these fires can be challenging to completely extinguish or suppress.

India's Forest Cover and Wild Fires Threat

India is one of the world's mega biodiversity zones, home to a wide variety of rare and unique plants and animals. 7,13,789 square kilometres of the nation are covered with forests, which makes up 21.71% of the total geographic area of the country (I.S.F.R., 2021). The area covered by Very Dense Forest is 99,779 Sq. Km (3.04%) and Moderately Dense Forest is 3,06,890 Sq. Km (9.33 %) and Open Forest is 3,07,120 Sq. Km. (9.34 %). Very Dense Forest and Moderately Dense Forest constitutes 57 % of the total forest cover of the country (I.S.F.R., 2021). On the other hand, 20,074.47 (2.81%) of the country's forest cover is extremely fire prone. Very highly prone to fire forest cover is 56,049.35 (7.85%), Highly prone to fire forest cover is 82,900 (11.61%), Moderately prone to fire forest cover is 94,126 (13.19%), and less prone to fire forest cover is 4,60,638.36 (64.54%) (I.S.F.R., 2021). States in the North Eastern region have the greatest rate of forest fire occurrence, and these states are located in the extremely to very highly prone to forest fire zone. Due to tremendous increase of population, the interval between forest fires has decreased. It has decreased from 20-30 years to 2-3 years, thus breaking ecosystems resilience (Puri *et al.*, 2011). States in North-Eastern region of India, including Mizoram, Tripura, Meghalaya, and Manipur, have the highest likelihood of experiencing a forest fire. Western Maharashtra, Southern Chhattisgarh, Central Orissa, and a small portion of Andhra Pradesh, Telangana, and Karnataka are among the states that have sections of extremely and very highly fire prone zones (I.S.F.R., 2021). Top five districts in terms of the number of forest fires that FSI's SNPP-VIIRS sensors identified during Nov. 2020- June, 2021were Gadchiroli (10,577), Kandhamal (6,156), Bijapur (5,499), Karbi Anglong (4,881), Kadapa (4,872). Almost 4% of the nation's forestland is incredibly prone to fire, whereas 6% is highly prone. Thus, a very high threat of forest fire exists for around 10% of the nation's forest area. In all, 36% of the nation's total forest cover is at risk of frequent forest fires (F.S.I.- T.I.S., 2019).

Forest Fire Incidences in India

Forest Survey of India, carried out vulnerability analysis based on the frequency of forest fire occurrences across the nation, the Forest Survey of India estimated that there were 8,645 forest fire incidences during the years 2004–2005, 20,567 during the years 2005–2006, 16,779 during the years 2006–2007, 17,264 during the years 2007–2008, 26,180 during the years 2008–2009, 30,892 during the years 2009–2010, and 13,898 incidences during the years 2010–2011, respectively. F.S.I. reported 15,937 forest fire alerts during 2015, 24,817 alerts during 2016 and 35,888 forest fires during 2017 (F.P.M., 2017). Maximum number of forest fire alerts was observed from Mizoram (2,468), Chhattisgarh (2,808) and Madhya Pradesh (4,781) during 2015, 2016 and 2017 respectively. India's forest cover increased by 0.48 % (between 2013-2021) and forest fire alerts grew by 186 % since 2013 (F.S.I., 2021).

F.S.I. Fire Monitoring System

The F.S.I. uses two different types of sensors to notify state departments about forest fires. These are the MODIS (Moderate Resolution Imaging Spectro-radiometer) and the more recent SNPP-

VIIRS sensor, which was included in the FSI fire monitoring system in 2017. The key distinction between the two devices is that VIIRS uses an imaging satellite in polar orbit and hence produces data with a higher resolution. Forest fire season 2019–2020 saw a total of 22,447 hot spots detected by MODIS Sensor and 1,24,473 by SNPP–VIIRS sensor, whereas season 2020–2021 saw a total of 52,785 hot spots detected by MODIS Sensor and 3,45,989 by SNPP–VIIRS sensor.

F.S.I.'S 2021 Report

According to the FSI'S 2021 report, Odisha experienced the highest volume of fire detections, with about 51,968 alarms from VIIRS. Madhya Pradesh (47,795) and Chhattisgarh came next (38,106). This number includes alarms for large, medium, and small fires. Andhra Pradesh, Assam, Chhattisgarh, Odisha, and Maharashtra are the states most vulnerable to high-intensity forest fire occurrences spurred on by rapid climatic change. Mizoram has had the largest number of forest fire incidents over the previous 20 years, with more than 95% of its districts serving as hotspots for wildfires. Districts that were formerly prone to flooding are now prone to drought as a result of climate changes. Over 75% of districts in India are hotspots for extreme weather, while over 30% of districts are hotspots for extreme forest fires. Top five states with large forest fires reported during November 2021- April 2022 were Madhya Pradesh (527), Chhattisgarh (305), Uttarakhand (292), Odisha (234) and Maharashtra (185).

Significant forest fires were reported in March, 2022 in states like Rajasthan, Madhya Pradesh, and Uttarakhand. The recent fire at Rajasthan's Sariska Tiger Reserve was similarly believed to be out of season because it spread more swiftly in the heat. Long-lasting fires were reported in the Kullu Valley of Himachal Pradesh, Uttarakhand, and Dzukou Valley (Nagaland and Manipur border) in January, 2021. According to research by the Council on Energy, Environment and Water (C.E.E.W.), India's forests have suffered significantly. Over 62% of Indian states are vulnerable to high-intensity forest fires, and there has been a ten-fold rise in forest fires over the previous two decades.

Challenges in Future

Climate change has posed new challenges to human beings. Around the world, variations in climatic conditions such as more frequent droughts, heat waves, warming of oceans, melting of glaciers and rise in sea level are posing serious threat. These changes can be prevented by protecting forest in nature. Forest is the major consumer of Carbon dioxide so if they are lost, this unused carbon dioxide will in turn heat the earth. Global warming exacerbates fires by drying out vegetation and soil, producing more fuel that spreads faster and faster. Decades of changing development patterns, land and fire management decisions, and climate change have caused fires to spread at an unprecedented rate and intensity. Climate change and wildfires are reinforcing each other, and the fires burning in many parts of the world today are larger, more intense and lasting longer than before. As droughts and heatwaves continue and greenhouse gas emissions increase, we expect more fires to occur in the coming years, especially as fire seasons increase. The United Nations Environment Program's fire report (2022), warns that although lightning and human negligence can cause wildfires but climate change, land-use change, and poor forest management are allowing them to burn longer and stronger than before. Climate change will increase wildfire frequency, size, and intensity. In the years and decades to come, wildfires are expected to get worse. Throughout the world, fires are used as a tool for forest management; however, rapid changes in climate and meteorological variables (high temperatures, insufficient rainfall and wind speed anomalies) are fuelling wildfires around the world as well as in the country (F.A.O., 2020).

References

❖ F. A. O. (2007). Fire Management- Global Assessment 2006. FAO Forestry Paper,151. Rome, Italy.
❖ I.S.F.R. (2015, 2021). Indian State of Forest Report, Forest Survey of India, MoEF, Government of India.
❖ Puri, K., Areendran, G., Raj, K., Mazumdar, S. and Joshi, P. K. (2011). Forest fire risk assessment in parts of Northeast

India using geospatial tools. *Journal of Forestry Research,* 22(4), 641–647.

❖ F.S. I- T. I. S. (2019). Identification of fire prone forest areas based on gis analysis of archived forest fire points detected in the last thirteen years. F.S.I, Ministry of Environment and Forests, Dehradun.

❖ F.P.M. (2017). Operational Guideline of Forest Fire Prevention & Management Scheme, Forest Protection Division, Ministry of Environment, Forest & Climate Change.

❖ U.N.E.P. (2022). Spreading like Wildfire: The Rising Threat of Extraordinary Landscape Fires.

❖ F.A.O. (2020). Global Forest Resources Assessment 2020 (Vol. 8).

Assistant Professor,
Department of Botany
Government M.S. College for Women, Bikaner,
Rajasthan, India.

14. Study The Effects of Sports Training on Iron Status, Physical and Physiological Variable of Female Athletes : Impact of Nutritional Manipulation

Debabrata Paria

Abstract

Athletic training is mainly practiced by athletic trainer or health care professionals who collaborate with physicians to optimize activity and participation of patients and clients. The main purpose of training of athletes is to increase the performance on the specific event. To achieve the best possible performance, training has to be formulated according to the principles of periodization. Anemia is the most common disorder of the blood, affecting about quarter the people worldwide. Iron-deficiency anemia is the greatest common type of anemia. It happens when the body does not have enough iron. Female athletes are considered to be at a greater risk of compromised iron status which may lead to iron deficiency (with or without anemia) due to negative iron balance contributed by insufficient dietary iron intake, menstruation, increased iron losses associated with hemolysis, sweating, gastrointestinal bleeding and exercise induced acute inflammation. Determining the prevalence of iron deficiency anemia and those factors associated with it among adolescent girls is crucial for initiation of effective intervention that improve their nutritional status to prevent occurrence of different risks during their adolescence, pregnancy, child birth, and beyond. Therefore, the aim of this study is to assess the prevalence of anemia and associated factors among school adolescent girls.

Keywords : Female athlete, Physical fitness, Nutritional status, Iron-deficiency anemia

Introduction

Athletic training is mainly practiced by athletic trainer or health care professionals who collaborate with physicians to optimize activity and participation of patients and clients. The main purpose of training of athletes is to increase the performance on the specific event. To achieve the best possible performance, training has to be formulated according to the principles of periodization [1]. Anemia is the most common disorder of the blood, affecting about quarter the people worldwide [2]. Iron-deficiency anemia is the greatest common type of anemia. It happens when the body does not have enough iron. Female athletes are considered to be at a greater risk of compromised iron status which may lead to iron deficiency (with or without anemia) due to negative iron balance contributed by insufficient dietary iron intake, menstruation, increased iron losses associated with hemolysis, sweating, gastrointestinal bleeding and exercise induced acute inflammation [3,4]. Iron plays an important role in oxygen transport and fuel consumption [5]. Iron affects peak physical performance and when an athlete functions without adequate iron, less oxygen is transported to the muscles, maximal oxygen consumption (VO_2max) falls, and physical performance is affected [6]. The female athletes are particularly important, not only as a health concern but also cause it may contribute to morbidity, diminished physical performance ad decrease in efficiency of the physiological adapting and responding mechanisms to training. Anemia if not treated can result in maternal mortality, weakness, diminished physical & mental capacity, increased morbidity from infectious diseases, peri-natal mortality, premature delivery, low birth weight etc. Children of mothers who have Anemia are much more likely to be Anemic. A woman with Anemia has a greater risk of obstructed labour, having a baby with a low birth weight, having adverse pregnancy outcomes, producing lower quality breast milk, death due to postpartum haemorrhage and illness for her and her baby.

So, there is a need for iron supplementation of adolescent girls which in turn will not only improve their physical and mental capacity but also improve their pre-pregnancy haemoglobin status and iron stores. In the later stage of their life, that will help in reducing the incidence of low birth weight of infants and maternal mortality rates. With this in background, to combat Anemia amongst Adolescent Girls, the Department of Health and Family Welfare

(DH&FW) initiated implementation of Adolescent Anemia Control Program (AACP).

Different researchers have conducted studies on anemia among adolescent girls from different part of the world. However, the age range which these scholars considered as adolescent differs among the studies and they were not the standard age category between 10 and 19 years. Since using the finding of studies that use different age ranges can negatively affect the impact of interventions, we argue that the studies should be conducted by selecting the appropriate age group. Furthermore, determining the prevalence of iron deficiency anemia and those factors associated with it among adolescent girls is crucial for initiation of effective intervention that improve their nutritional status to prevent occurrence of different risks during their adolescence, pregnancy, child birth, and beyond. Therefore, the aim of this study is to assess the prevalence of anemia and associated factors among school adolescent girls.

Review of Literature

(Iron deficiency must come first, followed by training and performance and the importance of anthropometry, physical and physiological variables. nutritional manipulation on improvement of iron status)

Adequate nutrient intake is essential for achieving optimal athletic performance. Female athletes generally meet macronutrient and micronutrient requirements with the exception of iron [a]. Female athletes are considered to be at a greater risk of compromised iron status which may lead to iron deficiency(with or without anemia) due to negative iron balance contributed by insufficient dietary iron intake, menstruation, increased iron losses associated with hemolysis, sweating, gastrointestinal bleeding and exercise induced acute inflammation [b]. The female athlete is at particular risk of iron deficiency due to menstruation and screening for iron deficiency is widely recommended for all athletes [c]. Iron deficiency anemia (IDA) requires medical intervention; however, increasingly sport scientists and nutritionists are measuring, monitoring and attempting to optimize iron status in athletes since it is closely connected to endurance performance [d]. Iron deficiency treatments include oral supplements, intramuscular or intravenous injections, and dietary iron treatments such as modification of diet through dietary advice and counselling, inclusion of iron fortified products or naturally iron-rich products into the daily diet. Although conventional treatments of oral iron supplements and injections improve iron status in athletes [e]. Those athletes with the most severe iron deficiency are most likely to respond positively to treatment [f]. Thus dietary modification is suggested as a preferred strategy for ensuring adequate iron intake, maintenance of iron status, and as the first line of action in the prevention of iron deficiency in female athletes [g].

Iron Balance in Females and Exercise Performance :

Haemoglobin, carried in the red blood cell, is a globular protein pigment molecule containing a non-protein haem group in its centre, carrying the iron ion at the site of oxygen binding. Haemoglobin is carried in red blood cells which are produced and cleared at a rate of approximately 2 million per second. The total haemoglobin mass (tHb-mass), a primary determinant of maximal oxygen uptake (V'O2max), is fundamentally reliant upon adequate iron stores [h]. A reduction in iron stores may therefore impact upon the capacity for both oxygen transport and utilisation, lead to fatigue, or cause under-performance. Appropriate identification and correction of iron deficiency can have a significant impact on athlete performance and wellbeing in endurance sports and team sports with a significant endurance component. The challenge therefore is to maintain an appropriate iron status, avoiding the negative consequences of either iron toxicity or iron deficiency. The reference nutrient intake (RNI) for adult females in the UK is 14.8 mg iron per day [i]. Additional iron is recommended for pregnant and lactating females, an increased iron allowance is not an official recommendation for female athletes. Some authors suggest that iron requirements for endurance female athletes, particularly distance runners, are increased by approximately 70 % [j]. If this suggestion was to be followed, a daily intake of 10 mg of iron would be added to the UK recommended value of 14.8 mg. Environmental factors, exercise volume and intensity, diet and supplementation are under the control of the athlete, whereas genetics, menstrual blood losses, the rate of iron absorption and compensatory physiological mechanisms are not.

The Effect of Iron Deficiency on Aerobic Exercise Performance :
IDA has a profound effect on performance, depending on the severity, however, the effect of iron deficient non-anemia (IDNA) is less clear. Some scientists has reported a relationship between sFer and 2 km time trial performance amongst female collegiate rowers at the beginning of a competition season, with those athletes who were IDNA reporting a 21s slower 2 km time trial times compared to those who were iron replete. Iron deficiency may also influence total training load, for example, IDNA female collegiate rowers performed significantly less weekly mileage than their iron replete counterparts [K]. Several iron supplementation studies have shown improvement in indices of aerobic capacity following treatment in female athletes [f]. However, there are also several studies that have reported no effects of iron treatments on exercise performance in female IDNA endurance athletes [l].

Identifying Iron Deficiency :
Symptoms of fatigue indicate potential iron deficiency. The gold standard for measuring iron stores is a bone marrow biopsy, but though there are various factors and variability and chances for lots of errors, so some scientist recommend alternative methods based on blood testing. Serum ferritin (sFer) has been used as a biomarker of iron stores since a direct correlation between plasma ferritin and whole body iron was established in the 1970s [m]. Periodic screening sFer and hemoglobin is recommended for all athletes by the International Olympic Committee [n]. Broadly, there are three stages of iron deficiency; firstly, a depletion of iron stores (i.e. a reduced serum ferritin) without any evidence of a haematological consequence; secondly, early signs of iron deficiency impacting upon haematological markers (for example, haemoglobin towards the lower end of the range, an elevated percentage microcytic reticulocytes and hypochromic reticulocytes), but these markers remaining within reference ranges and; finally, IDA characterised by multiple markers of low iron stores and haematological variables outside of reference ranges [o]. A diagnosis of IDNA can only be

confirmed definitively once a positive haematological response to treatment is observed and this approach has been advocated in recent studies [f].

Correcting The Iron Defeciency :

Where more severe iron deficiency exists and IDA is clearly present, iron treatment should be instigated under the guidance of a medical doctor. The response to the treatment should be tracked with measurements of red cell indices and tHb-mass where possible. It is reasonable to repeat tests as often as 2-week intervals to plot a positive response to treatment. If a clear improvement in tHb-mass is observed, the diagnosis of iron deficiency can be accepted and regular monitoring should continue.

Fig; A process for identifying and correcting iron deficiency in fatigued female athletes.

A. Effect of Iron Treatment on Iron Status :

Supplementing athletes with iron will increase sFer, at least transiently. Oral iron supplementation in doses ranging from 40–400 mg day–1, for 6–24 weeks and both intramuscular (IM) and intravenous (IV) injections have all resulted in significantly improved sFer values [p]. For individuals with IDA, iron treatments will increase sFer, tHb-mass and red cell indices resulting in an improved aerobic power and these indices will be maintained providing the cause for the anemia is identified and treated. Yet when individuals identified as IDNA are treated with IV iron the initial rise in ferritin will be present for only a number of weeks, after which sFer may return to pre-treatment levels [q]. A mean increase in tHb-mass of 11% was demonstrated in IDA athletes following 12 weeks of oral supplementation [f]. 2.7% and 1.9% improvements in tHb-mass have been reported 6 and 8 weeks following IV iron treatment without a change in HB [r].

B. Effect of Iron Treatment on Performance in Idna Athletes:

A number of studies have shown aerobic power to be unchanged following iron treatment in IDNA athletes [p]. Some study implies that iron treatments are effective for IDNA athletes and that IV treatments are more effective than oral supplements but the findings are limited by the lack of a control group. A randomized control trial examining the efficacy of a single 500 mg IV treatment showed no pre-to-post treatment changes inV˙O2max, VV˙O2max, running economy, speeds at 2 and 4 mmol L–1 blood lactate, or time to exhaustion, suggesting that IDNA had no effect on aerobic power or other laboratory measures that are commonly used to evaluate endurance athletes [l]. Sports science and medicine practitioners should be mindful that the effects of iron treatments are not be limited to a haematological response. Increased V˙O2max following iron treatment despite normal [Hb] has been reported [q]. There have been very few studies investigating the effects of IDNA on mitochondrial function in human subjects, particularly in athletes, probably because a muscle biopsy is required.

C. Dietary Iron :

Some studies showed that dietary iron is also poorly absorbed which constitutes a large portion of an athlete's training year and would be unwelcome given that iron deficiency may prevent athletes from coping with the required training load [k]. Some researchers also showed that a number of other foods and drugs may compromise iron absorption [r]. wheat products contain phytates (organic polyphosphates) which bind iron and reduce its absorption; Antacid therapy increased gastric pH and reduces iron absorption; Non-steroidal anti-inflammatory drug use may promote intestinal iron loss via microscopic bleedings.

D. Oral Iron Supplementation :

A recent study data suggests that up to 79% of elite athletes use iron supplements [s]. Supplementation is recommended where iron deficiency is suspected, with ongoing monitoring to avoid unnecessary supplementation. Although iron supplementation is considered safe, the effect of long-term iron supplement use is not known. However, increased intake of dietary iron is a primary risk factor in those with genetic abnormalities that predispose them to iron overload. the risk of clinically significant iron overload is increased, therefore caution should be applied with supplementation [t]. It has recently been shown that supplementing with Vitamin D3 significantly reduced hepcidin concentration in Vitamin D deficient but otherwise healthy adults [u]. Indicating the potential for a downstream effect on iron status. Such indirect means of addressing iron deficiency, without the aforementioned side effects, is an important area of future research.

Research Question

1. Whether iron deficiency affects the sports training and performance in female?
2. Whether iron status can influence the anthropometric, physical fitness and physiological variables of athletes?
3. Whether iron rich diet can improve iron status and sports performance in female athletes?

Hypothesis

1. Iron status can affect sports training and performance of female athletes.
2. Iron status, anthropometric, physical fitness and physiological variables may affect sports training and performance in female athletes.
3. Iron rich diet can improve iron status and sports performance in female athletes.

Aim and Objectives

The objectives of the project work are as follows-

➤ To find out the effect of sports training on iron status, anthropometric, physical fitness, and physiological variables of female athletes.

➤ To find out the age related change on iron status, anthropometric, physical fitness, and physiological variables of female athletes.

➤ To find out the impact of dietary modification on iron status, sports training and performance in female athletes.

Materials and Methods :

Material

Site of Study : The study will be conducted of different district in West Bengal.

Subjects : A total of four hundred fifty (n= 450) female volunteers within the age group 11-19 years will be randomly selected for the present study. The subjects will be equally divided into - (i) Control Group (CG, n= 150), (ii) Exercise Group (EG, n= 150), and (iii) Exercise and Dietary Modified Group (EGDM, n= 150). In each group the volunteers will be subdivided into 3 subgroups: (a) Pre pubertal (age 11-13 years), (b) Pubertal (age 14-16 years), and (c) Post pubertal (age 17-19 years). In each subgroup fifty subjects will be selected respectively for Control and Physically active groups. The detail of subjects and group distribution is given in table 1.

Table 1: Subjects and group distribution

Groups	Control Group	Exercise Group	Exercise + Dietary modified Group	Total
Pre pubertal (11-13 yrs.)	50	50	50	150
Pubertal (14-16 yrs.)	50	50	50	150
Post pubertal (17-19 yrs.)	50	50	50	150
Total	150	150	150	450

Inclusion Criteria : Subjects free from history of recent disease and illness will be included in the study. Subjects from the age of 11 to 19 years will be considered eligible for this study. This decision will be based on the medical examination performed by Physicians.

Exclusion Criteria : Participants will be excluded from the study if they had a history of disease and illness for at least 03 months prior to the commencement of the study. Other exclusion criteria include any medical or surgical conditions which may hinder physical performance e.g. evidence of inflammatory joint disease and lower limb pathology, recent fracture of the spine, past history of operative intervention for lower back problems, metastatic diseases, anxiety neurosis and depression. Women who were pregnant and those within 3 days before and 3 days after their menstruating will also be excluded.

Ethical Clearance : The subjects will be informed about the possible complications of the study and a written informed consent will be taken from them. Parental consent will be also taken if the participant is below 18 years of age. The ethical approval will be taken from the Institutional Research Committee for the present study.

Training and Testing :

The training session will be divided into three phase: (i) Transition Phase (TP, 0 week), (ii) Preparatory Phase (PP, 8 weeks), and (iii) Competitive Phase (CP, 4 weeks). The training session will be followed for 2 hours/day, 5 days/week for 12 weeks. The volume and intensities of the training components will also vary in each phase of the training and in different age groups. In the training programed will be followed only in the (i) Exercise Group and (ii) Exercise and Dietary Modified Group, where as in the Control Group no training will be given. The training programed will be followed according to the instructions of the qualified coaches. The selected anthropometric, physical fitness and physiological variables will be measured in each groups at the beginning of the training Transition Phase (TP, 0 week) and the end of Preparatory Phase (PP, 8 weeks), and Competitive Phase (CP, 4 weeks). The detail of the training schedule for the female athletes is given in table 2.

Table 2: General training schedule for the female athletes

Training Components	Transition Phase	Preparatory Phase	Competitive Phase
Continuous training	Low	High	Low
Interval training	Low	High	Maintenance
Strength training	Low	High	Low
Power training	Low	High	Maintenance
Speed training	Low	High	Maintenance
Flexibility training	Low	High	High
Skill training	Low	High	Maintenance

Assessment of Socioeconomic Status

The socio-economic status of the subjects will be assessed by questionnaire method by employing Kuppaswami scale (Guru Raj et al., 2015) and Prasad Socioeconomic Classification (2015).

Assessment of* Nutritional *Status

The nutritional status of the subjects will be assessed by questionnaire technique using 24 hour recall method (Gibson and Ferguson, 1999). The iron status of the subjects will also be evaluated through diet survey as well as by biochemical tests. Attempt will made to find out whether the subjects consume dietary iron as per the recommended dietary allowance (RDA). A modified diet rich in green leave vegetables, iron and vitamin-C will be advised for the subjects. The iron status will be estimated after 3 months interval.

Measurements

Measurement of Anthropometric Variables

Measurement of Height and Body Mass

The height (stature) and body mass will be measured using standard methodology (Jonson and Nelson, 1996).

Estimation of Body Composition

Body composition of the subject will be assessed by Body composition analyzer following the standard methodology. These include Body mass index (BMI), Body surface area (BSA), body fat and lean body mass (Jonson and Nelson, 1996). Simultaneously, a skin fold calliper will be used to assess the body fat percentage, from biceps, triceps, sub scapular and suprailiac sites. Body density will be calculated by the formulae of Durnin and Womersley (1974). Percentage body fat, total fat mass, LBM will be derived from the standard equation of Siri (1956).

Measurement of Waist to Hip Ratio

The waist to hip ratio of the subject's has been shown to be related to the risk of coronary heart disease. The measurements of hips and waist of the subject will be taken by a steel tape using standard procedure, and the hip to waist ratio will be determined by standard equation (Jonson and Nelson, 1996).

Measurement of Mid Upper Arm Circumference (MUAC)

The mid upper arm circumference (MUAC) is a measure of the nutritional status of the subject. The measurements of mid upper arm circumference (MUAC) of the subject will be taken by a steel tape using standard procedure (Jonson and Nelson, 1996).

Assessment of Physical Fitness

Assessment of Reaction Time by Ruler Drop Test

The reaction time of the subject will be assessed by ruler drop test using standard procedure (Jonson and Nelson, 1996).

Measurement of Grip and back Strength

The grip and back dynamometers will be used to record the strength of the grip and back muscles following a standard methodology (Jonson and Nelson, 1996).

Assessment of flexibility by Modified Sit & Reach Test

To monitor the development of the subject's hip and trunk flexibility modified sit and reach test will be applied using standard procedure (Jonson and Nelson, 1996).

Assessment of abdominal strength by Sit Ups Test

The sit ups test is used to monitor the development of the subject's abdominal strength. The test will be performed using standard procedure (Jonson and Nelson, 1996).

Assessment of elastic leg strength by Standing Long Jump Test

The standing long jump test is performed to monitor the development of the subject's elastic leg strength. The test will be performed using standard procedure (Jonson and Nelson, 1996).

Assessment of maximum speed by 30-metre Acceleration Test

The objective of this test is to monitor the development of the subject's ability to effectively and efficiently build up acceleration, from a standing start or from starting blocks, to maximum speed. The test will be performed using standard procedure (Jonson and Nelson, 1996).

Assessment of power by Margaria Kalamen Power Test

The objective of this test is to monitor the development of the subject's strength and speed (power). The test will be performed using the standard procedure. Standard equation will be used to evaluate the power of the subject (Margaria, 1996).

Assessment of Physiological Fitness

Assessment of heart rate and blood pressure

The subject will be asked to take rest for 15 minutes and the heart rate and blood pressure will be recorded. The heart rate will also be recorded during rest, maximal exercise and during recovery period using heart rate monitor (Astrand & Rodhal, 1986).

Measurement of Maximum Oxygen Uptake (VO_{2max})

The objective of the test is to monitor the development of the subject's cardiovascular system. VO_{2max} will be measured indirectly by Queen's College step test using standard procedure. Standard equation will be used for calculating the VO_{2max} (ml/kg/min) (McArdle et al. 1972).

Assessment of Lung Functions

The forced expiratory volume in 1 second (FEV1), forced vital capacity (FVC), peak expiratory flow rate (PEFR) of the subject will be measured using an electronic spirometer following a standard procedure (Mustajbegovic et al., 2003).

Estimation of Iron Status

A 5 ml of venous blood will be drawn from an antecubital vein after a 12-hours fast and 24 hours after the last bout of exercise for the subsequent determination of total red blood cells count, hematocrit, mean corpuscular volume (MCV), mean corpuscular hemoglobin (MCH), hemoglobin, serum ferritin (SF) and soluble transferrin receptor (sTfR) level (Mukharjee, 1997).

Statistical Analysis

All the values of socio-economic, nutritional, anthropometric, physical fitness, physiological variables, and iron status will be expressed as mean and standard deviation (SD). Analysis of Variance (ANOVA) followed by multiple comparison (Post Hoc) tests will be performed to find out the significant difference in selected socio-economic, nutritional, anthropometric, physical, physiological status, and iron status among the group and within the group. Pearson's correlation coefficient will be performed to find out the relationship between the socio-economic, nutritional, anthropometric, physical, physiological status, and iron status. In each case the significant level will be chosen at 0.05 levels. Accordingly, a statistical software package (SPSS) will be used.

Study Design :

The volunteers will be randomly selected and the group distribution will be performed. The following studies will be conducted in the present research.

i) Studies of socio-economic and nutritional status of female athletes.

ii) Study the age related change on iron status, anthropometric, physical fitness, and physiological variables of female athletes

iii) Study the effect of sports training on iron status, anthropometric, physical fitness, and physiological variables of female athletes.

iv) Study the impact of dietary modification on iron status, sports training and performance in female athletes.

Outcome of The Study

Iron deficiency is more common among physically active individuals compared with their sedentary counterpart. There are a few reasons why athletes are at a higher risk of experiencing iron deficiency compared to their non-athletic counterparts as higher requirements for iron use and increased risk of iron loss.

The findings of this study will provide new information about the current hemoglobin and iron status of female Indian athletes of different age groups. Also the study will help to get the good performance athlete by born, whose hemoglobin level and iron level is high, if they should train they will perform better in athletics. It means it may help in talent identification of the female Indian athletes.

Also it may found that iron deficiency anemia has any significant role on athletic training or not, also if that can be treated then it is possible to found good athletes for future.

Social Relevance

As the respondents are mostly from 10 to 20 years old girls, the iron deficiency will increase with the increasing age. And with the iron deficiency the hemoglobin deficiency will also increase and that will hamper the athlete's sports performance with the less oxygen carrying capacity.

So if the iron deficiency of the female athletes can be identified and if the iron status could be increase then the athletic sports performance of the female athletes will also be increase. And in case of in the lower level, the iron deficiency can be spotted and treated then it will also increase to increase one nation's sports performance.

Not only that but also it will help in talent identification of the athlete in early ages, that will help to get the best athletes from the society and that will increase the nation in worldwide in athletic performance.

References

1. Bompa TO. Periodization Training. In: Bompa TO (ed). *Periodization Training for Sports*. Champaign, IL: Human Kinetics, 1999; Pp:147-311.

A. Jonson BL, Nelson JK. *Practical measurements for evaluation in physical education*. London: Macmillan Publishing Co. 1996.

2. McLean E, Cogs well M, Egli I, Wojdyla D, de Benoist B (2009) Worldwide prevalence of anaemia, WHO Vitamin and Mineral Nutrition Information System, 1993-2005. Public Health Nutr 12(4): 444-454.

3. McClung JP, Gaffney-Stomberg E, Lee JJ. Female athletes: A population at risk of vitamin and mineral deficiencies affecting health and performance. J Trace Elem Med Biol, 2014; 28(4): 388-392.
4. Clenin G, Cordes M, Huber A, Schumacher YO, Noack P, et al. (2015) Iron deficiency in sports-definition, influence on performance and therapy. Swiss Med Wkly pp. 145.
5. Schumacher YO, Schmid A, Konig D, Berg A (2002) Effects of exercise on soluble transferrin receptor and other variables of the iron status. Br J Sports Med 36(3): 195-199.
6. Rockwell M, Hinton P (2005) Understanding iron. Training & Conditioning 15(8): 19-25.
B. Siri WE. The gross composition of the body. In: Tobias CA, Lawrence JH (ed). *Advances in Biological and Medical Physics*. New York: Academic Press, 1956; Pp:239-80.
C. Durnin JVGA, Womersley J. Body fat assessed from total body density and its estimation from skin fold thickness: measurements on 481 men and women from 16 to 72 years. *Br J Nutr.* 1974;32:77-97.
D. Kargotich S, Keast D, Goodman C, et al. Monitoring 6 weeks of progressive endurance training with plasma glutamine. *Int J Sport Med.* 2007;28:211-6.
E. Inbar O, Bar-Or O, Skinner JS. *The Wingate anaerobic test.* Champaign IL: Human Kinetics. 1996

Review of Literature References:
a. Alaunyte I, Stojceska V, Plunkett A, Derbyshire E. Dietary iron intervention using a staple food product for improvement of iron status in female runners. J Int Soc Sports Nutr. 2014;11:50.
b. McClung JP, Gaffney-Stomberg E, Lee JJ. Female athletes: a population at risk of vitamin and mineral deficiencies affecting health and performance. J Trace Elem Med Biol. 2014;28:388–92.
c. DellaValle, D. M. (2013). Iron supplementation for female athletes: Effects on iron status and performance outcomes. Current Sports Medicine Reports, 12(4), 234–239. doi:10.1249/JSR.0b013e31829a6f6b

d. Montero, D., Breenfeldt-Andersen, A., Oberholzer, L., Haider, T., Goetze, J. P., Meinild-Lundby, A. K., & Lundby, C. (2017). Erythropoiesis with endurance training: Dynamics and mechanisms. American Journal of Physiology – Regulatory, Integrative and Comparative Physiology, 312(6), R894–R902. doi:10.1152/ajpregu.00012.2017

e. Burden RJ, Morton K, Richards T, Whyte GP, Pedlar CR. Is iron treatment beneficial in, iron-deficient but non-anaemic (IDNA) endurance athletes? A meta-analysis. Br J Sports Med. 2014;0:1–10.

f. Wachsmuth, N. B., Aigner, T., Volzke, C., Zapf, J., & Schmidt, W. F. (2015). Monitoring recovery from iron deficiency using total hemoglobin mass. Medicine & Science in Sports & Exercise, 47 (2), 419–427. doi:10.1249/mss.0000000000000420

g. Hinton PS. Iron and the endurance athlete. Appl Physiol Nutr Metab. 2014;39:1012–8.

h. Higgins, J. M. (2015). Red blood cell population dynamics. Clinicsin Laboratory Medicine, 35(1), 43–57. doi:10.1016/j.cll.2014.10. 002

i. Department of Health Dietary Reference Values for Food, Energy and Nutrients for the United Kingdom. Report of the panel on dietary reference values of the committee on medical aspects of food policy. London, UK: H.M.S.O; 1991.

j. Whiting SJ, Barabash WA. Dietary reference intakes for the micronutrients: considerations for physical activity. Appl Physiol Nutr Metab. 2006;31:80–5.

k. Dellavalle, D. M., & Haas, J. D. (2012). Iron status is associated with endurance performance and training in female rowers. Medicine & Science in Sports & Exercise, 44(8), 1552–1559. doi:10.1249/MSS.0b013e3182517ceb

L. Burden, R. J., Pollock, N., Whyte, G. P., Richards, T., Moore, B., Busbridge, M., & Pedlar, C. R. (2015). Effect of intravenous iron on aerobic capacity and iron metabolism in elite athletes. Medicine & Science in Sports & Exercise, 47(7), 1399–1407. doi:10.1249/mss.0000000000000568

m. Jacobs, A., & Worwood, M. (1975). Ferritin in Serum. New England Journal of Medicine, 292(18), 951–956

n. Ljungqvist, A., Jenoure, P., Engebretsen, L., Alonso, J. M., Bahr, R., Clough, A., & Thill, C. (2009). The International Olympic Committee (IOC) Consensus Statement on periodic health evaluation of elite athletes March 2009. British Journal of Sports Medicine, 43(9), 631–643. doi:10.1136/bjsm.2009. 064394

o. Archer, N. M., & Brugnara, C. (2015). Diagnosis of iron-deficient states. Critical Reviews in Clinical Laboratory Sciences, 52(5), 256–272. doi:10.3109/10408363.2015.1038744

p. Burden, R. J., Morton, K., Richards, T., Whyte, G. P., & Pedlar, C. R. (2015). Is iron treatment beneficial in, iron-deficient but non-anaemic (IDNA) endurance athletes? A systematic review and meta-analysis. British Journal of Sports Medicine, 49(21), 1389–1397. doi:10.1136/bjsports-2014-093624

q. Pedlar, C. R., Whyte, G. P., Burden, R., Moore, B., Horgan, G., & Pollock, N. (2013). A case study of an iron-deficient female Olympic 1500-m runner. International Journal of Sports Physiology and Performance, 8(6), 695–698

r. Garvican, L. A., Saunders, P. U., Cardoso, T., Macdougall, I. C., Lobigs, L. M., Fazakerley, R., & Gore, C. J. (2014). Intravenous iron supplementation in distance runners with low or suboptimal ferritin. Medicine & Science in Sports & Exercise, 46(2), 376–385. doi:10.1249/MSS.0b013e3182 a53594

s. DellaValle, D. M., & Haas, J. D. (2014). Iron supplementation improves energetic efficiency in iron-depleted female rowers. Medicine & Science in Sports & Exercise, 46(6), 1204–1215. doi:10.1249/mss.0000000000000208

r. Clenin, G., Cordes, M., Huber, A., Schumacher, Y. O., Noack, P., Scales, J., & Kriemler, S. (2015). Iron deficiency in sports – definition, influence on performance and therapy. Swiss Medical Weekly, 145, w14196. doi:10.4414/smw.2015.14196.

s. Bruinvels, G., Burden, R., Brown, N., Richards, T., & Pedlar, C. (2016). The prevalence and impact of heavy menstrual bleeding (menorrhagia) in elite and non-elite athletes. PLoS One, 11(2), e0149881. doi:10.1371/journal.pone.0149881

t. Hollerer, I., Bachmann, A., & Muckenthaler, M. U. (2017). Pathophysiological consequences and benefits of HFE mutations:

20 years of research. Haematologica, 102(5), 809– 817. doi:10.3324/haematol.2016.160432

u. Smith, E. M., Alvarez, J. A., Kearns, M. D., Hao, L., Sloan, J. H., Konrad, R. J., & Tangpricha, V. (2017). High-dose vitamin D3 reduces circulating hepcidin concentrations: A pilot, randomized, double-blind, placebo-controlled trial in healthy adults. Clinical Nutrition, 36(4), 980–985. doi:10.1016/j.clnu. 2016.06.015

Department of Physiology,
Bajkul Milani Mahavidyalaya, Kismat Bajkul,
Purba Medinipur, West Bengal, India
email : debuparia1994@gmail.com

15. *Khushwant Singh As A Master and Creater of Mult-Idimentional Characters*

Dr. Bheemappa M.P.

Abstract

In Indian novels, Feministic ideas are familiar and recurrently taken by the Indian novelists. A large number of Indian writers have treated feministic views in their fiction as a modern creative exploration for multipurpose. There are many well-known literary jewels in Indian English Fiction. Perhaps, Khushwant Singh has privileged space as novelist of the front rank for his authentic writing and the conscious use of women characters in his fiction. Singh is a master of a unique in depicting the women characters of Indian society. He has a unique skill and ability to weave multi-dimensional characters into perfect, real and life-like situations, but has also given a sense of largeness to life. He has lent significance on the pictures of men and women world concerning to situations, human values with down-to-earth worldliness.

Singh has presented usually the women characters of two-dimensional and firmly interlinked with situation and atmosphere. The nature of characters and events enrage from a chronological responses to the happenings. The characters are primarily based on a principle of contrast which differentiated one character from another. They are also combined elements of contrast and parallelism. For instance, in his novel 'I Shall Not Hear the Nightingale', Sabhrai and Mrs. Taylor reveal parallelism in tendencies; the principal of contrast is the essential feature of the character portrayal in Champak and Sabhrai, Champak and Sita. He has shown special interest in creating the tempestuous, abnormal, sex-hungry Champak.

Khushwant Singh has a vision of changes and advancements in varied fields (not exception to any society). So, he has exposed the stark realism of men and women of the Indian society of all times in his novels. This paper is an attempt to show his representation and misrepresentation of women characters mainly in two novels of

Khushwant Singh as a unique achievement for his recognition not only in Indian literary scenario but also in the world literary scenario.

Keywords : Indian English fiction, Khushwant Singh, Gurudwara, Sikh, women characters, Champak, Shabrai, sex, love, I Shall not Hear the Nightingale, The Company of Women.......

Introduction :

Khushwant Singh, as an Indian fiction writer shines like a twinkling star in the galaxy of literary personalities of the Indian English fiction. Though he is the most widely read as controversial writer, he has been much revered and distinguished as a journalist, columnist and fiction writer in the field of Indian English literature. In his all novels, Singh is a master of a unique in depicting the women characters of Indian society. His mode is dramatic and presentation is graphic and lively. While reading a novel of Singh, it seems sometimes as if we are not reading the novel but we are watching an Indian movie showing the Indian society. He has a unique skill and ability to weave multi-dimensional characters into perfect, real and life-like situations, but has also given a sense of largeness to life of women characters. He has lent significance on the pictures of men and women world concerning to situations, human values with down-to-earth worldliness.

Singh has presented usually the women characters of two-dimensional and firmly interlinked with situation and atmosphere. The nature of characters and events enrage from a chronological responses to the happenings. His characters are primarily based on a principle of contrast which differentiated one character from another. They are also combined elements of contrast and parallelism. For instance, in his novel 'I Shall Not Hear the Nightingale', Sabhrai and Mrs. Taylor reveal parallelism in tendencies; but, we see the principal of contrast is the essential feature of the character portrayal in Champak and Sabhrai, Champak and Sita. He has shown special interest in creating the tempestuous, abnormal, sex-hungry Champak. Probably, the idea of the novelist to present her as a sex volcano in her person-apart from offering a sharp contrast to the moral values of Sabhrai- is to present a physical

155

counter-part to the politically unstable, violent, restless, aggressive world which upsets and inverts human relationships. Perhaps, she is a special character in the whole range of Indo-Anglican fiction.

Sabhrai embodies the instinctive understanding of life, the wisdom of the race, and possession of the sixth sense. She becomes a towering figure at the end of the novel. Sabhrai is illiterate, religiously orthodox, and devoted to God and her family. The novelist depicts her as a towering personality for her virtue of high moral and uprightness. Her whole time is spent only in telling the beads of rosary, chanting the prayers, visiting the Gurudwara, reading the 'Grantha Saheb'. She represents the devout and mystically inclined among the Sikh women. She has survived the worst moments of crisis. She maintains and retains peace all the time.

Sabhrai possesses a great redemptive character who inherits the ancient culture of her race. Perhaps she is a peerless character in the whole range of Indian English fiction. Khushwant Singh's early essay 'The Portrait of a Lady' looks forward to the lovable Sabhrai in this novel 'I Shall Not Hear the Nightingale'. Probably his innately good grandmother The Portrait of a Lady later becomes the dignified, gentle, and spiritually strong mother in 'I Shall Not Hear the Nightingale'. Even British officers admire and admit her dignity and decorum. She believes in pity, charity, faith, selfless service, and sacrifice. She sacrifices her life for her son, displaying a true mother's instinct by spending an entire cold night in Gurudwara praying and praying, and true to her faith and belief of prayers granted as her son released as Christian gift from the Taylors to her family. Her long hours stay at the Golden Temple for the grace and guidance of the Guru shows her spiritual strength. The feminine principle is absolutely embodied in her humanistic outlook personality. Her prayer and his release have been so timed as to lend a mystical to the event. She can find solace ultimately without any inputs from her husband and son speaks for the authenticity of her characters. Sabhrai is religious, traditional, true house-wife whose only concern is the welfare of the family. The act of immorality that is carried on by Champak and maid servant Shunno is bewildering, duplicity and contrast to her character.

The sex-hungry Shunno, and the tempestuous Champak are in same household of a pious, religious Sabhrai who is true to her husband and the family. The characters which represent in types in houses which otherwise remain surcharge with religious activities. As against all these, Sabhrai has the holy book as the source of all knowledge, solace, and enlightenment. All the characters of the novel speak and act on predictable lines. The only character who possesses some individuality is Sabhrai with her adherence to tradition and practices. She is depicted far higher in stature than other characters. No society is in the universe without love, sex, and illicit sexual relationships. These are some of the characteristics of a society. Some of them may open to public and some others will be withered or continued secretly without the knowledge of the people in the society. It is not exception even to the Indian society. Khushwant Singh takes an extraordinary zeal to discuss sex, weaving sex stories in his novels. He has exposed such aspects in all of his novels. In the novel, I SHALL NOT HEAR THE NIGHTINGALE he has put illicit sexual relationships in realistic detail. He has created a make believe world of sex-fantasy by skillfully painting the weakness in his characters who became daring in their sexual exploits.

The novelist has presented usually the characters of two-dimensional and firmly interlinked with situation and atmosphere. The nature of characters and events enrage from a chronological responses to the happenings. His characters are primarily based on a principle of contrast which differentiated one character from another. They are also combined elements of contrast and parallelism. For instance, we see the principal of contrast is the essential feature of the character portrayal in Sabhrai and Mrs. Taylor, Champak and Sabhrai, Champak and Sita,

Khushwant Singh has shown special interest in creating the tempestuous, abnormal, sex-hungry Champak. Probably, the idea of the novelist to present her as a sex volcano in her person-apart from offering a sharp contrast to the moral values of Sabhrai- is to present a physical counterpart to the politically unstable, violent, restless, aggressive world which upsets and inverts human relationships.

Perhaps, she is a special character in the whole range of Indo-Anglican fiction. The choice of names is also amazing in the hands of the novelist. They reflect their tendencies. For instance, Champaka is the name of an exotic flower containing over – powering fragrance. She always added 'my God' or 'by God' whenever she wanted to emphasize something. Champaka is very contrast to the name in the novel. The characterization of the novel is varied, paralleled, and contrasted. They are ironic and types of Indian society at the dawn of independence. They are the embodiments of social, cultural, moral, and political Indian society.

Of course the novel lacks a code hero, but it has code heroine in Sabhrai. The actual chief character of the novel is none other than Sabhrai. She is the savior of the lost souls. She occupies a dominant role in the novel. Her character appears as a three dimensional character.

The novelist is expert to arrest the attention of the readers with fully elaborative sex scenes. He brings in three lengthy paragraphs on sex in the novel. The novelist has pictured Champak as a nude exhibitionist. She gets pleasure in exposing her private parts. The novelist has sketched her exhibitionism to entertain the readers when she is examining herself before a full-length dressing table-mirror after shaving her pubic hair; her loosened hair, softy-rounded water-melon like buttocks, her dimples on either side of her rear waist, lifting of her breasts herself by palms of her hands, movement of her fingers around her nipples till they become like berries, wriggling of her lips in the manner hulala...hulala.... dancers. Probably Khushwant Singh's idea is that to show commonly every woman behaves like this in front of a mirror in her privacy. Her exhibitionism does not spare even minor teen-aged servant, Mundoo.

Singh exhibits in his novel, The Company of Women, familiar insights into everyday life in Delhi for those familiar with this sprawling and increasingly exciting Indian metropolis. Khushwant Singh presents Mohan Kumar as a hypothetical man who indulges in pleasures without a care for anything or anyone, without a thought for morality but shows now and then, how eventually, sex, money, prestige, comfort, convenience make him completely hollow from inside. His different sexual relationships with a veritable range of women from different parts are initially fulfilling but ultimately to disappointment. A relationship certainly would have called dead when its treatment of women as sexual objects for a momentary, physical, business like relationship of pleasure for money. At the surface level Mohan is a womanizer, debaucher and brings women only to use them for sex. But a closer examination of the individual encounters shows the feeling that it is he exploited by the womenfolk mainly for sex and money.

In describing the novel, Kapadia goes on to cite Buchi Emechetan's novel Gwendolen (1989) to expose how in African Literature also there is an instance in which an unusual sexual relationship is delineated. Kapadia finds this ramification of lust and saucy impertinence in the novels "Gwendolen" and "The Company of Women". According to him, both the novelists adopt a modernistic attitude the male-protagonists who are unable to control lustful needs. The psychology of the individual is examined instead of just projecting them as the men of evil incarnate. It is to be observed from the relationships of the protagonist; friendship may lead to love and lust but not love to friendship. The novelist warns people who lost in debauchery. The novel is quite accurate with regard to the social mores inherent in middle class Indian society which dictate that sexual relationships with unattached contemporaries of similar social standing are largely taboo. Cultural bearing on sex is an important factor that Mohan Kumar realizes in India. When he comes to Delhi from the States, he is encountered with a long chain of paraphernalia for having a bed-partner. In the States, he enjoyed sex freely every day. In India, he hankers for sex addition like a drug addict but he is conscious of having the socio-cultural hindrances in having sex.

Though Khushwant Singh has not taken the historical facts directly, he has touched historical places and personages in this novel. For instance, one evening being bored, instead of driving back home, Mohan decided to take a drive round the city. He had observed and done this for long time into Delhi. At that time, the novelist lists major historical places of the city- like Purana Quila, a statue of

King Goerge VI, India Gate, the majestic wall Memorial arch, the Rashtrapathi Bhavan, the entire panorama of buildings, lawns, water-tanks, and many more. The novelist shows his love for Delhi in these words-

"A sight for gods. Delhi was the only city in the world which gave him a sense of belonging".

In the following words, Khushwant Singh has taken the subject of religion in the novel The Company of Women through casual exchanges between various women characters and presents interesting perspectives. When Mohan went the woods with Jessica Browne in America she told him about many historical personages.

"........she told me about Martin Luther King and Malcolm X and the black Muslims, the Ku Klux Klan and the WASPs".

His choice of characters seemed to be advanced. In the classroom discussions at the University of Princeton, Singh has assimilated most religions (the Islam, Hinduism, Judaism, Christianity, Jainism, Buddhism and many more) of the world with their individual identities. So to say Yasmeen, a Muslim from Azad Kashmir dreaming about liberating Kashmir from the clutches of Hindus. She aggressively proclaims the superiority of the Islam religion and their Prophet as the greatest. She drags out many flaws in the Hindu society. A Jew asserts that Muslims have borrowed many things from the Judaism and they had nothing new. But surprisingly enough Mohan and Yasmeen share beds. At that time she reluctantly accepts that Islam provides for washing away of sins by a pilgrimage.

Similarly Molly Gomes from Goa tells Mohan that more number of Hindus than the Portuguese Catholics in Goa. The Hindus are richer but the Christians are more stylish and enjoy life. There are more cathedrals than temple, they attend in worships but don't intermarry. Susanthika from Sri Lanka tells Mohan a lot about Buddhism and its principles. But she accepts the strength of Hinduism and the Hinduism as a happy religion. Then the novelist has hugely inserted about the Holy Ganges. In this way the novelist has combined the religious discussions now and then and tried to give a lesson about the diversity. The novel is erotic and engrossing. The characters are real and relevant. This deals with elemental human passions.

Sex is not only a physical action but also related to human psyche and personality as a whole. Once in an interview, Vinod Mehta, the Editor-in-chief of Outlook, was in conversation with Singh, then the writer told about sex as-

"Indians have sex more often in their brains and not where it should be. Sex is an elemental passion. It's an integral part of our life. All human relationship is based on the desire to have sex. It's human to have desire for sex and when it is not fulfilled, it comes out in other forms. That is why celibacy does not work. The desire to have multiple partners is also normal. Married people commit adultery in their mind - happy married life is a façade. I have a collection of sex jokes, which I hope will be published posthumously".

Singh's treatment of sex reminds that of treatment in the novels of D.H. Lawrence. They explore psychological feelings through sex. Singh gives a factual account of each encounter with all possible details and banal description. He has surely a full claim to the artist's freedom of sensual creation to treat sex. This novel is like a documentary highlighting the evil effects of licentious sex is too simplistic.

It is difficult to say whether the novel is autobiographical or a work of fantasy and adult or an uninhibited, erotic, and endless entertainment of love, sex, and passion or a parody of the hedonistic upper middle class urban society. He has cleverly presented and highlighted masculine fantasies about seductive women. He emphasizes how such stereo types aggravate gender discrimination. He lashes out against this stereo type of modern society to which women fall victim. He analyses how women are obliged to fulfill certain roles that have embarked for them. He shows his analysis through the subtle use of repetition and irony.

Conclusion :

Khushwant Singh is parodying all the religious and moral taboos and codes of social responsibility on individuals in contemporary Indian upper class society. So his target could be an exposure of middle class aspirations, morality and moral hypocrisy of Indian society at present. Naturally, it belongs to the tradition of the critique of society novels. Singh's criticisms and comments on life and personalities of women characters aim at the humanistic ideal in his creative art. His writings are both creative as well as critical in representation of women characters. His approach towards their life is essentially sexual and liberal.

His writings on men and women characters have the art and artifice. They have the real microscopic view of touches to various ills and wills of our social life. He depicts in a humorous tone towards on-going issues of the Indian society. He presents the domestic as well as social backgrounds with physical transient relations and their deeper connotations largely, which is predominant in his last novel 'The Company of Women'. His treatment towards women reminds that of treatment in the novels of D. H. Lawrence. However, Singh's treatment of sex, narration is also very common and different. He gives a factual account of all possible details and banal description. In his delineation of women usually skin shows, body bares, and belly laughs. He has surely a full claim to the artist freedom of sensual creation to treat sex and exposing spontaneously and commonly. He exposes the innate smallness of the most of the people who camouflage their petty desires under righteous idealistic facades.

No doubt to say that Khushwant Singh deserves to be assessed adequately and fairly recognized as a master of ladies' psychologist. Though, he is regarded as having a complex personality, he managed to contradict himself not only in real life, but also in his different ways of writings prior to handling women characters in his fiction. He analyses the institutions and bare natures of women of society in his novels. This paper is an attempt to show his representation and misrepresentation of women characters as a unique achievement for his recognition not only in Indian literary scenario but also in the world literary scenario.

References :

➢ Singh, Khushwant, *Train to Pakistan,* New Delhi, India: Ravi Dayal, Viking Penguin, First published in 1956, ed., 1988, and 2007.

- *I Shall Not Hear the Nightingale*, New Delhi: Viking Penguin, First
published by Grove Press Inc., USA., 1959, First edition- 1997.
- --- *The Company of Women*, New Delhi: Ravi Dayal, Viking Penguin, 1999.
- Agrawal K. A., ed., *Indian Writing in English*: *A Critical Study*, New Delhi: Atlantic, 2003.
- Dhawan R.K., ed., *Commonwealth Fiction*- Volume-I, New Delhi: Karampura, Classical, 1988.
- --- '*Khushwant Singh: The Man and the Writer*', New Delhi: Prestige, 2001.
- Kar, Prafulla C., *"Khushwant Singh: Train to Pakistan", Major Indian Novels: An Evaluation*, ed., N. S. Pradhan, Delhi: Arnold-Heinemann, 1985.
- Mathur O.P., *New Critical Approaches to Indian English Fiction*, New Delhi: Dariya Ganj, Sarup and Sons, 2001.
- Mishra Manoj Kumar, *KHUSHWANT- The Misunderstood Khushwant*, New Delhi: Sarup and Sons, 2007.
- Nahal Chaman, *Three Contemporary Novelists*, ed., Dhawan R.K., New Delhi: Classical, 1985.
- Naik M. K., *Twentieth Indian English Fiction*, Ashok Vihar II, Delhi: Pen Craft International, 2004.
- Patil Mallikarjun ed., *"Khushwant Singh", Encyclopedia of Lterature In English*, New Delhi: M.K. Bhatnagar, Atlantic, 2001.
- Piciucco Pier Paolo, *A companion to Indian Fiction in English*, New Delhi: Rajouri Garden, Atlantic, 2004.
- Singh R. K., Anger in Action: *Explorations of Anger in Indian English Writing*, Sell: Series in English Language and Literature- New Delhi: Kalkaji, Bahri, 1997.

**Assistant Professor & Head,
DepartmentofEnglish,
Govt.FirstGradeCollegeForWomen,
Davangere. Karnataka-577004,
E-mail-bheemrajmp627@gmail.com**

16. Reproductive Toxicity of Commonly used Insecticides : A Review

*Mr.Neeraj Kumar,
Dr Praveen Goswami,
Ms Shilpi Damor

Abstract

There are large numbers of chemical residues are continually present in the air, food, and water we consume today. Pesticides are used widely in the world for increasing yielding and quality of crops. There are several types of insecticide or pesticides used by humans. Like, organochlorine, organophosphate, carbmate, pyrethroids. These are major types of pesticides. These are also categorized into various categories. Aim of this review is review the reproductive toxicity effect in men and women caused by commonly using insecticides like **DDT, Hexachlorocyclohexane, Chlorodecone, Mirex, Malathion, Parathion, Diazinon, Dichlorvos, Chlorpyrifos, Carbofuran, Carbaryl, Permethrin, Sumithrin, Allethrin, Permethrin.**

Keywords : *Reproductive toxicity, Sumithrin, Parathion, DDT, Hexachlorocyclohexane, Various insecticides.*

Introduction :

Pesticide is described by the Food and Agriculture Organization (FAO) as :

Any compound or combination of substances designed to prevent, destroy, or control any insect, including vectors of animal or human disease, unwanted plant or animal species, or causing damage during and or meddling with the yield, manufacturing, storage, transportation, or sales of food, agriculture commodities, wood, or wood products, or causing any harm during or otherwise interfering with the manufacture, preparation, preservation, transportation, or marketing of food, agriculture commodities, wood, or wood products. The term refers to compounds that are intended toto be used as a source of plant growth promoter, weedkiller, desiccant, or reagent that increase fruit size or prevent premature fruit fall. Also used as a pre- or post-harvest treatment for crops to prevent them against degradation during storage and transportation. [1]

Types of pesticides :

Pesticides are frequently referred to by the pests they kill. Pesticides are also categorized as compostable pesticides, which are simplify into harmless compounds by microorganisms and other natural organisms, or long-acting insecticides, which might take months or even years to break down: DDT's persistence, for example, Its concentration in the food web caused the death of top of the food-web birds.. Another approach to think regarding insecticides is to consider chemical pesticides that derive from a common factor or are manufactured in a similar way.[2]

1. Insecticides

Neonicotinoids are a type of neurotoxic pesticide with a chemical structure similar to nicotine. Imidacloprid, a neonicotinoid pesticide, is the highly used pesticides on the earth by humans. [3] The modes of action of carbamate and organophosphate insecticides are similar. They inhibit acetylcholinesterase activity, the enzyme that controls acetylcholine, at nerve synapses, affecting the nervous system of target pests (and non-target creatures). The para-sympathetic-nervous system is overstimulated as a result of this inhibition, which results in an increase in synaptic acetylcholine. [4]

2. Herbicides

Amidosulfuron, flazasulfuron, metsulfuron-methyl, rimsulfuron, sulfometuron methyl, terbacil, [5] nicosulfuron, [6] and triflusulfuron-methyl[7] are some of the sulfonylureas that have been produced for weed control. These herbicides work by preventing the enzyme acetoacetate synthase, which kills plants, weeds, and pests.

3. Biopesticides

Biopesticides are pesticides that are made from natural components such as living beings, animals, plants, microbes, and minerals. Canola oil and sodium bicarbonate (baking soda), e.g They have pesticidal activity and are called bio pesticides.

There are three types of biopesticides :

- Microbial insecticides :- Bacteria, entomopathogenic fungi, and viruses are used as microbial pesticides (and bacteria and fungi create metabolites, which are sometimes included.). Despite they are multicellular, entomopathogenic nematodes are frequently classified as microbial pesticides. [8]

- Biochemical or herbal pesticides :- Pesticides and microbiological diseases are controlled or monitored by pheromone by biochemical pesticides, which are naturally occurring chemicals.[9]
- Plant-incorporated protectants: - DNA or RNA from other species are incorporated into the genetic material of plant-incorporated protectants (PIPs) (i.e. Genetic modified crops). Their usage is fraught with controversy, particularly in several European nations. [10]

Classification of pest on basis of their types

Types	Action
Algicides	Control algae in water bodies like lakes, canals and swimming pools etc.
Antimicrobials	Kill bacteria and viruses and other microorganisms.
Attractants	These are used to attract pests,and allurement an insect or mouse to a trap. (food is not classified as an insecticide when used as an attractant.)
Biopesticides	These pesticides are obtained from natural objects like bacteria, animals, plants and some minerals.
Biocides	Kill microorganisms
Disinfectants and sanitizers	Inanimate items should have disease-producing bacteria deactivated or killed.
Fungicides	Control the fungi disease forms like rust, mildews, molds, blight.
Herbicides	Kill the unwanted plants and weeds, which grow anywhere.
Insecticides	These responsible for Kill insects and other arthropods
Miticides	These are responsible for inactivating or killing mites that grow on plants and animals.
Microbial pesticides	Microorganisms that inhibit competing pests, including insects or other microorganisms.
Molluscicides	Snails and slugs are killed by using products.
Nematicides	These are used in killing the nematodes or worms like animals that feed on plant's roots.
Ovicides	These are used to kill or inactivate the eggs of insects or mites.
Repellents	Useful in repelling pests, including insects, mosquitoes and cockroaches.
Rodenticides	These are used to control mice and rats.

Pesticides are divided into main groups are organochlorine, organophosphate, carbamate, and pyrethroid insecticides. [13]

Human exposure to organochlorine pesticides is a serious health concern. Concerns about all of these chemicals' capacity to accumulate and their possible public health effects have been raised due to their resistance to environmental degradation [11].

One of several processes can cause reproductive toxicants to have a negative effect. Some xenobiotics directly disrupt reproduction, either by chemical reactivity or structural resemblance to endogenous compounds, while others do so indirectly, either through metabolism to a direct-acting toxicant or through endocrine disruption. [12]

These pesticide's toxicity change depending on their molecular size, solubility, and impact on the CNS. Depending on the material and the situation, they might elicit either CNS depression or stimulation.[13]

The organochlorines are pesticides that consist of carbon, chlorine and hydrogen. Organochlorine compounds can be separated into 5 groups, as follows:

1. DDT (Dichlorodiphenyltrichloroethane), dicofol and methoxychlor
2. Hexachlorocyclohexane and isomers
3. Cyclodienes
4. Chlordecone
5. Toxaphene

A. Organochlorines :

Organochlorines (OC) are a family of chlorinated chemicals that are commonly employed as insecticides. These substances are categorized as persistent organic pollutants (POPs) because of their long-term persistence in the environment. OC insecticides were once effective in malaria and typhus prevention, but they are now prohibited in the majority of advanced nations. [14] Organochlorine pesticides like DDT, hexachlorocyclohexane (HCH), aldrin, and dieldrin is one of the most widely used pesticides in developing Asian nations due to its low cost and need against a variety of pests.[15]

1. **DDT** : DDT exposure decreased sperm volume on ejaculation, and decreased sperm counts in males[16]. DDT ingested in rats showed decreased weight of testis, sperm cell number and motility, as well as higher FSH and LH blood concentrations[17]. In rats exposed to DDT, a significant change of the spermatogenic process was seen, with a substantial reduction in the number of spermatozoa generated in the area of lumen of the seminiferous tubule [17]. As a result of the failure of the (-)ve feedback regulation on the hypothalamic pituitary axis, our findings suggest that DDT causes a decrease in the weight of the seminal vesicles due to a drop in the quantity of this hormone, resulting in an increasing serum FSH and LH.The well-known estrogen-like action of DDT and the inability of sertoli cells to produce inhibin, which modulates FSH secretion, might potentially explain the change in gonadotrophin secretion[18]. Furthermore, Methoxychlor is a substitute for DDT as a popular choice, lowered blood testosterone concentrations[19] and reduced steroid synthesis in growing Leydig cells[20].

2. **Hexachlorocyclohexane** : The only organochlorine insecticide still in use against pests and itching mites is HCH. HCH is broken down by the smooth ER cytochrome P450 system. In the case of HCH, insecticide-induced microsomal expression could potentially affect this subcellular fraction's oxygen production. Many investigations have revealed that lindane has an oxidative effect in many mammalian organs, including rat blood [21], brain [22], testis [23], and liver [21], and chick liver [29]; all these effects were duration- and age-dependent [24]. In the context of oxidative stress, increased lipid peroxidation, as well as changed levels of GSH and oxygen radical - scavenging- enzymes in the blood, are discussed [25]. There's also evidence that lindane causes an oxidative stress environment, which decreases uterine muscle contraction and myometrial gap junctions [26]. It's also worth noting that lindane hepatotoxicity in hyperthyroidism, which results in an increase in the liver's oxidative stress status, is depend on Kupffer cell function, that may also include the production of mediators that contribute to prooxidant and inflammatory processes[22].

3. **Chlorodecone :** Chlordecone exposure reduced sperm production and motility in males at the Hopewell factory, and experimental exposure in rodents had comparable results.[27]

4. **Mirex :** Algal growth was only minimally slowed by mirex and methoxychlor. The use of a 50 g/L mixture of mirex and methoxychlor had no influence on population increase. [28].

5. **Toxaphene :** Toxaphene's effects on reproduction in mammals and fish are largely unexplored. In mammals, toxaphene had few or no effects, indicating that it interfered with reproduction.[29]

B. Organophosphates : OPs are cholinesterase blocker that are mostly utilized as insecticides. Chemical warfare agents are also made from them (like nerve agents). All insecticides containing phosphorus generated from phosphoric acid are classified as OPs, and they are the most lethal insecticides to chordate animals. Carboxylic ester hydrolases such as chymotrypsin, acetylcholine-sterase (AChE), butyrylcholinesterase (BuChE), hepatic carboxylesterases, paraoxonases, and other non-specific esterases are inhibited by OPs and carbamates in the body. The suppression of AChE is among the most popular obvious clinical outcomes of OP poisoning.[30] The acute tubular necrosis that takes place as a result of OP poisoning has also been linked to reactive oxygen species and lipid peroxidation.[31]

1. Malathion : Malathion exposure has been linked to comparable testicular degeneration [32],[33]. The effects of MAL on the reproductive system have been observed [34]. Reactive oxygen species (ROS) generation and the activation of intracellular oxidative stress, which has been proposed to have various impacts, can affect cell growth and differentiation [35]. Oxidative stress is among the most common reasons of male infertility. At the spermatozoon level, DNA breakage and lipid peroxidation impair the spermatozoon's ability to sustain normal embryonic development and cell motility. As a result, oxidative stress can impair the germinal epithelium's capacity to distinguish normal spermatozoa at this stage [36].

2. Parathion : In the decidua, methyl parathion produces fibrosis and bleeding, as well as decidual cells with multinucleated nuclei and acidophilus cytoplasm and vascular congestion. Cytoplasm, and vascular congestion in the tract [37]. With the exception of the highest level of viability dose, there were no significant changes in reproductive indices such as pregnancy, parturition, live birth, and viability. However, there were significant changes in the duration of the estrous cycle, duration of the proestrus, and diestrus. [38]

3. Diazinon : DZN disrupted spermatogenesis, resulting in a significant drop in sperm quality. DZN at a dose in mice resulted in an increase in defective germ cells in the seminiferous tubule and morphological defects in sperm [39]. DZN was given to male rats at various doses by orally caused change in sperm mobility, viability, and morphology, indicating a reduction in reproductive function [40]. DZN-induced nuclear protamine phosphorylation leads to changes in sperm's chromatin network condensation and DNA integrity, both of which have a deleterious influence on male reproductive potential[41].

4. Dichlorvos : There is no literature on the side effects of dichlorvos on human reproduction. However, an intraperitoneal injection of dichlorvos into male mice resulted in a considerable decrease in sperm quantity and an increase in sperm abnormalities, according to a study[42]. Another study found that adult male rats fed dichlorvos-contaminated water had significantly lower testosterone levels. The researchers also discovered degrees of distortion in the cells of the seminiferous levels, as well as spermatogonia cell hypertrophy[43].

5. Chlorpyrifos : Certain sperm metrics, such as mobility, sperm count, and sperm onwards evaluations, were negatively affected by chlorpyrifos.[44] Clove oil or chlorpyrifos-treated rats had a greater rate of sperm abnormalities, especially in the tail and neck regions. Although the mechanical causes for these abnormalities are speculative, they could have been caused by an aberrant chromosome, tiny changes in testicular DNA, or faults during the spermatogenesis process [45].

C. Carbamates : Inhibits the enzyme AChE, which stimulates the hydrolysis of ACh, causing it to accumulate at neuromuscular junctions and nerve synapses, resulting in enhanced stimulation of these nerve terminals[46].

1. **Carbofuran** : Carbofuran is a very hazardous substance that causes degradation in sperm quality, a drop in fertility indices, and a drop in serum enzyme activity and testosterone levels. [47] Carbofuron causes epididymis, seminal-vesicles-gland, ventral-prostate, and coagulating-glands to lose weight. Rats had worse sperm motility, lower epididymal sperm count, and more morphological abnormalities in the head, neck, and flagellated tail of spermatozoa[48].

2. **Carbaryl** : Carbaryl has a wide range of activities. This is a carbamate insecticide. Carbaryl exposure impacts the number and quality of sperm generated by employees, according to two studies conducted at a carbaryl production plant. In one study, employees who were exposed to this toxin on a regular basis had significantly lower sperm counts than individuals who were not exposed. In a further investigation of the original sperm samples, the number of sperm abnormalities was shown to be greater among employees exposed to carbaryl[49]. According to Rani et al., carbaryl exposure resulted in deformed seminiferous tubules, altered spermatogenesis, buildup of cell-mass in tubule lumens, the interstitial spaces, and varied degrees of sperm loss in testes[50].

D. Pyrethroids : Pyrethroids and pyrethrins are both chemical substances extracted from pyrethrum flowers (Chrysanthemum cinerariaefolium and C. Coccineum). Pyrethrins get their insecticidal activities from chrysanthemic and pyrethroic acids' ketoalcoholic esters[51]. Pyrethroids block sodium channels, causing the organism to become paralysed. Pyrethroids have less of toxicities and a quick biodegradation rate. Nervousness, headaches, diarrhea, muscular cramping, poor energy, epilepsy, and unconsciousness may occur after exposure to extremely high quantities of the chemicals in the air, food, or water[52]. **Synthetic Pyrethroids** exposure during pregnancy and adolescence can cause damage to male F1 offspring or the male reproductive organs. Oxidative stress may be essential in the damage of the male reproductive organs. Finally, because Synthetic Pyrethroids are so widely used, humans are expected to interact with them. Synthetic Pyrethroids exposure was also linked to poor sperm quality in humans. [53]

1. **Permethrin :** Permethrin is a prominent insecticide used in agriculture, houses, gardens, and for the treatment of ectoparasites including bugs, lice, and scabies in humans and animals. Because permethrin is present in the reproductive system of male, it can cause disintegration of germ cells, loss of Leydig cells, degeneration of seminiferous tubules, decreased sperm count, and eventually reduced reproductive potential[54]. In ICR mice, oral treatment of cis-permethrin reduced epididymal sperm numbers and motility, as well as testosterone levels, while raising circulating LH levels[55].

2. **Sumithrin :** In 20–25 percent of couples, sperm concentration is low, weak motility, and/or aberrant sperm's morphology are the leading causes of infertility[56].

3. **Allethrin :** The expression pattern of stress response gene, p53, was altered in the epididymides and testes, whereas the mRNA expression of sperm maturation factors C-Kit and Scf remained largely unaltered, though decreased levels of Tgf-β1 was observed. Results of this study indicate that exposure to mosquito coil smoke for prolonged periods of time increases oxidative stress with concomitant changes in tumor suppressor response genes, thereby increasing the susceptibility to develop cancers of the male reproductive tract. Further, severe damage to the function of the reproductive tract of male may occur due to loss of organ and spermatozoa architectural integrity[57].

4. **Permethrin :** Two other synthetic pyrethroids, fenvalerate and permethrin, are routinely used to protect people against insects. However, nothing is known about the effects of pyrethroids on mammalian reproductive in vivo and in vitro.Fenvalerate has a negative outcome on the quality of mice's sperm, which might be linked to germ cell death[58]. The male reproductive organs in mice was affected by the low and long term permethrin treatment during prenatal and postpartum life, despite permethrin's minimal side effects to the mammals reproductive system. [59]

Conclusion :

Commonly used pesticides or insecticides are responsible for producing several side effects in mammals. Reviewed pesticides cause reproductive toxicity in mammals like decrease in sperm count, malfunction in sperm structure and adverse effect in reproductive organs. Some pesticides affect germ cells which leads to germ cell death. Continuing the utilization of these pesticides will cause a major adverse effect on the human population. While dealing with pesticides, social awareness, strict adherence to regulatory norms, monitoring and necessary preventive measures should be taken.

References :

[1]. *International Code of Conduct on the Distribution and Use of Pesticides" (PDF)*. (2002).

[2]. "Types of Pesticides". US EPA. Archived from the original on March 28, 2013. Retrieved February 20, 2013.

[3]. Yamamoto, I. (1997). *Nicotinoid Insecticides and the Nicotinic Acetylcholine Receptor* (I. Yamamoto & J. Casida, Eds.). Springer-Verlag.

[4].Colović, M. B., Krstić, D. Z., Lazarević-Pašti, T. D., Bondžić, A. M., & Vasić, V. M. (2013). Acetylcholinesterase inhibitors: pharmacology and toxicology. *Current Neuropharmacology*, *11*(3),   315–335. https://doi.org/10.2174/1570159X11311030006

[5]. Appleby AP, Müller F, Carpy S. Ullmann's Encyclopedia of Industrial Chemistry. Nicosulfuron" EXTOXNET Retrieved [Internet].   2002;9.   Available   from: http://dx.doi.org/10.1002/14356007.a28_165.ISBN978-3-527-30385-4

[6]. "Nicosulfuron". EXTOXNET. Retrieved 9 May 2013

[7]. "Conclusion regarding the peer review of the pesticide risk assessment of the active substance triflusulfuron". EFSA Journal. 7 (4): 195. 2009. doi:10.2903/j.efsa.2009.195r. ISSN 1831-4732

[8]. Coombs A. Fighting Microbes with Microbes. The Scientist. 2013;

[9]. Pal, G., & Kumar, B. (2013). Antifungal activity of some common weed extracts against wilt causing fungi, Fusarium oxysporum. *Archived from the Original on December, 2.*

[10]. Plant Incorporated Protectants (PIPs) / Genetically Modified Plants. (2017). In *US NPIC*.

[11]. Kirby, M. L., Barlow, R. L., & Bloomquist, J. R. (2001). Neurotoxicity of the organochlorine insecticide heptachlor to murine striatal dopaminergic pathways. *Toxicological Sciences: An Official Journal of the Society of Toxicology*, *61*(1), 100–106. https://doi.org/10.1093/toxsci/61.1.100

[12]. Mattison, D. R. (1983). The mechanisms of action of reproductive toxins. *American Journal of Industrial Medicine*, *4*(1), 65–79. https://doi.org/10.1002/ajim.4700040107

[13].Bhalla, M., & Thami, G. P. (2004). Reversible neurotoxicity after an overdose of topical lindane in an infant. *Pediatric Dermatology*, *21*(5), 597–599. https://doi.org/10.1111/j.0736-8046.2004.21515.x

[14]. Aktar, M. W., Sengupta, D., & Chowdhury, A. (2009). Impact of pesticides use in agriculture: their benefits and hazards. *Interdisciplinary Toxicology*, *2*(1), 1–12. https://doi.org/10.2478/v10102-009-0001-7

[15]. Bangkok: Regional Office for Asia and the Pacific. (2005). In *FAO. Proceedings of the Asia Regional Workshop*.

[16]. Ayotte, P., Giroux, S., Dewailly, E., Hernández Avila, M., Farias, P., Danis, R., & Villanueva Díaz, C. (2001). DDT spraying for malaria control and reproductive function in Mexican men. *Epidemiology (Cambridge, Mass.)*, *12*(3), 366–367. https://doi.org/10.1097/00001648-200105000-00022

[17]. Ben Rhouma, K., Tébourbi, O., Krichah, R., & Sakly, M. (2001). Reproductive toxicity of DDT in adult male rats. *Human & Experimental Toxicology*, *20*(8), 393–397. https://doi.org/10.1191/096032701682692946

[18] Weinbauer, G. F., Barlett, J., Fingscheid, U., Tsonis, C. G., Kretser, D., & Nieschlag, D. M. (1989). Evidence for a major role o inhibin in the feedback control of FSH in the male rat. *J Reprod Fertil*, *85*, 355–362.

[19] Lafuente, A., Márquez, N., Pousada, Y., Pazo, D., & Esquifino, A. I. (2000). Possible estrogenic and/or antiandrogenic effects of methoxychlor on prolactin release in male rats. *Archives of Toxicology*, *74*(4–5), 270–275. https://doi.org/10.1007/s002040000121

[20] Akingbemi, B. T., Ren-Shan, G. E., Klinefelter, G. R., Gunsalus, G. L., & Hardy, M. P. (2000). A metabolite of methoxychlor, 2,2bis(p-hydroxyphenyl)-1,1,1-trichloroethane, reduces testosterone biosynthesis in rat Leydig cells through suppression of steady-state messenger ribonucleic acid levels of the cholesterol side-chain cleavage enzyme. *Biol Reprod*, *62*, 571–578.

[21] Simon-Giavarotti, K. A., Giavarotti, L., Gomes, L. F., Lima, A. F., Veridiano, A. M., Garcia, E. A., Mora, O. A., Fernández, V., Videla, L. A., & Junqueira, V. B. C. (2002). Enhancement of lindane-induced liver oxidative stress and hepatotoxicity by thyroid hormone is reduced by gadolinium chloride. *Free Radical Research*, *36*(10), 1033–1039. https://doi.org/10.1080/1071576021000028280

[22]. Sahoo, A., Samanta, L., & Chainy, G. B. (2000). Mediation of oxidative stress in HCH-induced neurotoxicity in rat. *Archives of Environmental Contamination and Toxicology*, *39*(1), 7–12. https://doi.org/10.1007/s002440010073

[23]. Samanta, L., Sahoo, A., & Chainy, G. B. (1999). Age-related changes in rat testicular oxidative stress parameters by hexachlorocyclohexane. *Archives of Toxicology*, *73*(2), 96–107. https://doi.org/10.1007/s002040050593

[24] Bainy, A. C., Silva, M. A., & Kogake, M. (1994). Infl uence of lindane and paraquat on oxidative stress-related parameters of erythrocytes in vitro. *Hum Exp Toxicol*, *13*, 461–465.

[25]. Banerjee, B. D. (1999). The influence of various factors on immunotoxicity assessment of pesticides chemicals. *Toxicol Lett*, *107*, 21–31.

[26]. Iscan, M., Coban, T., Cok, I., Bulbul, D., Eke, B. C., & Burgaz, S. (2002). The organochlorine pesticide residues and antioxidant enzyme activities in human breast tumors: is there any association? *Breast Cancer Research and Treatment*, *72*(2), 173–182. https://doi.org/10.1023/a:1014828705281

[27]. Cohn, W. J., Boylan, J. J., Blanke, R. V., Fariss, M. W., Howell, J. R., & Guzelian, P. S. (1978). Treatment of chlordecone (Kepone) toxicity with cholestyramine. Results of a controlled clinical trial: Results of a controlled clinical trial. *The New England Journal of Medicine*, *298*(5), 243–248. https://doi.org/10.1056/NEJM197802022980504

[28]. Kricher, J. C., Urey, J. C., & Hawes, M. L. (1975). The effects of mirex and methoxychlor on the growth and productivity of Chlorella pyrenoidosa. *Bulletin of Environmental Contamination and Toxicology*, *14*(5), 617–620. https://doi.org/10.1007/bf01683381

[29].Chu, I., Secours, V., Villeneuve, D. C., Valli, V. E., Nakamura, A., Colin, D., Clegg, D. J., & Arnold, E. P. (1988). Reproduction study of toxaphene in the rat. *Journal of Environmental Science and Health. Part. B, Pesticides, Food Contaminants, and Agricultural Wastes*, *23*(2), 101–126. https://doi.org/10.1080/03601238809372591

[30]. Abdollahi, M., Jalali, N., & Sabzevari, O. (1999). Pesticide poisoning during an 18-month period (1995-1997) in Tehran, Iran. *Irn J Med Sci*, *24*, 77–81.

[31]. Poovala, V. S., Huang, H., & Salahudeen, A. K. (1999). Role of reactive oxygen metabolites in organophosphate-induced renal tubular cytotoxicity. *J Am Soc Nephrol*, *10*, 1746–1752.

[32]. Geng, X., Shao, H., Zhang, Z., Ng, J. C., & Peng, C. (2015). Malathion-induced testicular toxicity is associated with spermatogenic apoptosis and alterations in testicular enzymes and hormone levels in male Wistar rats. *Environmental Toxicology and Pharmacology*, *39*(2), 659–667. https://doi.org/10.1016/j.etap.2015.01.010

[33]. Bhardwaj, J. K., Saraf, P., Kumari, P., Mittal, M., & Kumar, V. (2018). N-Acetyl-cysteine mediated inhibition of spermatogonial cells apoptosis against malathion exposure in testicular tissue. *Journal of Biochemical and Molecular Toxicology*, *32*(4), e22046. https://doi.org/10.1002/jbt.22046

[34]. Moridi, H., Hosseini, S. A., Shateri, H., Kheiripour, N., Kaki, A., Hatami, M., & Ranjbar, A. (2018). Protective effect of cerium oxide nanoparticle on sperm quality and oxidative damage in malathion-induced testicular toxicity in rats: An experimental study. *International Journal of Reproductive Biomedicine (Yazd, Iran)*, *16*(4), 261–266. https://doi.org/10.29252/ijrm.16.4.261

[35]. Badr, A. M. (2020). Organophosphate toxicity: updates of malathion potential toxic effects in mammals and potential treatments. *Environmental Science and Pollution Research*

International, *27*(21), 26036–26057. https://doi.org/10.1007/s11356-020-08937-4

[36]. El-Atta, A., & Ahmed, H. (n.d.). Testicular dysfunction in malathion induced toxicity in male rats: Protective role of NAC and Silymarin. *Mansoura J Forensic Med Clin Toxicol, 2020,* 33–45.

[37]. Levario-Carrilo, M., Olave, M. E., Corral, D. C., Alderete, J. G., Gagioti, S. M., & Bevilacqua, E. (2004). Placental morphology of rats prenatally exposed to methyl parathion. *Experimental Toxicological Pathology, 55*(6), 489–496.

[38]. Sortur, S. M., & Kaliwal, B. B. (1999). Effect of methyl parathion formulation on estrous cycle and reproductive performance in albino rats. *Indian Journal of Experimental Biology, 37*(2), 176–178.

[39].Wang, D., Kamijima, M., Okamura, A., Ito, Y., Yanagiba, Y., Jia, X.-F., Naito, H., Ueyama, J., & Nakajima, T. (2012). Evidence for diazinon-mediated inhibition of cis-permethrin metabolism and its effects on reproductive toxicity in adult male mice. *Reproductive Toxicology (Elmsford, N.Y.), 34*(4), 489–497. https://doi.org/10.1016/j.reprotox.2012.07.007

[40]. El-Aziz, A., & Sahlab, M. I. (1994). Abd el-Khalik M. Influence of diazinon and deltamethrin on reproductive organs and fertility of male rats. *Dtsch Tierarztl Wochenschr, 101,* 230–232.

[41]. Salazar-Arredondo, E., de Jesús Solís-Heredia, M., Rojas-García, E., Hernández-Ochoa, I., & Quintanilla-Vega, B. (2008). Sperm chromatin alteration and DNA damage by methyl-parathion, chlorpyrifos and diazinon and their oxon metabolites in human spermatozoa. *Reproductive Toxicology (Elmsford, N.Y.), 25*(4), 455–460. https://doi.org/10.1016/j.reprotox.2008.05.055

[42]. Faris, S. K. (2008). Effects of dichlorvos pesticide on fertility of laboratory male mice (Mus musculus L.). *Bas J Vet Res, 7*(1), 9–18.

[43]. Ezeji, E. U., Ogueri, O. D., Udebuani, A. C., Okereke, J. N., & Kalu, O. O. (2015). Effects of Dichlorvos on the fertility of adult male albino rats. *Nature and Science, 13*(12), 1–5.

[44]. Bretveld, R., Brouwers, M., Ebisch, I., & Roeleveld, N. (2007). Influence of pesticides on male fertility. *Scandinavian Journal of Work, Environment & Health, 33*(1), 13–28. https://doi.org/10.5271/sjweh.1060

[45]. Giri, S., Prasad, S. B., Giri, A., & Sharma, G. D. (2002). Genotoxic effects of malathion: an organophosphorus insecticide, using three mammalian bioassays in vivo. *Mutation Research. Genetic Toxicology and Environmental Mutagenesis, 514*(1–2), 223–231. https://doi.org/10.1016/s1383-5718(01)00341-2

[46]. Gupta, R. C., Mukherjee, I., Doss, R. B., Malik, J. K., Milatovic, D., & Gupta, R. C. (2017). Chapter 35- Organophosphates and Carbamates. *Reproductive and Developmental Toxicology*, 609–631.

[47]. Kobeasy, M. I., Ashraf, Y., El-Naggara, A. A., & El-Naggara, A. A. (2015). El-Naggara, and Amr A. *Abdallah Journal of Chemical and Pharmaceutical Research*, 7(4), 1142–1148.

[48]. Pant, N., Prasad, A. K., Srivastava, S. C., Shankar, R., & Srivastava, S. P. (1995). Effect of oral administration of carbofuran on male reproductive system of rat. *Human & Experimental Toxicology, 14*(11), 889–894. https://doi.org/10.1177/096032719501401106

[49]. Wyrobek, A. J., Watchmaker, G., & Gordon, L. (1981). Sperm shape abnormalities in carbaryl- exposed employees. *Environ Health Perspect, 40*, 255–265.

[50]. Rani, A., Sahai, A., & Srivastava, A. K. (2007). Carbaryl induced histopathological changes in the testis of albino rats. *Journal of the Anatomical Society of India, 56*, 4–6.

[51]. Reigert, J. R., & Roberts, J. R. (1999). Organophosphate Insecticides. Recognition and Management of Pesticide Poisonings. U. S. Environmental Protection Agency, Office of Prevention, Pesticides and Toxic Substances. *Office of Pesticide Programs*, 5.

[52]. Goel A, Aggarwal P. Pesticide poisoning. Natl Med J India. 2007;20(4):182–9.

[53].Zhang, X., Zhang, T., Ren, X., Chen, X., Wang, S., & Qin, C. (2021). Pyrethroids toxicity to male reproductive system and offspring as a function of oxidative stress induction: Rodent

studies. *Frontiers in Endocrinology*, *12*, 656106. https://doi.org/10.3389/fendo.2021.656106

[54]. Patrick-Iwuanyanwu, K. C., & Udowelle, N. A. (n.d.). *Okereke Testicular toxicity and sperm quality following exposure to Solignum®:A Permethrin-containing wood preservative in adult male Wistar rats.*

[55]. Zhang, S. Y. (n.d.). *Permethrin may disrupt testosterone biosynthesis via mitochondrial membrane damage of Leydig cells in adult male mouse Endocrinology.*

[56]. Snick HK, Snick TS, Evers JL, Collins JA. The spontaneous pregnancy prognosis in untreated subfertile couples: the Walcheren primary care study. Hum Reprod [Internet]. 1997;12(7):1582–8. Available from: http://dx.doi.org/10.1093/humrep/12.7.1582

[57]. Golla Madhubabu and Suresh Yenugu, Ecotoxicology and Environmental Safety 208(10):111714.

[58]. Zhang, J., Hu, Y., Guo, J., Pan, R., Shi, R., Tian, Y., Zhou, Y., & Gao, Y. (2018). Fenvalerate decreases semen quality in puberty rat through germ cell apoptosis. *Andrologia*, *50*(9), e13079. https://doi.org/10.1111/and.13079

[59]. Saito, H., Hara, K., & Tanemura, K. (2017). Prenatal and postnatal exposure to low levels of permethrin exerts reproductive effects in male mice. *Reproductive Toxicology (Elmsford, N.Y.)*, *74*, 108–115. https://doi.org/10.1016/j.reprotox.2017.08.022

Department of Zoology,
Poddar International College,
Sector 7, Shipra Path,
Mansarovar, Jaipur, Rajasthan, India 302020.
email : Neerajparmar42@gmail.com,

17. "An Analysis to 'Environmental Pollution' and 'Development' with special reference to protect Child's Right to Life"

Dr. Upendra Nath

Abstract

Being the lifeline for the survivability of flora and fauna on this green planet, environment continues to be regarded as fragile and delicate natural component of our ecosystem. Human beings, in their quest to hegemony and development, by the dint of their intellectual skills and technological prowess has endeavored using the scarce natural resources towards making the civilization developed enough and subsequently aspires overhauling the very nature and character of our earth itself. However, such endeavor towards development does compromise with the basic natural 'right to life' equally available to every human beings, irrespective of their nationality, religion, race, sex, caste and alike. Environmental pollution, as an aftermath consequences of any of the state's developmental initiatives, do interferes with the natural processes that are inherently involved with a child's biological growth hampering thereby their inclusive rights pertaining to it. Albeit, development construe being the basic right of every sovereign nations; yet the same warrants being explores in a most judicious manner with the key aspects of socio-legal, economic, political and ethical elements of equity, reasonability, rationality, good conscience and alike. It is essentially desirable warding off the evil effect and menace of pollution which eventually continues abetting the persistent degradation of our fragile ecosystem threatening thereby the very existence of life on earth. Since the notion of development brings with itself the other related issues of urbanization, industrialization, population explosion, climate change with the increasing emission of greenhouse gases leading to environmental degradation; statutory global efforts are desired in the backdrop of the universal vis-à-vis equitable concept and notion of sustainable development that vies ensuring congenial balance between the imperativeness of development along with the sustenance of our serene ecological system itself. The paper aim analyzing the varied socio-legal and economic aspects of environmental pollution in the backdrop of the development which signifies the dynamism of human intellect towards ensuring not only their better livelihood but also vies to protect child's inclusive rights being an significant component of the human right to life on this planet as well.

Keywords : Development, Pollution, Environmental degradation, Human Rights, Child Right

Introduction

Nature has exclusively bestowed 'green environment' for the living beings not only to sustain, survive and flourish but also to ensure their perpetuity and growth on this 'green living planet' itself. However quest to acquire power and dominance over others remain being one of the basic undeniable socio-physiological instincts as part of their inherent traits amongst human beings living here at. Significantly, the latter's intellectual supremacy keep them engrossed with devising and exploring varied means through scientific feats & accomplishments towards ensuring progressive wellbeing of human civilization on this planet. However pragmatically viewed, often human initiatives, irrespective of its nature being either technologically or not, towards ensuring betterment of their own quality of life and livelihood, if not used rationally and reasonably, do cost our environment dearly in terms of rendering distortions & imbalance to its fragile ecological natural order. Eventually, the latter puts the entire flora and fauna at the risk of getting extinguished in the coming future. Sovereign states, being the custodian of ensuring 'environmental health' within its domain, ought to take measures- both legal, social, political & alike, with an ultimate motive and aim to protect the indispensible statutory 'right to life' of its populace. Vulnerable and marginalized socio-economic sections of populace like those of child, women, infirm and alike with their scanty means to survive suffers at the altar of development over the cost of environmental health itself. Child mortality rate from the preventable diseases across the world warrants specific attention and concern owing to the fact that many

181

of the factors associated with the environmental pollution proves to be the main cause for prevailing respiratory diseases amongst these target populace. It is worth mentioning that reducing neonatal mortality is one of the essential parts of the global 'third Sustainable Development Goal (SDG)' towards putting end to the preventable child deaths. As such, varied issues relating to environmental pollution warrants being addressed at the appropriate world forums designated for the same. Albeit, in the backdrop of ensuring inclusive human right protection to its citizen; states don't undermine underestimating the need for the inclusive development of both its populace and the state at large. As such, the statutory binding laws to protect environment becomes the need of hour for present space age era on his earth itself.

Human development may look good and impressive on paper and even when the same is apparently witnessed in its realistic parlance. But when its aftermath bearings on the human health and the requisite healthy surroundings for the same is taken into consideration then one would certainly force to question the viability of all the developmental projects that the state often undertakes, at the war footing, only at the ultimate cost of risking life and livelihood of the end user of the nation's target populace.

Meaning of Environmental Pollution

Basically, 'environmental pollution' may construe being an ecological concept that emphasizes the spate of degradation, in natural ecological surroundings, owing to the varied human activities that are consistently being carried out in an developmental pursuit eventually leading to imbalances in the natural component of environment that acts contrary to safeguard inclusive interests pertaining to one's health and survivability of lives here at. Invariably the term **'environment'** may vie connoting entire gamut of circumstances, objects, or conditions that surrounds living beings on this earth.. As such, in the context of our green planet, it may imply complex aggregation of physical, chemical and other biotic factors like those of climate, soil and other living things that somehow or rather have impact either upon an organism or an ecological community which eventually ensures determining both of its form and survivability. Herein, viable conditions may also remain apparently present not only for the development and growth of humanity and humane civilization but, even in an adverse scenario, simultaneously pose eminent threat and danger to the latter's survivability as well.

In the same vein, the term **'pollution'** implies introduction of contaminants into the natural environment that eventually results adverse change which brings destabilization into the ecological mechanisms to the detriment of life processes to exist on this planet at large. Pollution may either be chemical substances or energy variables in the form of noise, heat, light or alike. Pollutants, the basic components of pollution, can either include naturally occurring contaminants like those of volcanic ashes along with those of poisonous gases that get released into the atmosphere or other foreign substances, so inserted or emitted, into the latter as byproducts from many of the industrial activities that signifies a nation's mechanisms of development and growth. In fact, when the developmental activities are recklessly undertaken and natural resources get irretrievably exploited leading to natural imbalances; the resultant pollutants hamper wellbeing of the concerned. Overall, it's the human initiatives through their technological innovations that results altering the natural balance of ecological phenomenon within a state's vicinity. Pragmatically viewed, environmental pollution indeed affects the human quality of life, livelihood and sustenance. More specifically, child right to life suffers utmost due to environmental pollution since this target populace comprises the most vulnerable section of the society and warrants special preventive socio-economic, political and legislative measures towards ensuring their survivability and .inclusive wellbeing as well.

Relation between Development, Environment Pollution and Child Right

In our present age of technological innovations when human beings compete amongst themselves in terms of their intellectual talents, might and caliber towards ensuring quality of lives, livelihood and sustenance; then certainly some feats do results which eventually reflect the dynamism of human caliber & talents on this earth.

Role of Sustainable Development in Environmental Conservation

Today when the limits of horizon proves no bound for the human endeavor competing with the destiny; yet, our environment get affected in worst manner; ultimate victims for the same remains being the human themselves. There exists an adverse relationship between development and environmental pollution. Former being the human quest to enhance their quality of lives and livelihood through exploiting natural resources and on the other hand, latter denotes the adverse outcome of states' developmental activities undertaken, in irrational and unreasonable manners, without taking into consideration its negative impact for both the nature and humanity at large. Child signifies the future of human civilization and their inclusive rights to life ought to be protected by the state itself. Viewed pragmatically, no state can vie compromising any of its developmental initiatives and activities since these are considered as sine quo none for the ultimate growth, existence and sustainability of its citizenry and sovereignty at large. However, in the backdrop of the sustainable development doctrine; nations continue exploring to undertake inclusive developmental initiatives through the use of rational, reasonable and environmental friendly techniques for the same. In this respect, Honb'le Supreme Court of India has held that "Protection of 'life' under Art.21 with adherence of sustainable de elopement is sine quo non for maintenance of symbiotic balance between rights to development and environment. Right to development includes guarantee off fundamental human rights. Construction of dam or mega projects hence treats as integral component for development"[1]

However, it is worth mentioning that the nature's flora and faunas do get affected with human endeavor excessively exploiting natural resources, beyond permissible limit, towards furthering their own narrow interest to the detriment of global inclusive interests at large. Evidently the economic and technological notions of *'carbon emission'* along with the subsequent need for its curtailment remain being one of the root sources of concern and conflict amongst the global fraternity of nations vying to ensure that the earth's environment and its natural ecological balance remain maintained.

---

[1] N.D.Jayal v. Union of India AIR 2004 SC 867

Somehow or rather, *'carbon emission'* implies higher concentration of greenhouse gases comprising primarily those of carbon dioxide, methane, nitrous oxide, hydrochlorofluorocarbons (HCFCs), hydrofluorocarbons (HFCs),and ozone in the earth's lower atmosphere that invariably abet aggravating the ecological imbalances to the detriment of living beings and which are produced to either directly or indirectly support human activities. It usually expressed in equivalent tons of carbon dioxide. More or less, in our present industrialized world, this concept signifies the extent and level of socio-economic growth and development of both nations and its human constituents. More of its level, in a nation's atmosphere, is considered being a favorable indication of its industrialized stature and vice versa. In fact when a nation treads to the path of its inclusive development, then prima facie, it relies chiefly over exploiting the organic natural resources in terms of fossil fuels, like natural gas, crude oil, and coal, so existent within its domain, as a source to generate electricity. The latter invariably propels the engine of growth for the ultimate target constituents. While the rate of setting up industries and undertaking get accelerated; many other related initiatives too significantly abet altering the nation's socio-economic component in terms of generating employment opportunities for the inhabitants thereby enabling them to amicably sustain both their life and livelihood along with ensuring the nation's economic dynamism. Yet these entire processes and endeavors eventually results in deteriorating the state of environmental health itself owing to the rise in the level of pollutants and alike. Significantly these drastically affect uniformly the ultimate health of its beneficiaries themselves. Eventually it raises the cost of healthcare for safe and healthy livelihood. Along with those of the adult ones, child's right to life suffers heavily owing to malnourishment, diseases and increasing mortality rate due to non-availability of adequate timely medical care.

Moreover, towards addressing the aforesaid issue pertaining to ascertain the pragmatic linkage of development & pollution and its resultant impact on the life and livelihood of the human populace; as an apparent instance on the same, it is worth mentioning the visible negative impact of development on the inclusive environmental health in the cities of **Biha**r which erstwhile reflect an insignia of being one of the most backward Indian states in terms of the basic infrastructures and alike available here at. Owing to the socio-political and administrative zeal of the Bihar government, in the recent years, that the massive exercise towards developing the state's infrastructures was undertaken. The latter eventually covered it's almost the entire regions including those of the villages, so located even in the secluded remote corner of the state at large. These eventually lead to irrational planning of the developmental projects, in the state, without taking into consideration the root environmental issues related with the same. Significantly the state extensively lost its green cover. The latter being an indispensible lifeline to the environmental health serving as sink to the poisonous carbon pollutants that are present in the atmosphere itself.

Significantly, as reported in the print media,[2] the present Indian State of Bihar, with inheriting an illustrious ancient past, now draws the global attention but for the negative cause towards aggravating the already depleted environmental parameters threatening thereby the safe and healthy living and livelihood of the target populace here at. Significantly, Patna, the capital of Bihar, has been adjudged as the World's 7th most Polluted City and even ranking 6th in the country according to the reports released by 'Greenpeace Southeast Asia', a nongovernment environmental organization. According to 2018 World Air Quality Report, jointly compiled by IQAir, Air Visual and Greenpeace, the annual level of PM 2.5- particulate matter less than 2.5 microns in 2018 was raised to 119.7 micrograms per cubic meter in Patna which falls in the category of unhealthy air.

In fact, as per the aforesaid report, in Bihar, Patna remain followed by Muzaffarpur ranking 13th in the report with PM 2.5 concentration at 110.3 micrograms per cubic meter, followed by Gaya at the 18th rank with a yearly average of PM 2.5 concentration at 96.6 micrograms per cubic meter. In fact, it may be envisaged that PM 2.5 are construe being the tiny pollutants in air that causes the air to turn hazy, invade lungs and can even cause cancer. The World Health Organization [WHO] has already termed such air pollutants

[2] The Times Of India (TOI), Patna on 6th March 2019

as carcinogenic. It may be emphasized herein that the tiny pollutants are often considered as one of the major reason for the air pollution in the state capital. The spate of construction and building activities that are going on with rapid pace and either unregulated or unmonitored by the statutory environmental law enforcement machinery to ascertain whether these infrastructural developmental projects, either of private or public nature, are adhered to any of the environmental norms, statutorily provided for the same, have indeed made the situation more worrisome. It may further be ascertained that the aforesaid report has been compiled with data from around 3000 cities across the globe. Significantly, as per the guidelines of WHO, the annual average of PM 2.5 concentration in air should never cross the mark of annual average of 10 micrograms per cubic meter.

Moreover, Patna has consistently been topping the list when it comes to poor air quality index [AQI]. Also, as per the daily nationwide report prepared by Central Pollution Control Board [CPCB] in Patna, it was measured at 234, putting it in *'poor category'*. According to CPCB, the poor air quality often led to breathing discomfort to most of the people on prolonged exposure where the child's right to life suffers   It is further being ascertained that the AQI of the city often surges to over 400 during the peak winter months of December and January.

The reasons are cited for the abovementioned high level of PM 2.5. As such, according to the authorities of the Bihar State Pollution Control Board, [BSPCB], these include unregulated construction activities and alluvial soil on the banks of Ganges, which settles in the lower level of atmosphere. In this respect, it may be pointed out that even though the action plans to control pollution is being persistently chalked out by the State's pollution controlling authorities; the implementation for the same warrants equal participation of the society in these initiative. In latter's absence, the Board can only slate projecting its viability, on paper, with no result in sight and the target populace continue to suffer with consistent violation of their basic human right to life within a sovereign habitat.

Medical fraternity too frequently argue that due to the high concentration of the PM 2.5, the pollutant enter our respiratory system and settles in our alveolus, leasing to several respiratory issues like those of nasal blockage nasal infection, respiratory tract infection and asthma. These simply aggravates the rights to life of vulnerable populaces like those of children with their weak immune system suffers. Patna Municipal Corporation [PMC] has also initiated several steps to make air in the city clean. At least 10 dust sweeping machines are being used at night for the purpose. The machines are said to be highly efficient as they clean around 20 kg of dust settled in a street in a go. They even resort washing the streets towards ensuring prevention of dust particles getting further settled thereat.

Global Perspectives to Child Right amidst the issues of Development and Environmental Pollution

Basically the notion of 'development' may construe being an indication of human dynamism towards ensuring inclusive socio-economic growth and enhancement of lives and livelihood of the target populace within a sovereign state. It even tantamount to the natural right of human being to excel, prosper and build their personal stature amidst the basic ecological surroundings provided to them by the 'Mother Nature' itself. Somehow or rather, 'development' may also construe implying an active interference of the human beings with the balanced environmental ecosystem resulting thereby its distortions and imbalances to the eventual detriment of the human existence itself. It may also be envisaged that the existent of the Ministry of Environment & Forest in any of the sovereign nation construe the latter's prime concern to ensure that its policies and programs towards conservation of its natural resources including those of lakes, rivers, biodiversity, forests and wildlife remain implemented in its totality. It also aimed towards ensuring not only the welfare of animals but also to abet preventing and abatement of pollution, within the realm, as well. The ministry, in itself, remains guided by the indispensible principles of sustainable development and enhancement of human well-being.

Ensuring protection of Child right, being one of the key aspects of the larger human right, constitutes a significant issue of global concern amidst the perspective of a nation's developmental norms and initiatives and the resultant environmental pollution associated with the same. In this respect, 'Report to the Human Rights Council on the rights of children and the environment (2018)[3]', as submitted to the 37th session of the Council, too recognized the need to clarify some aspects of the human rights obligations pertaining to child right, relating to environment. It emphasized that no group is more vulnerable to environmental harm than to children. Air pollution, water pollution, and exposure to the toxic substances, together with the other types of environmental harm, cause 1.5 million deaths of children under the age of 5 every year and contribute to disease, disability and early mortality throughout their life. In addition, climate change and the loss of biodiversity threaten to cause long term effects that will disrupt children's lives for years to come. Making the matter worse, children are often not able to exercise their rights including those relating to information, participation and access to effective remedies.

Undoubtedly, pollution remains being one of the many environmental challenges that the world encounters in our present space age era. Its impact is apparently more severe in the developing countries in terms of ill health, death and disability in comparison to those of the developed ones; the latter being capable enough countering the same owing to their technological advancements along with the available rich economic resource for the same. However any of the initiative, to halt environmental pollution through ensuring curtailment of the level of carbon emissions would invariably result undermining the inclusive processes of economic growth and development in such sovereign economies across the world over and subsequently hamper them asserting their 'right to development' that continues to crystallize as a rule under the statutory domain of international law itself. In this respect, it is worth mentioning the significant *"Declaration on the Right to Development"* that was adopted by the UN General Assembly on 4th

---

[3] (A/HRC/37/58)

December, 1986.[4] Article 1 of the same invariably considers this right as an inalienable human right by virtue of which every human beings are entitled to participate in, contribute to, and enjoy further their economic, social, cultural and political development, in which all of their other available human rights and fundamental freedom can fully be realized.

Moreover, when issues pertaining to the legal aspect of pollution as an significant factor contributing violation of the people's right to a healthy life, in a natural environmental ecological system, owing to the negative consequences of the nation's economic developmental initiatives is taken up for consideration and analysis; it is indeed worth taking into account the imperativeness of such progress for the ultimate benefit and well-being of human civilization on this earth itself. However, the notion of 'sustainable development' is gaining currency in the present world order amidst the unhindered initiatives towards inclusive development by the target nations itself. It chiefly implies offsetting the negative consequences of development in terms of environmental pollution, deforestations, climate change, ecological imbalances and alike through undertaking positive initiatives to conserve natural ecology and abate further degradation of natural ecology at an altar of varied developmental work taken up both by the developed and developing nations as well. In fact, in March, 1988 itself, The United Nations Environmental Programme (UNEP), whilst adopting its strategy for environmental protection, had envisaged about the future role of the United Nations slate to focus on helping the countries to achieve an optimum level of sustainable development and subsequently aim reducing not only the impact of environmental degradation by pollution but simultaneously to abet rehabilitating those fragile ecosystems that has already been degraded and polluted by the various nations in its quest to inclusive developments.[5]

It may further be envisaged that at the global scale, the notion of 'environmental pollution, either due to the aftermath effect or

---

[4] General Assembly Resolution no. 41/128 Dt. 4th December, 1986
[5] "Action To Save Our Environment", U.N. Chronicle, Vol.XXV, No.2 (June 1988) Pg 43

consequences of any of the nation's initiative and varied activities towards ensuring inclusive development in its domain warrants being analyzed in the perspectives of international law pertaining to the same. Issues of transnational pollution or environmental degradations are often raised at an appropriate forum of international justices. The root concern remains being the contentious issue relating to the violation of fundamental right to life and environmental sovereignty of one nation due to the varied activities frequently undertaken by any other nation in the peripheral regional or global surroundings. Basically, in this respect, a fundamental principle of international law virtually limits action by one state that would cause injuries of multifarious dimensions and severity in the territory of another state.[6] In fact, there has been general recognition of the rule that no state ought to permit using its territory for such purposes that may prove injurious to the inclusive interests of other sovereign states. The aforesaid principle may construe being a reflection of the fundamental international law doctrine of "*sic utere tuo ut alienum non laedas*" implying '**one must use his own right so as not to do injury to another**'. Invariably ensuring protection to the basic human right to life also get recognized at the global level and ought not to be compromised at all under any circumstances and exigencies that may surfaces at one instance or the other in the course of any developmental initiatives undertaken by the target sovereigns.

Since, the menace of pollution warrants being checked worldwide for the ultimate sustainability of life on this living planet; the cumulative initiatives of comity of sovereigns, at the global level, are the demand of the timeline for the same. Even though statutory measures, at the international level, towards ensuring conservation of earth's scarce natural resources and protection of environment from getting further degraded owing to the persistent emission of pollutants and many other greenhouse gases into it, are existent in the form of 'environmental treaties and conventions'; the same cannot be expected to deliver effective results in the absence of monitoring machinery along with the inherent intentions & motives for it from the global sovereigns itself.

---

[6] Corfu Channel Case, (1949) I.C.J. Rep.4

Role of Sustainable Development in Environmental Conservation

In India, the state governments do undertake measures to contain the menace of environmental pollution. For instance, the state government of Bihar has drawn up an action plan to curb pollution, from various sources in the city such as vehicles, construction sites, road dust, industries and garbage fire. The focus remains on curbing suspended particulate matter less than 2.5 micron (pm 2.5) which is the deadliest and biggest contributor to air pollution. The measure include refusing permission to diesel-operated auto rickshaws, ban on cutting of trees for road construction, blanket ban on burning of solid waste and mandatory covering of construction sites among others. Civic authorities are also directed to sprinkle water on roads to prevent dust particles.

Such measures to control air pollution warrant being emulated by any other sovereigns around the world as well. Apart from it, alternative sore of energy like those of wind, solar and hydropower warrants being promoted on the larger scale. "*Polluter Pays Principle*"[7] should also be effectively implemented at the global level under the aegis of international organs like those of 'UN Security Council' for imposing monetary an strategic sanctions on the violators of environmental norms. In fact, the aforesaid principle imposes statutory liability on a person, responsible for polluting the environment, through any of his deeds or activities, to compensate for the ultimate damage caused and eventually vies returning the environment to its original state regardless of the intent for the same. Even the '*Principle*' has been incorporated within the legal domain of our Indian Judicial system that invariably considers it being a part of the nation's 'Environmental Law Regime' and the same is evident from many of the judgments passed by the competent Judicial Authorities. Some of the landmark cases, decided on the basis of the aforesaid '*Principle*', by the Apex Court of India do include:-

➤ Indian Council for Enviro-Legal Actions vs Union of India 1996(3) SCC 212

---

[7] incorporated in the Rio Declaration (Principle 16)- 'polluter should bear the cost of pollution

➢ Vellore Citizen's Welfare Forum vs Union of India 1996(5) SCC 647
➢ The Oleum Gas Leak Case (M.C.Mehta vs Union of India air 1987 SC 1086
➢ M.C.MehtaVs Kamal Nath&Othrs (1997) 1 SCC 388

Further, it is worth mentioning that millions of children across the world suffer violations of their right to health, food, water, and other rights because either of problematic government responses or inaction to environmental degradation and climate changes. Worst affected are the children from the marginalized groups, especially those children from the indigenous communities, are often particularly affected. In addition, national environmental laws and policies infrequently address the rights of children. And international environmental agreements too have long ignored a human rights approach; wherein the child right constitutes a key component. This gap invariably hinders rights-based approaches to environmental problems affecting children. However, the Paris Agreement on Climate Change and the Sustainable Development often take a more integrated approach to address varied aspects of human rights and environmental issues.

Moreover, the Global Children's Environmental Rights Initiatives (CERI), aimed furthering to promote the children's right to a healthy and sustainable environment, set up a follow-up processes to the aforesaid report pertaining to children's right and the environment. In fact, with an object to accomplish Sustainable Development Goals relating to the issue in question, this initiative aims to boost recognition and implementation of   children's right to healthy and sustainable environment by;

• empowering children and youth in relation to their rights regarding the environment
• increasing awareness and building capacity among national regional and global decision-makers about the relationship on children's rights and environment, including state obligations in this respect
• convening key stakeholders and facilitating dialogue and stronger cooperation in relation to fulfilling children's right to a healthy environment

- shaping and securing international recognition of a global set of guiding principles on children's environmental rights, and informing standard-setting and policy development at global , regional and national levels.

It is worth mentioning that CERI also organizes digital consultations, provides technical guidance and capacity building tools, and even undertakes advocacy to promote children's right to a safe and healthy environment in many of its key forums as well.

Impact of Environmental Harm on Children's Right

According to the World Health Organization (WHO), 1.7 million children under the age of 5 died in 2012 owing to the reason that they lived in an unhealthy environment.[8] Children, across the world, frequently get exposure to hazardous substances, particularly, lead zinc, silica, mercury and alike, while playing on the ground, bathing in rivers, going to school, eating or drinking, or working. It is ascertained that many off the hazardous substances have particularly harmful consequences for children, whose developing bodies absorb them more readily than those of adults and are especially vulnerable to certain toxins, leading in some cases to irreversible long-term damage, disability and even death.

Business activity too has been considered as one of the prime source of significant environmental damage that somehow or rather harms children through air pollution, poor quality drinking water, and other routes of exposure. In this respect, governments often fail to regulate companies towards taking precaution against it. For example, children living near or working in leather tanneries very frequently get exposed to chemicals that flowed off tannery floors into open gutters of nearby streets. They show even health problems, including those of fevers, diarrhea, respiratory problems, and chronic infections in skin, stomach, and eye conditions. Similarly, smelters and battery factories have caused lead poisoning in children in chins and Kenya, and protests by parents have been met with government

---

8 World Health Organization, "An estimated 12.6 million deaths each year are attributable to unhealthy environments," March 15, 2016, http://www.who.int/mediacentre/news/releases/2016/deaths-attributable-to-unhealthy-environments/en/ (accessed March 3 , 2023).

repression.[9] In agriculture too, child labors have been exposed to fertilizers and pesticides in Indonesia, the United States, ad Israel/Palestine. Similar is the case for the children who work in tobacco farming. They suffer from the symptoms that are consistent with nicotine poisoning[10].

It is also worth pointing out that children's health often get severely affected owing to their being exposed to chemicals from the large-scale and small-scale mining operations. In one of the worst environmental health disasters, over 400 children died in Nigeria from exposer to lead contaminated dust produced inadvertently during artisanal and small-scale gold mining. Similarly, in small-scale gold mining regions of Mali, Ghana, Tanzania, the Philippines, and elsewhere, children continues being exposed to toxic mercury used to process gold, and in some of the cases, developed symptoms that are consistent with mercury poisoning are even detected[11].Further, governments, in many nations also have failed to protect children from hazardous chemicals, like arsenic, in the ground, groundwater, or water-supply system. For instance, in Canada, indigenous communities, mostly children, have persistently been exposed to water containing naturally occurring uranium[12],

---

[9] Jane Cohen (Human Rights Watch), "Dispatches: Hope for Kenya's Lead Poisoning Victims," August 13, 2014, https://www.hrw.org/news/2014/08/13/dispatches-hope-kenyas-lead-poisoning-victims.

[10] Human Rights Watch, Teens of the Tobacco Fields: Child Labor in United States Tobacco Farming, December 2015, https://www.hrw.org/report/2015/12/09/teens-tobacco-fields/child-labor-united-states-tobacco-farming; Human Rights Watch, "The Harvest is in My Blood": Hazardous Child Labor in Tobacco Farming in Indonesia, May 2016, https://www.hrw.org/report/2016/05/24/harvest-my-blood/hazardous-child-labor-tobacco-farming-indonesia.

11 Human Rights Watch, A Poisonous Mix: Child Labor, Mercury, and Artisanal Gold Mining in Mali, December 2011, https://www.hrw.org/report/2011/12/06/poisonous-mix/child-labor-mercury-and-artisanal-gold-mining-mali;

[12] Human Rights Watch, Make It Safe: Canada's Obligation to End the First Nations Water Crisis, June 2016,

Significantly, climate change also impacts children's access to water food, and healthcare. It warrants that governments need to address the human rights consequences of climate change on children. The latter from ingenious communities are often vulnerable because their culture and livelihood is tied to their land, and such marginalized groups typically lack the resources and government support to effectively respond to the effects of climate change on their lives and livelihood. In this respect, it may be asserted that climate change along with other related environmental, political, and economic developmental challenges, has, to a large extent, limited local indigenous communities' access to food and clean water. As a result, may children often fall sick owing to the inability off their families to provide them with sufficient food and clean drinking water. Girls often walk extremely long distances to dig for water in dry riverbeds, exposing them to dangers along the route and leaving them with lesser time to attend their school or rest. Even the scientific studies have shown that recurring draught and food insecurity can also have indirect effects on health.

Conclusion and Suggestions

Intellectual prowess and dynamism construe being the key to human civilization taking strides exploring the various facets of this green planet ranging from its surface both beneath the land, ocean and zeal showing their inherent intentions to undertake human imperialist initiatives towards conquering the secrets of deep space, universe and even beyond it. However, beginning for the same ought to be made from the earth and its surrounding living atmosphere. In these processes, human have encountered varied socio-economic, legal, political, technological and other related allied issues that signifies the various facets of the growth and development of human civilization accomplishing the present feat of achievement for their ultimate survivability, sustenance and existence on this earth at large.

But, pragmatically viewed, such zeal has eventually costs dearly the ecological health of this planet itself. And the same get manifested in the form of issues like those of urbanization, industrialization, population explosion, depletion of earth's scarce natural resources owing to its over exploitation for human development, pollution to land, air & water along with the menace of deforestation causing increase of poisonous greenhouse gases in the atmosphere to the detriment for the lives of both flora and fauna existent here at. At the same time, growing human consciousness about their inclusive right to development and growth have galvanized the global comity of sovereigns, representing varied interests of their populace, to come across and explore the rational, viable and humane concept of sustainable development as a panacea arresting the pace of further deletion of environment at the altar of human aspirations and competitiveness for assertive global hegemony. The doctrine of judicial activism on the issues of pollution, in any of the sovereign nation, could viably be regarded as a statutory tool forcing the target nation to implement all the provisions available to it under the aegis of Environmental Laws; either domestic or the international ones.

It is worth mentioning that the inclusive processes of development emphatically brings with it the grave issues of environmental pollution which somehow or rather hampers the right of citizenry to healthy environment, life and livelihood. Health of the vulnerable and marginalized sections of the populaces comprising those of children suffers due to hazardous byproducts in the environment. These issues warrant being addressed adequately at an appropriate international forum. Governments should ensure that their laws, policies and actions pertaining to development and environment explicitly include measures relating to child rights. The latter include protection from environmental harm such as toxic pollution and climate change as well. Efforts should also be made to strengthen accountability for the past violations and to require companies to conduct due diligence, in supply chain, with regards to the harmful effects of environment damage on child rights.

However, emphasizing the role and imperativeness of development in the context of environmental pollution; whilst speaking before the U.N. Conference on Human Environment at Stockholm, late Prime Minister Mrs. Indira Gandhi had said that "for the developed countries development might be the cause of destruction of environment, but for a country like India it was primary means for improving the standard of living, to make available food products, water, cleanliness, shelter, to bring about greenery in deserts and to make hills and mountains worth living". As such India has always served as the voice of both developing and underdeveloped nations, and vied implementing the notion of sustainable development, when issues pertaining to development and pollution comes before the international comity of nations for an effective deliberations on the same.

It is further worth pointing out that the advantage of any of the developmental initiatives can be enjoyed in the true sense only when these do not cause adverse impact on environment. It would certainly be rationale asserting that those states which are apparently found responsible for causing adverse impact on environment should be compelled to make reparations and the funds so received ought to be invested for improving the environment itself and subsequently to abet freeing the same from the ill effects of pollution thereby making it healthy vis-à-vis congenial for the civilization to live, excel and flourish on this living green planet at large.

Reference :
i) "Action To Save Our Environment", U.N. Chronicle, Vol.XXV, No.2 (June 1988) Pg 43
ii) All India Reporter, published by All India Reporter Pvt. Ltd. Nagpur- 440012
iii) General Assembly Resolution no. 41/128 Dt. 4th December, 1986
iv) Human Rights Watch Reports on child right violations
v) Intergovernmental Panel on Climate Change, "Climate Change 2007": Synthesis Report
vi) The Times Of India (TOI), Patna

Assistant Professor,
Faculty of Law, Patna Law College,
Patna University, Patna, Bihar, (INDIA)
email : dr.unath46@gmail.com

18. E-Waste and Circular Economy : Opportunities and Challenges for Electronic Product Design and Remanufacturing

Dr. Ruchir Saxena[1],
Dr. Praveen Goswami[2]
Mr. Shashikant Sharma[3],
Ms. Pooja Saxena[4],
Ms. Shalini Gill[5]

E-waste

E-waste, or electronic waste, is a term used to describe discarded electronic devices, such as computers, mobile phones, and televisions. It is one of the fastest-growing waste streams globally, with an estimated 53.6 million metric tons generated in a year, according to the Global E-waste Monitor report.

The increasing number of electronic devices in use, coupled with the decreasing lifespan of these devices, has led to a growing amount of e-waste generated annually. Improper disposal of e-waste can lead to environmental and health hazards, as many electronic devices contain hazardous substances such as lead, mercury, and cadmium, which can leach into the soil and water and harm human health and the environment.

The management of e-waste is a complex issue that involves various stakeholders, including governments, manufacturers, recyclers, and consumers. There is a need to develop sustainable and effective e-waste management strategies to minimize the negative impact of e-waste on the environment and human health.

Definition of Circular Economy

Circular economy refers to an economic system that aims to keep products and materials in use for as long as possible, by reducing waste, pollution, and resource depletion. The circular economy is based on three key principles: designing out waste and pollution, keeping products and materials in use, and regenerating natural systems. This means designing products that are durable, easy to repair, and can be disassembled and reused or recycled at the end of their life. It also involves developing new business models that prioritize the use of renewable energy, the sharing of resources, and the use of waste as a resource.

The circular economy offers several benefits, including the reduction of waste, the creation of new jobs and economic opportunities, and the promotion of sustainable resource use. By reducing waste and pollution, the circular economy can also help to mitigate climate change and improve public health. The circular economy is increasingly being adopted by businesses, governments, and individuals worldwide as a means of achieving sustainable development and addressing pressing environmental challenges.

Importance of Circular Economy for e-waste Management

The circular economy is essential for e-waste management for several reasons:

- Reducing e-waste generation: The circular economy aims to keep products and materials in use for as long as possible, which can help to reduce the amount of e-waste generated. By designing products that are durable, easy to repair, and can be disassembled and reused or recycled, the circular economy can help to extend the lifespan of electronic products and reduce their environmental impact.

- Promoting resource efficiency: The circular economy prioritizes the use of renewable energy, the sharing of resources, and the use of waste as a resource. This can help to reduce the depletion of natural resources and promote sustainable resource use, which is crucial for the long-term management of e-waste.
- Creating economic opportunities: The circular economy can create new jobs and economic opportunities in areas such as repair, refurbishment, and remanufacturing. This can help to promote local economic development and reduce the environmental impact of e-waste.
- Mitigating environmental and health hazards: E-waste often contains hazardous substances that can leach into the soil and water and harm human health and the environment. The circular economy promotes sustainable e-waste management practices that can help to mitigate these environmental and health hazards.

The circular economy provides a framework for sustainable e-waste management that focuses on reducing waste generation, promoting resource efficiency, creating economic opportunities, and mitigating environmental and health hazards. By adopting circular economy principles, businesses, governments, and individuals can help to address the growing problem of e-waste and promote a more sustainable future.

E-Waste Generation and Management

Overview of e-waste Generation

E-waste, or electronic waste, refers to the discarded electronic devices and components that are no longer in use or have reached the end of their lifespan. E-waste is a rapidly growing waste stream, driven by the increasing demand for electronic devices, the shortening lifespan of these devices, and the rapid pace of technological advancement.

E-waste can come from various sources, including households, businesses, governments, and institutions. The most common electronic products that contribute to e-waste generation include mobile phones, computers, televisions, and other electronic devices. Other sources of e-waste include electronic accessories, batteries, and electronic components.

The improper management of e-waste poses significant environmental and health hazards, as electronic devices often contain hazardous substances such as lead, mercury, and cadmium that can leach into the soil and water and harm human health and the environment. Therefore, the proper management of e-waste is crucial to minimize its negative impact on the environment and human health and promote sustainable resource use.

Types and Sources of e-waste

There are several types of e-waste, which can be broadly classified into two categories:

- Large Household Appliances: This category includes electronic devices that are used for domestic purposes, such as refrigerators, air conditioners, washing machines, and dishwashers. These devices often contain hazardous substances such as refrigerants and insulation foam, which can harm the environment if not disposed of properly.
- Information Technology (IT) and Telecommunications Equipment: This category includes electronic devices used for communication and information processing, such as computers, laptops, printers, mobile phones, and televisions. These devices often contain hazardous substances such as lead, mercury, and cadmium, which can pose environmental and health hazards if not disposed of properly.

Other types of e-waste include electronic components, batteries, and electronic accessories such as keyboards, mouse, and cables. These devices also contain hazardous substances and should be managed properly to prevent environmental contamination.

It is essential to dispose of e-waste safely and responsibly to prevent the release of hazardous substances into the environment. Recycling, refurbishment, and remanufacturing are some of the ways to manage e-waste and extract valuable resources from discarded electronic devices.

E-waste can come from various sources, including :

- Households: As more people use electronic devices in their daily lives, households are becoming an increasingly significant source of e-waste. Discarded electronic devices such as mobile phones, laptops, and televisions contribute significantly to e-waste generation.

- Businesses and Institutions: Companies and organizations regularly upgrade their electronic devices and equipment, leading to the disposal of older models. This process generates a significant amount of e-waste. Additionally, electronic devices used in offices, hospitals, and schools, such as printers, scanners, and projectors, contribute to e-waste generation.
- Governments: Governments are a significant source of e-waste, primarily due to the replacement of old and outdated electronic devices used in public services such as hospitals, schools, and administrative offices.
- Manufacturing: The production of electronic devices generates waste, including faulty or damaged components, manufacturing scrap, and excess inventory. These wastes contribute to e-waste generation and should be managed appropriately.
- Online Shopping: The rise of e-commerce has led to an increase in the sale of electronic devices online. This has contributed to the generation of e-waste due to the rapid replacement of older devices by consumers.

It is essential to manage e-waste properly to prevent environmental and health hazards. Governments, businesses, and individuals can adopt sustainable practices such as reducing waste generation, reusing and recycling electronic devices, and adopting circular economy principles to minimize the environmental impact of e-waste.

Current e-waste Management Practices

Current e-waste management practices involve a combination of approaches, including disposal, recycling, and reuse. However, the effectiveness of these practices varies significantly across regions and countries due to differences in regulatory frameworks, infrastructure, and financial resources.

- Disposal: Disposal involves the landfilling or incineration of e-waste. However, this practice is not environmentally friendly, as it can lead to the release of hazardous substances into the soil, air, and water. Moreover, landfills can be a source of greenhouse gas emissions.

- Recycling: Recycling involves the recovery of valuable materials from e-waste. Recycling can help to reduce waste, save resources, and mitigate environmental pollution. The recycling process involves the collection, sorting, and processing of e-waste to extract valuable metals such as copper, gold, and silver.
- Reuse: Reuse involves extending the lifespan of electronic devices by refurbishing or repairing them. This practice can help to reduce e-waste generation and conserve resources. However, it requires skilled labor and adequate infrastructure to be effective.

Currently, most countries rely on a combination of disposal and recycling to manage e-waste. However, the recycling and reuse of e-waste remain low in many regions due to inadequate infrastructure, a lack of awareness, and insufficient regulatory frameworks. Inadequate financing and technology also limit the adoption of more sustainable e-waste management practices.

To improve e-waste management, there is a need for strong regulatory frameworks that promote sustainable practices, provide incentives for industry players, and ensure proper disposal of hazardous substances. Additionally, increased public awareness, investment in recycling infrastructure, and the promotion of circular economy principles can help to reduce the environmental and health impacts of e-waste.

Challenges Associated with e-waste Management

There are several challenges associated with e-waste management, including:

- Lack of awareness and education: Many people are not aware of the environmental and health risks associated with improper e-waste disposal. Lack of awareness can lead to incorrect disposal practices, including dumping e-waste in landfills or incinerators, which can release hazardous substances into the environment.
- Inadequate regulatory frameworks: In many regions, regulatory frameworks for e-waste management are weak or nonexistent. This can lead to ineffective waste management practices and uncontrolled dumping of e-waste.
- Insufficient infrastructure: Recycling facilities and other e-waste management infrastructure are often insufficient or nonexistent in

many regions. This can make it difficult to collect, sort, and process e-waste safely and effectively.

- Limited financing: E-waste management is often expensive, and financing is a significant challenge, especially for developing countries. This can limit the adoption of sustainable e-waste management practices.
- Complex composition of electronic devices: Electronic devices contain a complex mix of materials that are difficult to separate, making it challenging to recover valuable materials from e-waste.
- Informal sector involvement: The informal sector, which includes waste pickers and scrap dealers, plays a significant role in e-waste management in many regions. However, the informal sector can lead to unsafe and uncontrolled waste handling practices, putting workers' health at risk.
- Global trade: E-waste is often traded across borders, leading to the transfer of hazardous substances to countries with weak e-waste management systems. This can lead to environmental and health risks in receiving countries.

Addressing these challenges will require a coordinated effort from governments, industry, civil society, and consumers to promote sustainable e-waste management practices. This includes developing and implementing effective regulatory frameworks, improving infrastructure, increasing public awareness, and promoting the adoption of circular economy principles.

Environmental and Health impacts of e-waste

E-waste has significant environmental and health impacts. When electronic devices are disposed of improperly, they release hazardous substances into the environment, leading to pollution of the soil, water, and air. These substances can include heavy metals, such as lead, cadmium, and mercury, as well as flame retardants and other toxic chemicals. These substances can persist in the environment for a long time and can bioaccumulate in the food chain, leading to adverse health effects in humans and animals.

Some of the environmental and health impacts of e-waste include:

- Soil pollution: Heavy metals and other hazardous substances released from e-waste can contaminate the soil, making it unsuitable for agriculture and other land uses.

- Water pollution: Improper disposal of e-waste can lead to the release of hazardous substances into water bodies, leading to pollution and harm to aquatic life.
- Air pollution: Burning of e-waste or incineration of electronic devices can release toxic substances into the air, leading to respiratory and other health problems.
- Health impacts: Exposure to hazardous substances from e-waste can lead to a range of health problems, including neurological damage, reproductive problems, cancer, and other illnesses.
- Occupational hazards: Workers involved in the informal e-waste sector are particularly vulnerable to health risks, including exposure to hazardous substances and physical injuries from handling electronic devices.
- Climate change: E-waste disposal contributes to greenhouse gas emissions, leading to climate change and its associated impacts.

To address the environmental and health impacts of e-waste, it is essential to promote sustainable e-waste management practices, including the reduction of e-waste generation, safe disposal, and the recovery of valuable materials through recycling and reuse. Adopting circular economy principles can also help to reduce the environmental and health impacts of e-waste by promoting resource efficiency, reducing waste generation, and mitigating climate change.

Circular Economy and its relevance to e-waste Management
What is circular economy

Circular economy is an economic model that aims to keep resources in use for as long as possible, by minimizing waste and maximizing the use of renewable resources. In a circular economy, products and materials are designed to be reused, repaired, or recycled, rather than disposed of after use. This involves closing the loop of material flows, by recovering and regenerating materials and products at the end of their lifecycle. The goal of a circular economy is to create a sustainable and resilient system, where economic growth is decoupled from resource consumption and environmental degradation.

Principles and Strategies of Circular Economy

The principles and strategies of circular economy include:

- Design for circularity: Products and materials are designed with the intention of keeping them in use for as long as possible. This involves designing products that are easy to repair, reuse, and recycle, and avoiding the use of hazardous or non-recyclable materials.
- Reduce, reuse, and recycle: The circular economy aims to minimize waste and maximize the use of renewable resources. This involves reducing the amount of materials used in products, reusing products and materials as much as possible, and recycling materials at the end of their lifecycle.
- Regenerate natural systems: The circular economy aims to support the regeneration of natural systems, such as forests and oceans, by using renewable resources and minimizing the use of non-renewable resources.
- Foster collaboration and innovation: The circular economy requires collaboration between stakeholders, including businesses, governments, and civil society. Collaboration can help to identify new opportunities for circular solutions and foster innovation.
- Consider the whole value chain: The circular economy considers the entire value chain, from raw material extraction to end-of-life disposal. This involves working with suppliers and customers to promote circular solutions and reduce waste throughout the value chain.
- Create new business models: The circular economy requires new business models that promote resource efficiency, such as product-as-a-service, where customers pay for access to a product rather than owning it, or closed-loop supply chains, where products are recovered and reused at the end of their lifecycle.

By adopting these principles and strategies, the circular economy aims to create a more sustainable and resilient system, where economic growth is decoupled from resource consumption and environmental degradation.

Role of Circular Economy in e-waste Management

The role of circular economy in e-waste management is significant. E-waste is a growing problem worldwide, and the traditional linear approach to e-waste management, which involves disposal and incineration, is not sustainable. The circular economy offers a solution to this problem by promoting resource efficiency, reducing waste generation, and mitigating climate change. The circular economy principles can be applied to e-waste management in the following ways:

- Design for circularity: The circular design principles can be applied to electronic product design, with the aim of designing products that are easy to repair, upgrade, and disassemble. This can increase the lifespan of electronic products and reduce the amount of e-waste generated.
- Reuse and refurbishment: Electronic devices that are still functional can be reused or refurbished, rather than being disposed of. This can extend the lifespan of electronic devices and reduce the demand for new products, leading to a reduction in e-waste generation.
- Recycling and material recovery: Recycling and material recovery can help to recover valuable materials from e-waste, such as metals and plastics, which can be reused in the production of new products. This can reduce the demand for virgin materials, leading to a reduction in resource consumption and greenhouse gas emissions.
- Extended producer responsibility: Extended producer responsibility (EPR) schemes can be implemented, where manufacturers are responsible for the end-of-life management of their products. This can encourage manufacturers to design products with circularity in mind, and to take responsibility for the environmental impact of their products throughout their lifecycle.

By adopting circular economy principles, e-waste can be transformed from a waste stream into a resource stream. The circular economy can help to reduce the environmental and health impacts of e-waste, promote resource efficiency, and support sustainable economic growth.

Examples of Successful Circular Economy initiatives in the Electronics Industry

There are several successful circular economy initiatives in the electronics industry that demonstrate the potential of circular solutions to e-waste management. Here are some examples:

- Fairphone: Fairphone is a social enterprise that produces smartphones with a focus on ethical sourcing, repairability, and longevity. The company uses modular design, which allows users to easily repair and upgrade their devices, reducing the need for new devices and lowering e-waste generation. The company also works with suppliers to source materials from conflict-free and fair sources, promoting social and environmental responsibility in the electronics industry.
- Dell: Dell has implemented a closed-loop supply chain for its products, which involves recovering and reusing materials from end-of-life products in the production of new products. The company uses recycled plastics and metals in its products, and has committed to sourcing 100% of its packaging from sustainable materials by 2030. Dell's closed-loop supply chain has helped to reduce waste generation and resource consumption in the electronics industry.
- Apple: Apple has implemented a recycling program for its products, which allows users to return their old devices for recycling. The company uses a robot, named Daisy, to disassemble and recover materials from old devices, which are then used in the production of new products. Apple has also made commitments to use recycled materials in its products, and has set a goal of achieving a closed-loop supply chain for its products.
- The Ellen MacArthur Foundation: The Ellen MacArthur Foundation is a non-profit organization that works to promote the circular economy. The Foundation has launched several initiatives in the electronics industry, including the Circular Electronics Initiative, which aims to accelerate the transition to a circular economy in the electronics industry. The initiative brings together stakeholders from across the value chain to develop circular solutions to e-waste management.

- HP: HP has implemented a closed-loop recycling program for its ink cartridges, which allows users to return their used cartridges for recycling. The company uses recycled plastic from these cartridges to produce new cartridges, reducing waste and resource consumption.
- Philips: Philips has developed a range of circular lighting products, including LED bulbs and luminaires, that are designed for easy disassembly and repair. The company also offers a take-back program for end-of-life products, which allows customers to return their old products for recycling or refurbishment.
- Toshiba: Toshiba has implemented a circular economy program called "Close the Loop," which aims to promote sustainable practices throughout the product lifecycle. The program includes initiatives such as material reuse and recycling, product take-back programs, and design for disassembly and repair.
- IKEA: While not strictly in the electronics industry, IKEA's commitment to the circular economy is worth mentioning. The company has set a goal of becoming a circular business by 2030, and has launched several circular initiatives, including a take-back program for furniture and a circular textile collection that uses recycled materials.

These are just a few examples of successful circular economy initiatives in the electronics industry. These initiatives demonstrate the potential of circular solutions to e-waste management, and the benefits of designing products with circularity in mind.

Opportunities for Electronic Product Design in the Circular Economy

Product Design and its impact on e-waste

Product design plays a crucial role in the generation of electronic waste (e-waste). The design of electronic products determines their lifespan, repairability, upgradability, and recyclability, which in turn determines how much e-waste is generated and how it can be managed.

Poor product design can lead to premature obsolescence, making it difficult or impossible to repair or upgrade products, resulting in more e-waste generation. In addition, products that are difficult to disassemble or recycle can end up in landfills, where they pose a risk to the environment and human health.

On the other hand, product design that is focused on circular economy principles can help reduce e-waste generation and promote sustainable resource use. Products designed for repair, upgradability, and disassembly can extend their lifespan, reducing the need for new products and the associated resource consumption and waste generation.

Furthermore, products designed for recyclability can enable the recovery of valuable materials, reducing the need for new resource extraction and waste disposal. By incorporating circular economy principles into product design, companies can create more sustainable and responsible products that have a positive impact on the environment and society.

Therefore, it is crucial for companies to consider the impact of their product design on e-waste generation and management, and to prioritize circular economy principles in their design processes. This can involve designing products for durability, ease of repair, upgradability, and disassembly, as well as considering the use of sustainable and recyclable materials.

Strategies for designing Products for circularity

Designing products for circularity involves incorporating principles of the circular economy into the design process, with the aim of reducing waste, extending product lifetimes, and promoting sustainable resource use. Here are some strategies that can be used to design products for circularity:

- Design for durability: Products that are designed to be durable and long-lasting are less likely to be discarded and contribute to e-waste. This involves choosing high-quality materials, designing products for robustness and longevity, and testing products for durability before they are released.
- Design for repair: Products that are designed for easy repair can extend their lifespan and reduce the need for new products. This involves designing products with modular components that can be replaced, making repair manuals available to customers, and using standard components that are easy to source.

- Design for upgradability: Products that can be upgraded with new components or features can extend their lifespan and reduce the need for new products. This involves designing products with replaceable components, making it easy for customers to upgrade their products, and using interfaces and connectors that are compatible with future technologies.
- Design for disassembly: Products that are designed for easy disassembly can be more easily recycled at the end of their life, reducing the amount of waste generated. This involves designing products with removable parts, minimizing the use of adhesives and glues, and using materials that can be easily separated and sorted.
- Design for recyclability: Products that are designed for recyclability can ensure that valuable materials can be recovered and reused, reducing the need for new resource extraction. This involves using recyclable materials, designing products with a limited number of materials and avoiding complex material combinations, and avoiding hazardous substances that can hinder recycling.

By incorporating these strategies into product design, companies can create products that are more sustainable, circular, and contribute to reducing e-waste.

Remanufacturing and Refurbishment of Electronic Products
Remanufacturing and Refurbishment

Remanufacturing is the process of restoring used products to like-new condition, using a combination of reuse, repair, and replacement of parts. The goal of remanufacturing is to extend the lifespan of products, reduce waste, and promote sustainable resource use. In remanufacturing, the product is disassembled, cleaned, and rebuilt with new or refurbished components. The end result is a product that is as good as new, with the same functionality and performance.

Refurbishment, on the other hand, is the process of restoring used products to a good working condition, but not necessarily to a like-new condition. Refurbishment typically involves cleaning, repairing, and testing products to ensure that they meet the manufacturer's specifications. Refurbished products may have some cosmetic blemishes or signs of wear and tear, but they are fully functional and meet the same standards as new products. Refurbishment is often used in the electronics industry to extend the lifespan of products and reduce waste.

Benefits of Remanufacturing and Refurbishment for e-waste Management

Remanufacturing and Refurbishment are important strategies for managing e-waste and promoting sustainable resource use. By extending the lifespan of products and conserving resources, these strategies can help to reduce the environmental impact of e-waste and support a more circular economy. Remanufacturing and refurbishment offer several benefits for e-waste management:

- Extended product lifespan: By restoring used products to like-new or good working condition, remanufacturing and refurbishment can significantly extend the lifespan of products. This reduces the need for new products to be manufactured, which reduces the amount of waste generated.

- Resource conservation: Remanufacturing and refurbishment promote sustainable resource use by reducing the need for new raw materials. Instead, existing products and components are reused and recycled, conserving resources and reducing the environmental impact of resource extraction.

- Reduced waste: By extending the lifespan of products, remanufacturing and refurbishment reduce the amount of waste generated. This helps to reduce the environmental impact of e-waste and conserve valuable resources.

- Cost savings: Remanufacturing and refurbishment can be more cost-effective than manufacturing new products. This is because the cost of producing new products is often higher than the cost of refurbishing or remanufacturing existing products.

- Job creation: Remanufacturing and refurbishment can create jobs in the repair and maintenance sectors. This can help to support local economies and provide opportunities for skilled workers.

Challenges Associated with Remanufacturing and Refurbishment

Remanufacturing and refurbishment are important strategies for managing e-waste, but they also come with some challenges. Some of the key challenges include:

- Quality control: Remanufacturing and refurbishment require careful testing and quality control to ensure that the products meet the same standards as new products. This can be challenging, especially for complex electronic devices that require specialized expertise and equipment.
- Parts availability: Remanufacturing and refurbishment require a steady supply of high-quality parts and components. In some cases, it can be difficult to source these parts, especially if the original manufacturer no longer produces them.
- Technical expertise: Remanufacturing and refurbishment require skilled technicians with expertise in repairing and maintaining complex electronic devices. This expertise can be difficult to find, especially in areas where the repair and maintenance industry is not well-developed.
- Customer perception: Some customers may be hesitant to purchase remanufactured or refurbished products, as they may perceive them as lower quality or less reliable than new products. This can be a challenge for companies that are trying to promote these products as a sustainable and cost-effective alternative to new products.
- Regulatory issues: Remanufacturing and refurbishment may be subject to different regulations than new products. Companies may need to navigate complex regulatory frameworks and obtain permits and certifications to ensure that their products meet legal requirements.

These challenges can make it difficult to scale up remanufacturing and refurbishment programs, and may limit their effectiveness as a strategy for managing e-waste. However, by addressing these challenges and developing innovative solutions, companies and governments can promote the growth of a more sustainable and circular economy.

Examples of Successful Remanufacturing and Refurbishment initiatives in the Electronics Industry

There are several successful remanufacturing and refurbishment initiatives in the electronics industry. Here are a few examples:

- Dell: Dell has implemented a successful refurbishment program for its computer products. The program includes a rigorous testing process, in which all components are thoroughly inspected, cleaned, and tested before being reassembled. The refurbished products are sold at a discounted price, and come with the same warranty as new products. The program has been successful in reducing e-waste and conserving resources, while also providing cost savings for customers.
- Xerox: Xerox has implemented a successful remanufacturing program for its toner cartridges. The program involves disassembling used cartridges, cleaning and testing each component, and replacing any worn or damaged parts. The remanufactured cartridges are then sold at a discounted price, and come with a satisfaction guarantee. The program has been successful in reducing the environmental impact of toner cartridge waste, while also providing cost savings for customers.
- Caterpillar: Caterpillar has implemented a successful remanufacturing program for its heavy equipment products. The program includes a rigorous testing process, in which all components are disassembled, inspected, cleaned, and tested before being reassembled. The remanufactured products are sold at a discounted price, and come with the same warranty as new products. The program has been successful in reducing the environmental impact of heavy equipment waste, while also providing cost savings for customers.
- Apple: Apple has implemented a successful refurbishment program for its iPhone products. The program involves disassembling used iPhones, cleaning and testing each component, and replacing any worn or damaged parts. The refurbished iPhones are then sold at a discounted price, and come with a one-year warranty. The program has been successful in reducing e-waste and conserving resources, while also providing cost savings for customers.

Overall, these initiatives demonstrate the potential for remanufacturing and refurbishment to promote sustainable resource use and reduce the environmental impact of e-waste. By developing innovative solutions and implementing best practices, companies can help to support a more circular economy and promote a more sustainable future.

Economic and Policy drivers for Circular Economy in e-waste Management

To support the transition to a circular economy in e-waste management, governments can implement policies such as extended producer responsibility (EPR) and eco-design regulations. EPR requires manufacturers to take responsibility for the environmental impact of their products throughout their entire lifecycle, from design to disposal. Eco-design regulations require products to be designed with sustainability in mind, such as by using recyclable materials and making products easy to disassemble for repair and recycling.

There are several economic and policy drivers for promoting a circular economy in e-waste management. These include:

- Resource conservation: By adopting circular economy principles, companies can reduce their reliance on virgin resources and instead utilize existing materials and components. This can help to conserve natural resources and reduce the environmental impact of resource extraction and processing.
- Cost savings: Circular economy initiatives can also result in cost savings for companies. By reusing and remanufacturing materials and products, companies can reduce their waste disposal costs and avoid the expense of purchasing new materials.
- Market demand: There is increasing consumer demand for sustainable and environmentally-friendly products. Companies that adopt circular economy principles can meet this demand and gain a competitive advantage in the market.
- Regulatory pressure: Governments around the world are implementing regulations to promote sustainable resource use and reduce waste. Circular economy initiatives can help companies to comply with these regulations and avoid fines and penalties.
- Job creation: The circular economy can also create new job opportunities in industries such as remanufacturing, refurbishment, and recycling.

Promoting a circular economy in e-waste management can bring economic, environmental, and social benefits. By implementing innovative solutions and collaborating across industries and sectors, we can create a more sustainable future for generations to come.

Case Studies of successful Policies and regulations promoting Circular Economy in e-waste Management

There are several examples of successful policies and regulations promoting circular economy in e-waste management. India as well as European union, Japan, France and many more has implemented several policies and regulations to promote circular economy in e-waste management. These policies and regulations demonstrate commitment to promoting a circular economy in e-waste management. By implementing regulations that require producers to take responsibility for their products and incentivizing sustainable design, we can reduce waste and promote sustainable resource use. Here are some case studies:

- E-waste Management Rules, 2016: The E-waste Management Rules, 2016, were implemented to promote the sustainable management of e-waste in India. The rules require producers to take responsibility for the entire lifecycle of their products, from design to disposal. This includes financing the collection and treatment of e-waste, as well as ensuring that products are designed for repair, reuse, and recycling. The rules have led to an increase in e-waste recycling rates in India.

- Extended Producer Responsibility (EPR) Scheme: The EPR scheme was implemented under the E-waste Management Rules, 2016, to hold producers responsible for the collection and disposal of their products. The scheme requires producers to submit a plan for managing their e-waste, including financing the collection and treatment of e-waste. The scheme has led to an increase in e-waste recycling rates in India and has created new job opportunities in the e-waste recycling industry.

- Swachh Bharat Mission: The Swachh Bharat Mission was launched in 2014 to promote cleanliness and sanitation in India. As part of the mission, the government has implemented several initiatives to promote the sustainable management of e-waste, including awareness campaigns and the establishment of e-waste

217

collection centers. The mission has led to an increase in public awareness about the importance of e-waste management and has helped to reduce the amount of e-waste that ends up in landfills.

- Green E-certification: The Green E-certification program was launched by the Ministry of Electronics and Information Technology in 2017 to promote the sustainable management of e-waste in India. The program provides certification to electronic products that meet certain environmental standards, including energy efficiency and recyclability. The program has incentivized manufacturers to design products that are more sustainable and has helped to reduce the environmental impact of e-waste in India.

- European Union's Waste Electrical and Electronic Equipment (WEEE) Directive: The WEEE Directive was implemented in 2003 to reduce the environmental impact of e-waste and promote the circular economy. The directive requires manufacturers to take responsibility for the entire lifecycle of their products, from design to disposal. This includes financing the collection and treatment of e-waste, as well as ensuring that products are designed for repair, reuse, and recycling. Since its implementation, the directive has led to an increase in e-waste recycling rates in Europe.

- Japan's Act on Promotion of Recycling of Small Waste Electrical and Electronic Equipment: This act, implemented in 2013, requires manufacturers to take responsibility for the collection and recycling of small e-waste items, such as smartphones and digital cameras. Manufacturers must also ensure that their products are designed for easy disassembly and recycling. The act has resulted in a significant increase in small e-waste recycling rates in Japan.

- California's Electronic Waste Recycling Act: The act, implemented in 2003, requires manufacturers of certain electronic products sold in California to finance the collection and recycling of their products. The act has led to an increase in e-waste recycling rates in California and has helped to create new jobs in the e-waste recycling industry.

- France's Anti-Waste Law: This law, implemented in 2020, requires manufacturers to implement measures to extend the lifespan of their products and reduce waste. This includes measures such as making spare parts available for repair and ensuring that products are designed for repair and reuse. The law also requires manufacturers to finance the collection and recycling of their products. The law aims to reduce waste and promote a circular economy in France.

These policies and regulations demonstrate the importance of government intervention in promoting a circular economy in e-waste management. By implementing regulations that require manufacturers to take responsibility for their products throughout their entire lifecycle, we can reduce waste and promote sustainable resource use.

Economic benefits of Circular Economy for e-waste Management

Circular economy practices can provide economic benefits for businesses and communities by creating new job opportunities, reducing production costs, and increasing resource security. By adopting circular economy practices in e-waste management, we can create a more sustainable and prosperous future for all.

Circular economy has several economic benefits for e-waste management. Here are some of them:

- Job creation: Circular economy practices such as remanufacturing and refurbishment can create new job opportunities in the e-waste management industry. This is because these practices require skilled labor to repair and refurbish electronic products, which can stimulate local economic development.
- Cost savings: By designing products for circularity and implementing practices such as remanufacturing and refurbishment, businesses can reduce their production costs by using fewer virgin materials and decreasing waste disposal fees.
- New revenue streams: Circular economy practices such as remanufacturing and refurbishment can create new revenue streams for businesses. For example, remanufactured products can be sold at a lower price point than new products, which can appeal to cost-conscious consumers.

- Resource conservation: Circular economy practices can help conserve resources such as energy, water, and materials, which can reduce production costs and increase resource security. For example, remanufacturing a product can save up to 80% of the energy and materials required to produce a new product.
- Increased competitiveness: Implementing circular economy practices can improve a business's competitiveness by increasing their brand value and reputation. Consumers are increasingly interested in sustainable products and are willing to pay more for products that are designed for circularity.

Conclusion and Future Directions

1. E-waste is a growing problem that poses significant environmental and health risks if not managed properly.
2. Circular economy is an economic model that aims to eliminate waste and promote the sustainable use of resources.
3. Circular economy can play a crucial role in e-waste management by promoting the reuse, refurbishment, and recycling of electronic products.
4. Successful circular economy initiatives in the electronics industry include product design for circularity, remanufacturing, and refurbishment.
5. Circular economy practices can provide economic benefits for businesses and communities by creating new job opportunities, reducing production costs, and increasing resource security.

However, there are challenges associated with e-waste management, circular economy practices, and the implementation of policies and regulations that promote circular economy.

Some Potential Recommendations for Future Research in e-waste:

1. Develop more accurate and comprehensive data collection methods to better understand e-waste generation, disposal, and management practices on a global scale.
2. Explore the potential of emerging technologies such as blockchain, artificial intelligence, and the Internet of Things to improve e-waste management practices and promote circular economy.

3. Investigate the environmental and health impacts of e-waste recycling practices, including the potential for exposure to hazardous materials and air pollution.
4. Study the economic and social benefits of circular economy practices in e-waste management, including job creation, resource security, and community development.
5. Examine the role of consumer behavior in e-waste generation and explore strategies for promoting sustainable consumption patterns.
6. Investigate the potential of circular economy practices in reducing the environmental impact of other waste streams beyond e-waste, such as food waste, plastics, and construction waste.
7. Study the effectiveness of policies and regulations promoting circular economy in e-waste management and identify best practices for policy implementation and enforcement.

By exploring these research areas, we can deepen our understanding of e-waste management and identify new strategies for promoting a more sustainable and circular economy.

Reference :

1. Baldé, C. P., Forti, V., Gray, V., Kuehr, R., & Stegmann, P. (2017). The global e-waste monitor 2017: Quantities, flows, and resources. United Nations University, International Telecommunication Union & International Solid Waste Association.
2. Ellen MacArthur Foundation. (2019). Circular economy. https://www.ellenmacarthurfoundation.org/circular-economy/concept
3. Ghisellini, P., Cialani, C., & Ulgiati, S. (2016). A review on circular economy: The expected transition to a balanced interplay of environmental and economic systems. Journal of Cleaner Production, 114, 11-32.
4. Gupta, S., & Dey, S. (2019). Circular economy practices in the electronics industry: A review. Resources, Conservation and Recycling, 148, 54-71.

5. Khetriwal, D. S., Nema, A. K., & Jha, M. K. (2018). E-waste management: A review of recent patents on emerging solutions. Recent Patents on Engineering, 12(1), 20-34.

6. Lepawsky, J. (2018). Reassembling rubbish: Worlding electronic waste. MIT Press.

7. Robinson, B. H. (2009). E-waste: An assessment of global production and environmental impacts. Science of The Total Environment, 408(2), 183-191.

8. Geissdoerfer, M., Savaget, P., Bocken, N. M., & Hultink, E. J. (2017). The Circular Economy–A new sustainability paradigm? Journal of Cleaner Production, 143, 757-768.

9. Wang, J., Chen, J., & Chen, S. (2021). Circular economy for e-waste management: A review. Resources, Conservation and Recycling, 167, 105431.

10. Akenji, L., & Hotta, Y. (2010). E-waste management in Japan and China: an overview. Journal of material cycles and waste management, 12(1), 1-12.

11. European Commission. (2020). Closing the loop: Commission adopts new circular economy action plan – main measures. Retrieved from https://ec.europa.eu/commission/presscorner/detail/en/IP_20_42 0

12. Chancerel, P., Meskers, C. E. M., Hagelüken, C., & Rotter, V. S. (2015). Circular economy: improving the management of waste mobile phones. Waste Management, 45, 254-264.

13. Geng, Y., Fu, J., Sarkis, J., Xue, B., & Zeng, X. (2019). Towards a national circular economy indicator system in China: An evaluation and critical analysis. Journal of Cleaner Production, 225, 627-638.

14. Wang, X., & Chen, H. (2019). Environmental impacts of e-waste recycling in China: A case study of Guiyu. Journal of Cleaner Production, 222, 56-65.

15. Stahel, W. R. (2016). The circular economy. Nature News, 531(7595), 435-438.

16. Nnorom, I. C., & Osibanjo, O. (2008). Overview of electronic waste (e-waste) management practices and legislations, and their

poor applications in the developing countries. Resources, Conservation and Recycling, 52(6), 843-858.

[1]Associate Professor, Department of Information Technology, Poddar Management & Technical Campus, Jaipur Rajasthan.
[2]Professor, Poddar International College, Jaipur Rajasthan.
[3]Assistant Professor, Department of Information Technology, Poddar Management & Technical Campus, Jaipur Rajasthan.
[4]Assistant Professor, University Five Year Law College, University of Rajasthan, Jaipur Rajasthan.
[5]Assistant Professor, Department of Information Technology, Poddar International College, Jaipur Rajasthan.

19. Financial Inclusion and Role of Fintech Companies in India

[1]Govind Singh
[2]Dr. Lokesh Verma
[3]Pushpender Singh

Abstract

Financial inclusion is about providing affordable banking services to the majority of the low-income disadvantaged. The main focus of financial inclusion in India is to promote sustainable development and create jobs in rural areas for rural people. Of her 19.9 million households in India, only her 6.82 billion households have access to banking services. As for rural areas, only 4.16 million of her 13.83 million households in India have access to basic banking services. In urban areas, only her 49.52% of urban households have access to banking services. Over 41% of India's adult population does not have a bank account. There are many factors affecting access to financial services by vulnerable segments of Indian society. The Reserve Bank of India and the government have taken several steps to bring economically excluded people into formal banking services. A 100% financial inclusion campaign is underway nationwide. The State Level Banking Commission (SLBC) advised him to identify one or more districts for 100% financial inclusion. To date, SLBC has certified 100% financial inclusion in 431 districts. As of March 31, 2009, 204 districts in 18 states and 5 federal territories have reported achievement. In view of the enormous tasks involved, the Financial Inclusion Commission has launched, in mission mode, the National Rural Financial Inclusion Plan (NRFIP) was established. We excluded rural households by 2012 and the rest by 2015.

1. Keywords

Financial Inclusion, Inclusive Growth, Bank, RBI, Finance

2. Introduction

Financial inclusion is described as a way of providing banking and financial solutions and services to all individuals in society without any form of discrimination. It primarily aims to include everyone in society by providing basic financial services, regardless of personal income and savings. Financial inclusion is primarily focused on providing economically disadvantaged members of society with unfairly trusted financial solutions. It is intended to provide financial solutions without signs of inequality. We are also committed to transparency while providing financial support without any hidden transactions or costs.

Financial inclusion wants everyone in society to be involved and wisely involved in financial management. There are many poor families in India who do not have access to domestic financial services. They are not familiar with banks and their functions. Even if they know banks, many poor people do not have access to banking services.

You may not meet the minimum eligibility requirements set by your bank, so you will not be able to use their services. Banks have requirements such as minimum income, minimum credit rating, age criteria and minimum years of service. Banks will only allow deposits or loans to applicants if they meet these criteria. Many of the poor may be unemployed with no previous employment record due to lack of education, lack of resources, lack of money, etc.

These economically disadvantaged members of society may not have the proper documentation to present to banks to verify their identity and income. Every bank has certain mandatory documents that must be provided during the loan application process or during the bank account creation process. Many of these people do not realize the importance of these documents. Nor can you apply for government-approved documents.

Financial inclusion aims to remove these barriers and provide low-cost financial services to less affluent segments of society. This allows them to become financially self-sufficient without resorting to charities or other means to raise funds that are inherently unsustainable. Financial inclusion also aims to spread awareness of financial services and financial management among members of society. Additionally, she wants to develop a formal and systematic credit route for the poor. For several years, only the middle and upper classes of society acquired formal forms of credit. Poor people have been forced to rely on unorganized and informal forms of credit. Many of them were uneducated and lacked basic knowledge of finance, so they were duped by the greedy and wealthy members of society. Several poor people have been exploited for years in the context of financial assistance.

3. Financial Inclusion Schemes in India

The Indian government has introduced some exclusive programs aimed at financial inclusion. These schemes are designed to provide social security to less wealthy segments of society. After extensive planning and research by several financial experts and policy makers, the government has launched a program with financial inclusion in mind. These programs have been in place for many years. Take a look at the list of financial inclusion programs in the country. :

❖ Pradhan Mantri Jan Dhan Yojana (PMJDY)
❖ Atal Pension Yojana (APY)
❖ Pradhan Mantri Vaya Vandana Yojana (PMVVY)
❖ Stand Up India Scheme
❖ Pradhan Mantri Mudra Yojana (PMMY)
❖ Pradhan Mantri Suraksha Bima Yojana (PMSBY)
❖ Sukanya Samriddhi Yojana
❖ Jeevan Suraksha Bandhan Yojana
❖ Credit Enhancement Guarantee Scheme (CEGS) for Scheduled Castes (SCs)
❖ Venture Capital Fund for Scheduled Castes under the Social Sector Initiatives
❖ Varishtha Pension Bima Yojana (VPBY)

4. Objectives of Financial Inclusion

❖ Financial inclusion aims to ensure that people have access to affordable financial services and products such as deposits, money transfer services, insurance and payment services.
❖ It aims to create adequate financial institutions that meet the needs of the poor. These institutions must have clear regulations and maintain high standards in the financial industry.
❖ Financial inclusion aims to build and maintain financial sustainability.
❖ Financial Inclusion also intends to have a large number of institutions offering affordable financial assistance so that there is sufficient competition and that customers have many options to

choose from. There are traditional banking options on the market. However, the number of institutions offering cheap financial products and services is very small.

❖ Financial inclusion aims to raise awareness of the benefits of financial services among economically disadvantaged members of society.

❖ The financial inclusion process works to create financial products suitable for disadvantaged members of society.

❖ Financial inclusion aims to improve the financial literacy and financial awareness of the public. Financial inclusion aims to provide digital financial solutions to economically disadvantaged people in the country.

❖ Mobile He also plans to launch banking and financial services to reach out to the poorest people living in the country's extremely remote areas.

❖ It aims to provide poor people with customized financial solutions, tailored to their individual financial situation, household needs, preferences and income levels.

❖ There are many government agencies and non-governmental organizations dedicated to promoting financial inclusion. These agencies focus on improving access to obtain government-approved documents. Many poor people cannot open bank accounts or apply for loans because they do not have identification. There are so many people living in rural areas and tribal villages who know nothing about documents such as PAN, Aadhaar, driver's license and voting cards. As a result, many of the services provided by government and private organizations are not available. Without these documents, you cannot claim government subsidies.

5. Goals of Financial Inclusion for Women Empowerment

Financial inclusion is the involvement of women, especially in the financial management of the home. Financial inclusion believes that women can manage household finances more effectively than men. Financial inclusion activities therefore target women by helping them engage in financial management. Many households do not allow women to manage money. They are managed by the men of the house and are supposed to do only household chores. Many conservatives in India believe that women cannot handle money. With the help of financial inclusion, governments and non-governmental organizations want to eliminate this mindset. Financial inclusion encourages women to pursue more employment opportunities and become financially independent. It also explains that women do not depend on men for money. No need to wait for the man's permission. Financial inclusion aims to empower women by increasing the economic awareness of women in low-income groups. Women are also taught simple ways to save money for the future. Get access to some affordable savings tools. You will also learn about the different forms of credit available in the market. These forms of credit help them start a new small business or complete an apprenticeship to apply for a new job. This will also increase your monthly income.

Financial inclusion has encouraged many women to buy mobile phones for themselves. In some parts of the country, only men had their own mobile phones, and women depended on him. In recent years, women have started owning mobile phones and using them for work, business, and financial purposes. Many of them have started using digital money and other financial transactions with the help of their mobile phones. This made transactions simpler and faster.

The idea of financial inclusion encourages banks and other financial institutions to help the unbanked segment of society. Many of these agencies also focus on financial support for women by offering special rates, special discounts and other perks. Many banks charge women subsidized or discounted interest rates on their loan products. In savings accounts offered by certain banks and non-bank financial institutions, female depositors receive higher interest on deposits than male depositors.

6. Financial Inclusion with The help of Financial Technology (Fintech)

Financial technology (FinTech) refers to the use of advanced technology in the financial industry or sector. The emergence of financial technology and FinTech has significantly improved financial inclusion around the world. India also has many FinTech companies that are constantly working to simplify the process of providing financial services to potential clients. Fintech companies are also successful in providing financial services and products at minimal cost. This is very helpful for customers as they spend less and their savings can be directed towards other needs. Financial technology companies are enabling rural people to apply for loans and open bank accounts using their mobile phones. In rural India, some people have mobile phones or even have access to the internet on their mobiles. Fintech services can therefore be used to provide reliable financial services.

The latest FinTech options used by individuals include crowdfunding, digital payment systems, peer-to-peer (P2P) and e-wallets. Many people in rural and urban areas use these advanced banking options. However, there are many people who have no experience in banking or other financial institutions and are unfamiliar with it. Accessing mobile-based financial services is difficult for such people.

When many of these poor people make financial transactions with checks or cash, they are usually tricked by financial fraudsters. Also, when you go to a bank branch or NBFC branch to open a savings account or apply for a loan, you may have to pay high fees at the branch. These fees or charges may be processing fees, transaction fees, exchange fees, etc. To save the poor from the high cost of financial services, banks, NBFCs and FinTech companies are working together to find simpler and faster banking processes that eliminate unnecessary fees and charges. Developing such a process will help engage both banked and unbanked members of society.

7. Financial Inclusion Through Digitalpayment Systems

You can also pay for products and services in your local area with the help of electronic payment wallet systems. The Indian government has launched several e-wallet schemes via smartphone apps such as Bharat Interface for Money (BHIM), Aadhaar Pay.

Electronic wallets or e-wallets refer to wallets that can be used using electronic means such as mobile phones. These wallets replace physical wallets. Users can make cashless payments both online and offline. You will need to download an e-wallet app on your mobile phone and use it to make transactions. These e-wallets can be used for mobile top ups, utility payments, grocery stores, e-commerce portals, and more.

Many digital financial tools offer deals and discounts when people use these tools. They are very helpful and new to economically disadvantaged segments of society. Enjoy offers, get cashback options and bonuses. These incentives help users save a lot of money.

8. Impact of Demonetization on Financial Inclusion

Aiming to make India completely cashless within a few years, the government has rolled out low-cost e-wallet options to ensure the country's underprivileged population is not excluded from going cashless. It has regional languages in addition to English. Users can choose the language they know to use the app conveniently. Some of these e-wallets allow users to make payments as well as transfer funds from one bank account to another.

The implementation of a demonstration process in India in 2016 has increased the need for digital financial services. The ban on the use of Rs.500 and Rs.1,000 notes has increased demand for alternative payment methods for goods and services. Therefore, the number of digital wallets in the country has grown exponentially. The Indian government's goal is to make the country cashless, so a number of digital wallets will help the government achieve its goals. In addition, the transaction limit for e-wallets has been increased to Rs. 20,000. . This is good news for both users and e-wallet businesses. Many low-income people have also started using e-wallets because they had no other choice. It is true that many of them initially struggled with the demonization process. When the demonization process suddenly took effect, some middle and lower class people were stuck. However, the launch of multiple digital banking and financial services has been a major boon for all economic classes of society.

A few low-income, unemployed people (including illiterate people) living in both rural and urban areas can learn how to open a bank account, apply for a loan, use technology for banking services, access I started learning about Access financial services without waiting in long lines and transact without carrying cash.

9. Financial Inclusion in India through Digitalization of Monetary Transactions

The Government of India is using Unified Payment Interface (UPI), Unstructured Supplementary Service Data (USSD) banking methods, Immediate Payment Service (IMPS) and National Electronic Funds Transfer (NEFT) to make hundreds of payments now and in the coming years. It plans to execute 10,000 digital financial transactions.), Aadhaar Pay, Debit Card, BHIM, Credit Card.

Additionally, the government would like to require fertilizer warehouses, block offices, petrol pumps, road transport authorities, hospitals, colleges and universities, etc. to accept payments for services and products via digital payment systems. is especially meaningful when customers have to pay large sums to these institutions and offices. The government intends to achieve this by issuing mandates to the above agencies. Separately, the government would like to mandate that government receipts are provided only in digital mode. Many administrative procedures are now carried out digitally, and customers are encouraged to provide payment receipts digitally. However, this was not effective enough in all parts of the country. To attract more users to digital cash, governments are doing their best to eliminate or reduce service fees that businesses charge for electronic transactions.

These digital financial apps help eliminate corruption on top of financial inclusion. These apps aim to achieve financial inclusion by offering interesting and attractive bonuses to their users and traders. Customers using these cashless payment tools can enjoy a referral bonus program and merchants can earn cashback rewards and points by allowing their customers to transact through these cashless systems. .

Besides introducing digital financial systems to the poor, some banks are releasing mobile vans and trucks to reach the interior and pristine areas of the country. In these areas, people do not have access to transportation, communications, or financial services.

In addition to government payment apps, there are many private mobile electronic wallet systems (e wallets) developed by private companies and banks. Most of these apps allow bank transfers. All of these e-wallets allow users to make payments digitally and conveniently. Even if an individual runs out of cash, they are not stuck anywhere. With money in an e-wallet, you can safely make financial transactions without depending on someone else's money. Most of these apps are available for Android and iOS smartphones. There are also some apps available for phones running Windows.

One of the leading e-wallets in India is Paytm. Available for Android, Blackberry, iOS, Ovi, Windows and more. Other popular e-wallet apps include Freecharge, MobiKwik, Citrus Wallet, Oxigen Wallet, ItzCash, Axis Bank Lime, Jio Money, HDFC PayZapp, SBI Buddy, mRupee, Vodafone M-Pesa, PayMate, PayUmoney, Juspay, Ezetap And so on. Citi MasterPass, MomoeXpress, Ola Money, Mswipe, etc.

10. Need for Financial Inclusion

Financial inclusion comprehensively strengthens a country's financial system. It enhances the availability of economic resources. Most importantly, it strengthens the concept of savings among the poor living in both urban and rural areas. In this way, it makes a lasting contribution to economic progress.

Many poor people are prone to fraud, and because poor people are vulnerable, they can even be exploited by wealthy landlords and unlicensed moneylenders. With the help of financial inclusion, we can change this serious and dangerous situation.

Financial inclusion involves involving the poor in formal banking with the aim of securing a minimum amount of funds for future use. Many households do not have adequate facilities for farmers and artisans to save their hard-earned money.

11. Financial Inclusion Programmes Organised by The Reserve Bank of India (Rbi)

Reserve Bank of India is working on exclusive programs and plans to make financial inclusion effective in the country. It employs a bank-led strategy to enable frictionless financial inclusion. The Central Bank of India has also issued strict regulations that all banks must follow. RBI also provides eligible support to all banks in the country in order to achieve its financial inclusion goals.

The RBI has mandated that all banks maintain Basic Savings Bank Deposits (BDSD) accounts for economically vulnerable segments of society. These are no-frills accounts that do not require account holders to maintain a minimum balance or deposit. These account holders can withdraw cash from ATMs or bank branches. They should also be given the opportunity to receive and transfer money to others using electronic payment channels.

The RBI has also asked banks to introduce Simple Know Your Customer (KYC) rules for disadvantaged members of society. There are many rural people who cannot open a bank account due to strict KYC standards. Therefore, RBI wants banks to simplify KYC requirements, especially if low-income individuals are interested in opening bank accounts with amounts below Rs 50,000. We also ask for minimum KYC standards for him if the total account balance in his one year does not exceed 1 million rupees. Banks are being asked to accept her Aadhaar card as proof of identity and address, as most people belonging to the low-income group have her Aadhaar card issued in their name these days.

Faced with a shortage of bank branches in rural areas, the RBI urged all banking institutions to open more and more branches in villages across the country to provide better banking services to villagers. There are many remote villages with no banks and poor transport links. It is very difficult for residents of these areas to travel to remote bank branches for banking services. Therefore, due to RBI's compulsory rule, banks distribute and balance the ratio of banks in villages and towns.

According to the concept of financial inclusion, from a credit standpoint, a low-income person should have reasonable access to emergency loans, consumer loans, home loans, business his living loans at affordable interest rates. In terms of wealth accumulation, poor people need to be able to save well and have access to reliable investment opportunities that generate high returns. All low-income households must also have basic financial skills and a clear understanding of financial risk concepts.

Under the contingency plan of the financial inclusion system, the poor should have access to funds that can only be used in the future. It is not enough for these people to just have the funds to improve their income and improve their lifestyle. We also need the right resources to prepare for the future, especially as we age. Many poor people may not be aware of retirement plans. They should be offered an affordable retirement plan that will give them good returns later in life. You should also get insurable contingencies to protect and protect yourself. Many poor people don't even think about life or auto insurance because of the high cost. Insurers should offer insurance options for economically weaker classes at subsidized premiums. These policies provide protection and prevent you from paying exorbitant compensation costs if an unforeseen event or misfortune happens to you or your family.

The Reserve Bank of India encourages the establishment of Financial Literacy Centers (FLCs). Many changes and revisions have been made to the structure of the Financial Literacy Center (FLC). The various planned local branches of commercial banks and financial literacy centers are asked to raise financial awareness on a larger scale and strengthen financial literacy activities by organizing easy and simple financial literacy camps. These camps can be held outdoors under trees or other open spaces by conducting monthly or more frequent financial awareness camps. Financial education camps aim to provide financial education and provide easy access to finance for low-income members of society.

With the aim of decentralizing the proposed commercial bank (SCB) branches, the RBI has instructed the bank to set up branches in Tier 2 to Tier 6 centers with less than 1,000 residents in her. These branches can be opened with general approval from the RBI. In Sikkim and the northeastern states, the proposed commercial banks can open branches without RBI approval. You are free to open branches in those states. RBI is also working to liberalize the way commercial banks operate, with the exception of Rural Banks (RRBs), to open branches in Tier 1 centers with general permits.

The country's central bank has also asked banks to discuss and prepare a financial inclusion plan (FIP). These plans include the staff employed, the branches opened, the facilities provided at each of those branches, and the measures taken to transform the non-bank segment of society into individuals with basic access to banking services. It includes details such as the measures taken. Plans include no-frills accounts opened at public or private banks. The

RBI is committed to reviewing each bank's FIP and providing constructive feedback.

RBI also asked banks to install stationary intermediate structures between their head offices and other branches. This should be done for purposes such as organizing and managing cash, handling customer complaints, systematically collecting and maintaining essential documents, and monitoring branch activities. This particular intermediate branch can be an inexpensive building with basic infrastructure, a passbook printer, a bank terminal, an ATM, or even a safe to store large amounts of cash.

RBI has also invested heavily in banking service technology and is able to integrate innovative technologies to make banking processes simple, fast and cost-effective. Planned commercial banks were asked to use information and communication technology (ICT) to provide affordable digital banking services. Banks are also starting to use technology to offer bank accounts, loans, and other financial services at their doorstep. Moreover, with the advent of banking technology, it is okay for customers to be illiterate. They use technical devices and can work with biometrics. This also allows customers to make secure transactions with no room for fraud or deception. This also leads to dependence on the banking system by the non-banking sector of society.

The Reserve Bank of India has made it possible for designated commercial banks to obtain Business Correspondents (BC) and Business Facilitators (BF). These BCs and BFs act as intermediaries providing banking services to customers nationwide. The Business Correspondent strategy facilitates the delivery of banking products to the customer's doorstep. It also offers cash transactions, making it easily accessible to people living in rural areas where there are not many bank branches and convenient transportation to commute to nearby towns and cities.

These business correspondents are not only individuals, but also organizations or companies that act as intermediaries between banks and their customers. There are many individuals and organizations willing to take on the role of business correspondent. Both non-profit organizations and commercial enterprises are permitted to act as business correspondents. This is an important milestone in the banking industry. In a rural environment, economic correspondents usually receive support from the Village Panchayat (the local authority of a particular village) to develop a strong system consisting of Common Service Centers (CSCs). The Common Service Center is a locally operated electronic hub. This center has computers and is connected to the Internet. This system provides e-business services and e-governance to people living in rural areas. It also provides an opportunity for local people to become innovative and smart. People can develop their own ideas and technical solutions to create and improve business processes, marketing efforts, and recurring sales increases.

12. Financial Inclusion in India

In the Indian subcontinent, the concept of financial inclusion was first popularized in 2005 with the release of the Annual Policy Statement by the Reserve Bank of India. The concept quickly spread throughout the country. It was introduced mainly to touch every corner of the country without ignoring remote areas. This concept addressed the lack of formal financial and banking systems to meet the money needs of the poor.

In 2005, the Khan Commission's report was published, mainly discussing rural credit and microfinance. It spoke of the number of people in the country missing out on the benefits of a professional licensed banking system.

Khan's commission report focuses on providing access to essential financial services, helping people open bank accounts without frills and complications. All banks are asked to minimize regulation of the account creation process for economically vulnerable segments of society. Several banks have been asked to work together towards 100% financial inclusion by participating in a campaign launched by the RBI.

The Government of India has also launched the 'Pradhan Mantri Jan Dhan Yojna' with the sole purpose of motivating and encouraging the poor to open bank accounts. The program aims to have at least 75 million people open bank accounts by 2015.

13. Chief Aspects of an Integral Financial Integral Strategy

Every country has a financial integration strategy to build a comprehensive financial sector and keep it stable for years. This strategy also works to strengthen the economy's financial system when there are fluctuations in the financial markets.

Her three key components of an essential financial strategy are financial literacy or education, financial stability, and financial inclusion.

Financial literacy or education refers to spreading awareness and knowledge of the financial services offered by banks and other financial institutions. Financial inclusion refers to providing reasonable access to multiple financial services for all economic classes in society. This therefore suggests that financial literacy explains the demand angle by increasing people's financial literacy. Financial inclusion, on the other hand, addresses the supply side by ensuring that financial services are delivered to end users. These two factors help build financial stability.

As for finance, there is a financial tripod with these three elements forming a triangle that shows how each element contributes to strengthening the financial sector of the economy.

14. Special Financial Products Offered for attaining Financial Inclusion

Noting that low-income people living in rural and urban areas have very limited access to financial products and services. Many of them only know basic financial services such as savings plans, savings accounts, personal loans, crop loans and microfinance.

However, because banks do not have access to instant credit, they are directed to issue low-cost credit cards to low-income segments of society. The specific financial products offered to them are:

❖ **General Credit Cards (GCC)** : The bank has been asked by her RBI to introduce and offer general credit card facilities up to Rs 25,000 at its branches in semi-urban and rural areas.

❖ **Kissan Credit Cards (KCC)** : The Reserve Bank of India also warns banks that small-scale farmers with very low incomes, very limited funds, and who are unable to invest in suitable agricultural equipment, fertilizers, pesticides, seeds, tractors, and land-based agriculture. We have instructed farmers to issue Kissan credit cards only. They are forced to rely on other wealthy landowners for sowing land. These Kissan credit cards are designed to help farmers get instant purchases when they need them. Farmers often do not buy work-related items due to lack of money.

❖ **ICT-Based Accounts via BCs** : The Reserve Bank also plans to help banks reach out to the unbanked in society by providing information and communication technology (ICT)-based bank accounts using Business Correspondence (BC) was formulated. These accounts allow users to withdraw cash, make deposits, and apply for loans and other forms of credit through electronic forms. This type of account makes banking cheap and easy.

❖ **Increase in ATMs** : The Reserve Bank of India also reports that many rural areas of the country do not have enough ATMs (ATMs), which hinders many trading operations by people living in those areas. To make physical cash available to these people, the number of ATMs has increased significantly.

15. Financial Inclusion Through Microfinance

Microfinance is a highly effective way of funding economically disadvantaged segments of society. Microfinance refers to the provision of microloans or microcredits to disadvantaged entrepreneurs and small businesses. This kind of financing has greatly contributed to India achieving financial inclusion in a cost-effective manner. It has affected the lives of the poorest people in the country. This includes providing loans, savings tools, and other financial tools to earn more money and save efficiently for multiple purposes. There are some poor people in the country who do not have access to sources of funds and do not know how to get out of their desperate financial situation. With simple microfinance, they get the chance to start a business, find a better job, or improve their lifestyle. It is a great boon to them as it gives them the opportunity to use it for their own lucrative purposes and repay it conveniently over a period of time.

16. Financial Inclusion with The help of Private Companies

Private companies have also launched programs to help achieve financial inclusion in the country. These private companies planned and implemented projects to involve low-income people in development projects.

These programs include DCM's Haryali Kisan Bazaar, ITC's E-Choupal or E-Sagar, and Hindustan Unilever's Project Shakti.

In recent years, financial inclusion has become a very important aspect of public policy to develop economies in a sustainable way. It plays an important role in keeping the funding institutions in a very stable and stable state. Banks enjoy greater stability once financial inclusion is achieved.

It also brings financial institutions closer to their customers and helps maintain healthy relationships. Financial inclusion gives all economic players in the country access to formal financial services and the opportunity to move towards the overall development of the economy.

References
[1]   https://www.slideshare.net/vijaykumarsarabu/financial-inclusion-in-india-an-over-view
[2]   Microsoft Word - Financial_Inclusion (jsscacs.edu.in)
[3]   https://download.oliveboard.in/pdf/Financial-Inclusion.pdf
[4]   Financial Inclusion in India – Objectives, Schemes & Operations (bankbazaar.com)
[5]https://www.ijmra.us/project%20doc/2018/IJRSS_DECEMBER2018/IJRSS%20Dec18AnjaliKK.pdf

1Assistant Professor,
Department of Commerce & Finance,
Quantum University, Roorkee
2Associate Professor,
Department of Management,
Quantum University, Roorkee
3Associate Professor,
Department of Management,
Quantum University, Roorkee

20. Study of Physical Motor Fitness

Dr.Markand Choure

Abstract

The main aim of physical education to improve the effeciney & functionposition of the Body. The increasement of physical growth to improvement of patience heart & respiratory tract with the help of different programe like as fitness programe. Physical training programe, conditioning programe etc. undesirable conditions are of two types like as efficiency of Body & Motor efficiency. The fact of motor development efficiency is a control part of eligibility The different types of exercise to improvement of different types of functioning condition of the body.

Keyword : Motor,Ability,Fitness,Agility,Strength.

Introduction :

Motor efficiency which introduce to the patience of shoulders, power of Shoulder, Flexibility, Balance & movement etc. these are the component of motor development The Starting of Running which shows that the different types of activities like as motor by man, Gym, Lift, Alight, Swim & Lift of heavy weight etc.

To define the above definition to free of differnet struggle of life like as Tension free life & problems of life and Emergency condition of life.

			Physical Fitness					
			Motor Fitness					
	General		Motor			Ability		
Arm & Eye Coordination	Muscular Power	Agility	Muscular Strength	Muscular Endurance	Cardio Respiratary Endurance	Flexibility	Speed	Foot-Eye Coordination

Motor Developmentt Elements
Muscular Strength Muscular Endurnace and Cardio respiratory endurance
Physical Fitness is defined as the combined performance factors of muscular Strength. Muscular endurance cardio Vascular endurance. Power and flexibility.

High Function
1) Agility
2) Co-ordinationa
3) Speed
4) Balance

Intermediate Function
1) Flexibility
2) Power
3) Cardio Vascular Endurance
4) Muscular Endurance
5) Muscular Strength

Motor Fitness

Physical Fitness

Low Function
1) Motor Response
2) Perception
3) Sensory input
4) Reflexes
5) Inborn Neural Character

Basic Motor Development

Motor Fitness Components
1) Muscular Strength
2) Muscular Endurance
3) Cardio Vascular Edurance
4) Freedom From obesity
5) Flexibility
6) Power
7) Speed
8) Agility
9) Balance
10) Reaction time

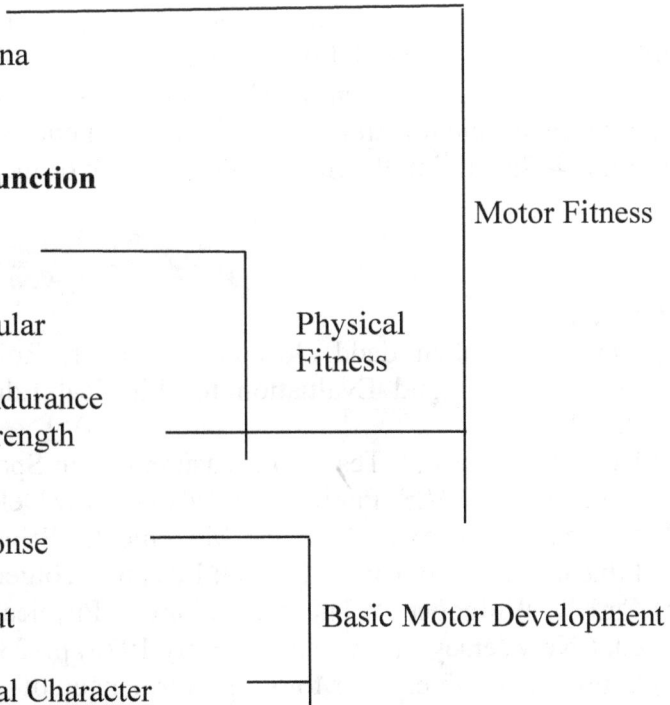

Conclusion :

Motor efficiency is a Stage of child to improve the movement of Hand, Neak, eye and movement of other organs to introduce the quantitative eligibility and it is to introduce the man efficiency of life intellegency, and efficiency of work. These are depend upon the component of Spiritual, Social imotional, mental and physical efficiency and eligibility of do the work.

All component to connect with each other It is to indicate the motor efficiency of the above definition to show the complete efficiency or It is the line man efficiency. These are considered the component like motor efficiency shows that the component as spiritual, Metal imotional, Social, intelligence of the body life of the man.

Reference :

1) Don R. Kiroken dadd, Joseph J. Gruber, Robert E. Johnson 'Measurement and Evaluation for Physical Education" 2nd ed. P.102

2) Devinder Kausal, " Test and Measurement in Sports and Physical Education" (D.V.S. Publication Kalkaji. New Delhi) 1st ed. P.3.

3) Haroda M. Barrow. " Man and Movement, : Principle of Physical Education. 3rd Ed. (Philadelphia: Lea and Febiger 1977) P 307.

4) Carl E. Willgoose. " The curriculum in Physical Education" 3rd ed. (New Jersey Prentice hall. Cratty 1979) p.123.

5) Lauro Geraidine. " Motor performance of Primary Grade Children." Completed Research in Health Physical Education and Recreation 10 (1968). 15.

(Offi.Principle)
Director of Physical Education.
S.Chandra Mahila Mahavidyalaya Ashti,
Dist-Gadchiroli Maharashtra,India 442707
email : dr.markandchoure@gmail.com

www.ingramcontent.com/pod-product-compliance
Lightning Source LLC
Chambersburg PA
CBHW050223270326
41914CB00003BA/549